Developing Analytic Talent

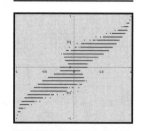

Developing Analytic Talent

Becoming a Data Scientist

Vincent Granville, Ph.D.

WILEY

Developing Analytic Talent: Becoming a Data Scientist

Published by
John Wiley & Sons, Inc.
10475 Crosspoint Boulevard
Indianapolis, IN 46256
www.wiley.com

Copyright © 2014 by John Wiley & Sons, Inc., Indianapolis, Indiana

Published simultaneously in Canada

ISBN: 978-1-118-81008-8
ISBN: 978-1-118-81004-0 (ebk)
ISBN: 978-1-118-81009-5 (ebk)

Manufactured in the United States of America

10 9 8 7 6 5 4 3 2 1

For general information on our other products and services please contact our Customer Care Department within the United States at (877) 762-2974, outside the United States at (317) 572-3993 or fax (317) 572-4002.

Wiley publishes in a variety of print and electronic formats and by print-on-demand. Some material included with standard print versions of this book may not be included in e-books or in print-on-demand. If this book refers to media such as a CD or DVD that is not included in the version you purchased, you may download this material at http://booksupport.wiley.com. For more information about Wiley products, visit www.wiley.com.

Library of Congress Control Number: 2013958300

For my loving wife, Paris, my wonderful daughter, Capri, and son, Zinal, for their constant support. In loving memory of my father, Roger, who introduced me to mathematics when I was a kid.

About the Author

Vincent Granville, Ph.D., is a visionary data scientist with 15 years of big data, predictive modeling, digital, and business analytics experience. Vincent is widely recognized as the leading expert in scoring technology, fraud detection, and web traffic optimization and growth. Over the last 10 years, he has worked in real-time credit card fraud detection with Visa, advertising mix optimization with CNET, change point detection with Microsoft, online user experience with Wells Fargo, search intelligence with InfoSpace, automated bidding with eBay, and click fraud detection with major search engines, ad networks, and large advertising clients. Vincent also manages the largest big data and analytics data science group on LinkedIn, with more than 100,000 members.

Most recently, Vincent launched Data Science Central, the leading community for big data, business analytics, and data science practitioners. Vincent is a former post-doctorate of Cambridge University and the National Institute of Statistical Sciences. He was among the finalists at the Wharton Business Plan Competition and at the Belgian Mathematical Olympiad. Vincent has published 40 papers in statistical journals and is an invited speaker at international conferences. He also developed a new data mining technology known as hidden decision trees, owns multiple patents, published the first data science book, and raised $6M in start-up funding. Vincent is one of the top 20 big data influencers according to Forbes, and was featured on VentureBeat, MarketWatch, and CNN. Vincent can be reached on Twitter @Analyticbridge.

About the Technical Editor

Joni Ngai is a Digital Evangelist who works with senior executives at Fortune 500 companies to develop digital vision and leverage technology and data to intelligently engage customers in today's connected world. She has extensive experience leading agencies and customers to develop new practices across digital, CRM, online media, analytics, and technology development. Joni started her digital consulting career with Razorfish in New York in 2000. Since then, she has worked with a number of top digital agencies, such as MRM Worldwide and Havas Digital, across the Asia-Pacific region for many global brands like Intel, Microsoft, and P&G. Joni was appointed as Vice-Chair at I-COM China, an industry- backed global forum in digital measurement, to facilitate participation in standardizing online measurements to help industries grow.

Joni graduated from the University of Waterloo majoring in Electrical Engineering with an option in Management Science. She also received an Executive MBA degree from the Kellogg School of Management at Northwestern University and Hong Kong University of Science and Technology. Joni also teaches graduate courses for the Master of Science in New Media program at the Chinese University of Hong Kong.

Credits

Executive Editor
Carol Long

Project Editor
Christina Haviland

Technical Editor
Joni Ngai

Production Editor
Christine Mugnolo

Copy Editor
San Dee Phillips

Editorial Manager
Mary Beth Wakefield

Freelancer Editorial Manager
Rosemarie Graham

Associate Director of Marketing
David Mayhew

Marketing Manager
Ashley Zurcher

Business Manager
Amy Knies

**Vice President and
Executive Group Publisher**
Richard Swadley

Associate Publisher
Jim Minatel

Project Coordinator, Cover
Todd Klemme

Compositor
Cody Gates,
Happenstance Type-O-Rama

Proofreaders
Shannon Coohill, Word One New York
Louise Watson, Word One New York
Candace Cunningham

Indexer
Robert Swanson

Cover Designer
Ryan Sneed/Wiley

Acknowledgments

I would like to thank Chris Haviland and Carol Long from Wiley for making this book happen; for taking the risk; and for turning a vast amount of valuable but unstructured and scattered text, published online, into a coherent, comprehensive, and useful book. In many ways, this complex process is similar to turning unstructured into structured data, a challenge many data scientists face on a regular basis, with solutions provided in this book. Also, I would like to thank my business partner and co-founder, Tim Matteson, who helped grow Data Science Central to a point where it has become not only the leading data science community, but also a modern, lean start-up focused on delivering value. Finally, I want to thank all the members of our community for their numerous comments and support. Without them, this book would not exist.

Contents at a Glance

Contents

Introduction

This book is a type of "handbook" on data science and data scientists, and contains information not found in traditional statistical, programming, or computer science textbooks. The author has compiled what he considers some of the most important information you will need for a career in data science, based on his 20+ years as a leader in the field. Much of the text was initially published over the last three years on the Data Science Central website, which is read by millions of website visitors. The book shows how data science is different from related fields and the value it brings to organizations using big data.

This book has three components: a multi-layer discussion of what data science is and how it relates to other disciplines; technical applications of and for data science including tutorials and case studies; and career resources for practicing and aspiring data scientists. Numerous career and training resources are included (such as data sets, web crawler source code, data videos, and how to build APIs) so you can start practicing data science today and quickly boost your career. If you're a decision maker, you will find information to help you make decisions on how to build a better analytic team, whether and when you need specialized solutions, and which ones will work best for your need.

Who This Book Is For

This book is intended for data scientists and related professionals (such as business analysts, computer scientists, software engineers, data engineers, and statisticians) who are interested in shifting to big data science careers. It is also for the college student studying a quantitative curriculum with the goal of becoming a data scientist. Finally, it is for managers of data scientists, and people interested in creating a startup business or consultancy around data science.

These readers will find valuable information throughout the book, and specifically in the following chapters:

- **Data science practitioners** will find Chapters 2, 4, 5, and 6 particularly valuable because they contain material on big data techniques (clustering and taxonomy creation) and modern data science techniques such as combinatorial feature selection, hidden decision trees, analytic APIs, and when MapReduce is useful. A number of case studies (fraud detection, digital analytics, stock market strategies, and more) are detailed enough to allow the reader to replicate the analyses when facing similar data in the real world when doing their jobs. However, it is also explained in simple words, not spending too much time on technicalities, code, or formulas, to make it accessible to high level managers.

- **Students** attending computer science, data science, or MBA classes will find Chapters 2, 4, 5, and 6 valuable for their purposes. In particular, they will find more advanced material in Chapters 2, 4, and 5, such as practical data science methods and principles, most of it not found in textbooks or taught in typical college curricula. Chapter 6 also provides real life applications and case studies, including more in-depth technical details.

- **Job applicants** will find resources about data science training and programs in Chapter 3. Chapters 7 and 8 provide numerous resources for job seekers including interview questions, sample resumes, sample job ads, a list of companies that routinely hire data scientists, and salary surveys.

- **Entrepreneurs** who want to launch a data science startup or consultancy will find sample business proposals, startup ideas, and salary surveys for consultants in Chapter 3. Also, throughout the book, consultants will find discussions on improving communication in data science work, lifecycles of data science projects, book and conference references, and many other resources.

- **Executives** trying to assess the value of data science, where it most benefits enterprise projects, and when architectures such as MapReduce are useful will find valuable information in Chapters 1, 2, 6 (case studies), and 8 (sample job ads, resumes, salary surveys). The focus of these chapters is usually not technical, except, to a limited extent, in some parts of Chapters 2 and 6, where new analytic technologies are introduced.

What This Book Covers

The technical part of this book covers core data science topics, including:

- Big data and the challenges of applying traditional algorithms to big data (Solutions are provided, for instance in the context of big data clustering or taxonomy creation.)

- A new, simplified, data science–friendly approach to statistical science, focusing on robust model-free methods
- State-of-the-art machine learning (hidden decision trees and combinatorial feature selection)
- New metrics for modern data (synthetic metrics, predictive power, bumpiness coefficient)
- Elements of computer science that are needed to build fast algorithms
- MapReduce and Hadoop, including numerical stability of computations performed with Hadoop

The focus is on recent technology. You will not find material about old techniques such as linear regression (except for anecdotal references), since such are discussed at length in all standard books. There is some limited discussion on logistic-like regression in this book, but it's more about blending it with other classifiers and proposing a numerically stable, approximate algorithm (approximate solutions are often as good as the exact model, since no data fits perfectly with a theoretical model).

Besides technology, the book provides useful career resources, including job interview questions, sample resumes, and sample job ads. Another important component of this book is case studies. Some of the case studies included here have a statistical/machine learning flair, some have more of a business/decision science or operations research flair, and some have more of a data engineering flair. Most of the time, I have favored topics that were posted recently and very popular on Data Science Central (the leading community for data scientists), rather than topics that I am particularly attached to.

How This Book Is Structured

The book consists of three overall topics:

- What data science and big data is, and is not, and how it's different from other disciplines (Chapters 1, 2, and 3)
- Career and training resources (Chapters 3 and 8)
- Technical material presented as tutorials (Chapters 4 and 5, but also the section on Clustering and Taxonomy Creation for Massive Data Sets in Chapter 2, and the section on New Variance for Hadoop and Big Data in Chapter 8), and in case studies (Chapters 6 and 7)

The book provides valuable career resources for potential and existing data scientists and related professionals (and their managers and their bosses), and generally speaking, to all professionals dealing with increasingly bigger, more complex, and faster flowing data. The book also provides data science recipes, craftsmanship, concepts (many of them, original and published for the first time), and cases studies illustrating implementation methods and techniques that have proven successful in various domains for analyzing modern data — either manually or automatically.

What You Need to Use This Book

The book contains a small amount of sample code, either in R or Perl. You can download Perl from `http://www.activestate.com/activeperl/downloads` and R from `http://cran.r-project.org/bin/windows/base/`. If you use a Windows machine, I would first install Cygwin, a Linux-like environment for Windows. You can get Cygwin at `http://cygwin.com/install.html`. Python is also available as open source and has a useful library called Pandas.

For most of the book, one or two years of college with some basic quantitative courses is enough for you to understand the content. The book does not require calculus or advanced math — indeed, it barely contains any mathematical formulas or symbols.

Yet some quite advanced material is described at a high level. A few technical notes spread throughout the book are for those who are more mathematically inclined and interested in digging deeper. Two years of calculus, statistics, and matrix theory at the college level are needed to understand these technical notes. Some source code (R, Perl) and data sets are provided, but the emphasis is not on coding.

This mixture of technical levels offers the opportunity for you to explore the depths of data science without advanced math knowledge (a bit like the way Carl Sagan introduced astronomy to the mainstream public).

Conventions

To help you get the most from the text and keep track of what's happening, we've used a number of conventions throughout the book.

NOTE Notes, tips, cross-references, and asides to the current discussion are offset and placed in features like this.

As for styles in the text:

- We *highlight* new terms and important words when we introduce them.
- We show keyboard strokes like this: Ctrl+A.

- We show filenames, URLs, and code within the text like so: `persistence.properties`.

- We present code like this:

```
We use a monofont type with no highlighting for most code examples.
```

What Is Data Science?

Sometimes, understanding what something *is* includes having a clear picture of what it *is not*. Understanding data science is no exception. Thus, this chapter begins by investigating what data science is not, because the term has been much abused and a lot of hype surrounds big data and data science. You will first consider the difference between true data science and fake data science. Next, you will learn how new data science training has evolved from traditional university degree programs. Then you will review several examples of how modern data science can be used in real-world scenarios.

Finally, you will review the history of data science and its evolution from computer science, business optimization, and statistics into modern data science and its trends. At the end of the chapter, you will find a Q&A section from recent discussions I've had that illustrate the conflicts between data scientists, data architects, and business analysts.

This chapter asks more questions than it answers, but you will find the answers discussed in more detail in subsequent chapters. The purpose of this approach is for you to become familiar with how data scientists think, what is important in the big data industry today, what is becoming obsolete, and what people interested in a data science career don't need to learn. For instance, you need to know statistics, computer science, and machine learning, but not everything from these domains. You don't need to know the details about complexity of sorting algorithms (just the general results), and you don't need to know how to compute a generalized inverse matrix, nor even know what a generalized inverse matrix is (a core topic of statistical theory), unless you specialize in the numerical aspects of data science.

> **TECHNICAL NOTE**
>
> This chapter can be read by anyone with minimal mathematical or technical knowledge. More advanced information is presented in "Technical Notes" like this one, which may be skipped by non-mathematicians.

CROSS-REFERENCE You will find definitions of most terms used in this book in Chapter 8.

Real Versus Fake Data Science

Books, certificates, and graduate degrees in data science are spreading like mushrooms after the rain. Unfortunately, many are just a mirage: people taking advantage of the new paradigm to quickly repackage old material (such as statistics and R programming) with the new label "data science."

Expanding on the R programming example of fake data science, note that R is an open source statistical programming language and environment that is at least 20 years old, and is the successor of the commercial product S+. R was and still is limited to in-memory data processing and has been very popular in the statistical community, sometimes appreciated for the great visualizations that it produces. Modern environments have extended R capabilities (the in-memory limitations) by creating libraries or integrating R in a distributed architecture, such as RHadoop (R + Hadoop). Of course other languages exist, such as SAS, but they haven't gained as much popularity as R. In the case of SAS, this is because of its high price and the fact that it was more popular in government organizations and brick-and-mortar companies than in the fields that experienced rapid growth over the last 10 years, such as digital data (search engine, social, mobile data, collaborative filtering). Finally, R is not unlike the C, Perl, or Python programming languages in terms of syntax (they all share the same syntax roots), and thus it is easy for a wide range of programmers to learn. It also comes with many libraries and a nice user interface. SAS, on the other hand, is more difficult to learn.

To add to the confusion, executives and decision makers building a new team of data scientists sometimes don't know exactly what they are looking for, and they end up hiring pure tech geeks, computer scientists, or people lacking proper big data experience. The problem is compounded by Human Resources

(HR) staff who do not know any better and thus produce job ads that repeat the same keywords: Java, Python, MapReduce, R, Hadoop, and NoSQL. But is data science really a mix of these skills?

Sure, MapReduce is just a generic framework to handle big data by reducing data into subsets and processing them separately on different machines, then putting all the pieces back together. So it's the distributed architecture aspect of processing big data, and these farms of servers and machines are called the *cloud*.

Hadoop is an implementation of MapReduce, just like C++ is an implementation (still used in finance) of object oriented programming. NoSQL means "Not Only SQL" and is used to describe database or data management systems that support new, more efficient ways to access data (for instance, MapReduce), sometimes as a layer hidden below SQL (the standard database querying language).

CROSS-REFERENCE See Chapter 2 for more information on what MapReduce can't do.

There are other frameworks besides MapReduce — for instance, graph databases and environments that rely on the concepts of nodes and edges to manage and access data, typically spatial data. These concepts are not necessarily new. Distributed architecture has been used in the context of search technology since before Google existed. I wrote Perl scripts that perform *hash joins* (a type of NoSQL join, where a join is the operation of joining or merging two tables in a database) more than 15 years ago. Today some database vendors offer hash joins as a fast alternative to SQL joins. Hash joins are discussed later in this book. They use hash tables and rely on *name-value pairs*. The conclusion is that MapReduce, NoSQL, Hadoop, and Python (a scripting programming language great at handling text and unstructured data) are sometimes presented as Perl's successors and have their roots in systems and techniques that started to be developed decades ago and have matured over the last 10 years. But data science is more than that.

Indeed, you can be a real data scientist and have none of these skills. NoSQL and MapReduce are not new concepts — many people embraced them long before these keywords were created. But to be a data scientist, you also need the following:

- Business acumen
- Real big data expertise (for example, you can easily process a 50 million-row data set in a couple of hours)
- Ability to sense the data
- A distrust of models
- Knowledge of the curse of big data
- Ability to communicate and understand which problems management is trying to solve

- Ability to correctly assess lift — or ROI — on the salary paid to you
- Ability to quickly identify a simple, robust, scalable solution to a problem
- Ability to convince and drive management in the right direction, sometimes against its will, for the benefit of the company, its users, and shareholders
- A real passion for analytics
- Real applied experience with success stories
- Data architecture knowledge
- Data gathering and cleaning skills
- Computational complexity basics — how to develop robust, efficient, scalable, and portable architectures
- Good knowledge of algorithms

A data scientist is also a generalist in business analysis, statistics, and computer science, with expertise in fields such as robustness, design of experiments, algorithm complexity, dashboards, and data visualization, to name a few. Some data scientists are also data strategists — they can develop a data collection strategy and leverage data to develop actionable insights that make business impact. This requires creativity to develop analytics solutions based on business constraints and limitations.

The basic mathematics needed to understand data science are as follows:

- Algebra, including, if possible, basic matrix theory.
- A first course in calculus. Theory can be limited to understanding computational complexity and the O notation. Special functions include the logarithm, exponential, and power functions. Differential equations, integrals, and complex numbers are not necessary.
- A first course in statistics and probability, including a familiarity with the concept of random variables, probability, mean, variance, percentiles, experimental design, cross-validation, goodness of fit, and robust statistics (not the technical details, but a general understanding as presented in this book).

From a technical point a view, important skills and knowledge include R, Python (or Perl), Excel, SQL, graphics (visualization), FTP, basic UNIX commands (sort, grep, head, tail, the pipe and redirect operators, cat, cron jobs, and so on), as well as a basic understanding of how databases are designed and accessed. Also important is understanding how distributed systems work and where bottlenecks are found (data transfers between hard disk and memory, or over the Internet). Finally, a basic knowledge of web crawlers helps to access unstructured data found on the Internet.

Two Examples of Fake Data Science

Here are two examples of fake data science that demonstrate why data scientists need a standard and best practices for their work. The two examples discussed here are not bad products — they indeed have a lot of intrinsic value — but they are not data science. The problem is two-fold:

- First, statisticians have not been involved in the big data revolution. Some have written books about applied data science, but it's just a repackaging of old statistics courses.

- Second, methodologies that work for big data sets — as big data was defined back in 2005 when 20 million rows would qualify as big data — fail on post-2010 big data that is in terabytes.

As a result, people think that data science is statistics with a new name; they confuse data science and fake data science, and big data 2005 with big data 2013. Modern data is also very different and has been described by three *V*s: velocity (real time, fast flowing), variety (structured, unstructured such as tweets), and volume. I would add veracity and value as well. For details, read the discussion on when data is flowing faster than it can be processed in Chapter 2.

CROSS-REFERENCE See Chapter 4 for more detail on statisticians versus data scientists.

Example 1: Introduction to Data Science e-Book

Looking at a 2012 data science training manual from a well-known university, most of the book is about old statistical theory. Throughout the book, R is used to illustrate the various concepts. But logistic regression in the context of processing a mere 10,000 rows of data is not big data science; it is fake data science. The entire book is about *small* data, with the exception of the last few chapters, where you learn a bit of SQL (embedded in R code) and how to use an R package to extract tweets from Twitter, and create what the author calls a word cloud (it has nothing to do with cloud computing).

Even the Twitter project is about small data, and there's no distributed architecture (for example, MapReduce) in it. Indeed, the book never talks about data architecture. Its level is elementary. Each chapter starts with a short introduction in simple English (suitable for high school students) about big data/data science, but these little data science excursions are out of context and independent from the projects and technical presentations.

Perhaps the author added these short paragraphs so that he could rename his "Statistics with R" e-book as "Introduction to Data Science." But it's free and it's a nice, well-written book to get high-school students interested in statistics and programming. It's just that it has nothing to do with data science.

Example 2: Data Science Certificate

Consider a data science certificate offered by a respected public university in the United States. The advisory board is mostly senior technical guys, most having academic positions. The data scientist is presented as "a new type of data analyst." I disagree. Data analysts include number crunchers and others who, on average, command lower salaries when you check job ads, mostly because these are less senior positions. Data scientist is not a junior-level position.

This university program has a strong data architecture and computer science flair, and the computer science content is of great quality. That's an important part of data science, but it covers only one-third of data science. It also has a bit of old statistics and some nice lessons on robustness and other statistical topics, but nothing about several topics that are useful for data scientists (for example, Six Sigma, approximate solutions, the 80/20 rule, cross-validation, design of experiments, modern pattern recognition, lift metrics, third-party data, Monte Carlo simulations, or the life cycle of data science projects. The program does requires knowledge of Java and Python for admission. It is also expensive — several thousand dollars.

So what comprises the remaining two-thirds of data science? Domain expertise (in one or two areas) counts for one-third. The final third is a blend of applied statistics, business acumen, and the ability to communicate with decision makers or to make decisions, as well as vision and leadership. You don't need to know everything about six sigma, statistics, or operations research, but it's helpful to be familiar with a number of useful concepts from these fields, and be able to quickly find good ad hoc information on topics that are new to you when a new problem arises. Maybe one day you will work on time-series data or econometric models (it happened unexpectedly to me at Microsoft). It's okay to know a little about time series today, but as a data scientist, you should be able to identify the right tools and models and catch up very fast when exposed to new types of data. It is necessary for you to know that there is something called *time series*, and when faced with a new problem, correctly determine whether applying a time-series model is a good choice or not. But you don't need to be an *expert* in time series, Six Sigma, Monte Carlo, computational complexity, or logistic regression. Even when suddenly exposed to (say) time series, you don't need to learn everything, but you must be able to find out what is important by doing quick online research (a critical skill all data scientists should have). In this case (time series), if the need arises, learn about correlograms, trends, change point, normalization and periodicity. Some of these topics are described in Chapter 4 in the section Three Classes Of Metrics: Centrality, Volatility, Bumpiness.

The Face of the New University

Allow me to share two stories with you that help to illustrate one of the big problems facing aspiring data scientists today. I recently read the story of an adjunct professor paid $2,000 to teach a class, but based on the fee for the course and the number of students, the university was earning about $50,000 from that class. So where does the $48,000 profit go?

My wife applied for a one-year graduate program that costs $22,000. She then received a letter from the university saying that she was awarded a $35,000 loan to pay for the program. But if she needed a loan to pay for the program, she would not have pursued it in the first place.

The reason I share these two stories is to point out that the typically high fees for U.S. graduate and undergraduate programs are generally financed by loans, which are causing a student debt crisis is the United States. The assumption is that traditional universities charge such high fees to cover equally high expenses that include salaries, facilities, operations, and an ever-growing list of government regulations with which they must comply. Because of this, traditional universities are facing more and more competition from alternative programs that are more modern, shorter, sometimes offered online on demand, and *cost much less* (if anything).

> **NOTE** Not all countries have educational costs as high as those encountered in the United States. It could make sense for an American student to attend a data science program abroad — for instance, in China or Europe — to minimize costs while still having access to high-quality material and gaining international experience.

Since we are criticizing the way data science is taught in some traditional curricula, and the cost of traditional university educations in the United States, let's think a bit about the future of data science higher education.

Proper training is fundamental, because that's how you become a good, qualified data scientist. Many new data science programs offered online (such as those at Coursera.com) or by corporations (rather than universities) share similar features, such as being delivered online, or on demand. Here is a summary regarding the face of the new data science "university."

The new data science programs are characterized by the following:

- Take much less time to earn, six months rather than years
- Deliver classes and material online, on demand
- Focus on applied modern technology
- Eliminate obsolete content (differential equations or eigenvalues)
- Include rules of thumb, tricks of the trade, craftsmanship, real implementations, and practical advice integrated into training material
- Cost little or nothing, so no need to take on large loans
- Are sometimes sponsored or organized by corporations and/or forward-thinking universities (content should be vendor-neutral)

- No longer include knowledge silos (for instance, operations research versus statistics versus business analytics)

- Require working on actual, real-world projects (collaboration encouraged) rather than passing exams

- Include highly compact, well-summarized training material, pointing to selected free online resources as necessary

- Replace PhD programs with apprenticeships

- Provide substantial help in finding a good, well paid, relevant job (fee and successful completion of program required; no fee if program sponsored by a corporation: it has already hired or will hire you)

- Are open to everyone, regardless of prior education, language, age, immigration status, wealth, or country of residence

- Are even more rigorous than existing traditional programs

- Have reduced cheating or plagiarism concerns because the emphasis is not on regurgitating book content

- Have course material that is updated frequently with new findings and approaches

- Have course material that is structured by focusing on a vertical industry (for instance, financial services, new media/social media/advertising), since specific industry knowledge is important to identifying and understanding real-world problems, and being able to jump-start a new job very quickly when hired (with no learning curve)

Similarly, the new data science "professor" has the following characteristics:

- Is not tenured, yet not an adjunct either

- In many cases is not employed by a traditional university

- Is a cross-discipline expert who constantly adapts to change, and indeed brings meaningful change to the program and industry

- Is well connected with industry leaders

- Is highly respected and well known

- Has experience in the corporate world, or experience gained independently (consultant, modern digital publisher, and so on)

- Publishes research results and other material in online blogs, which is a much faster way to make scientific progress than via traditional trade journals

- Does not spend a majority of time writing grant proposals, but rather focuses on applying and teaching science

- Faces little if any bureaucracy

- Works from home in some cases, eliminating the dual-career location problem faced by PhD married couples

- Has a lot of freedom in research activities, although might favor lucrative projects that can earn revenue

- Develops open, publicly shared knowledge rather than patents, and widely disseminates this knowledge

- In some cases, has direct access to market

- Earns more money than traditional tenured professors

- Might not have a PhD

CROSS-REFERENCE Chapter 3 contains information on specific data science degree and training programs.

The Data Scientist

The data scientist has a unique role in industry, government, and other organizations. That role is different from others such as statistician, business analyst, or data engineer. The following sections discuss the differences.

Data Scientist Versus Data Engineer

One of the main differences between a data scientist and a data engineer has to do with ETL versus DAD:

- **ETL** (Extract/Load/Transform) is for data engineers, or sometimes data architects or database administrators (DBA).

- **DAD** (Discover/Access/Distill) is for data scientists.

Data engineers tend to focus on software engineering, database design, production code, and making sure data is flowing smoothly between source (where it is collected) and destination (where it is extracted and processed, with statistical summaries and output produced by data science algorithms, and eventually moved back to the source or elsewhere). Data scientists, while they need to understand this data flow and how it is optimized (especially when working with Hadoop) don't actually optimize the data flow itself, but rather the data processing step: extracting value from data. But they work with engineers and business people to define the metrics, design data collecting schemes, and make sure data science processes integrate efficiently with the enterprise data systems (storage, data flow). This is especially true for data scientists working in small companies, and is one reason why data scientists should be able to write code that is re-usable by engineers.

Sometimes data engineers do DAD, and sometimes data scientists do ETL, but it's not common, and when they do it's usually internal. For example, the data engineer may do a bit of statistical analysis to optimize some database processes, or the data scientist may do a bit of database management to manage a small, local, private database of summarized information.

DAD is comprised of the following:

- **Discover**: Identify good data sources and metrics. Sometimes request the data to be created (work with data engineers and business analysts).

- **Access**: Access the data, sometimes via an API, a web crawler, an Internet download, or a database access, and sometimes in-memory within a database.

- **Distill**: Extract from the data the information that leads to decisions, increased ROI, and actions (such as determining optimum bid prices in an automated bidding system). It involves the following:

  - Exploring the data by creating a data dictionary and exploratory analysis

  - Cleaning the data by removing impurities.

  - Refining the data through data summarization, sometimes multiple layers of summarization, or hierarchical summarization)

  - Analyzing the data through statistical analyses (sometimes including stuff like experimental design that can take place even before the Access stage), both automated and manual. Might or might not require statistical modeling

  - Presenting results or integrating results in some automated process

Data science is at the intersection of computer science, business engineering, statistics, data mining, machine learning, operations research, Six Sigma, automation, and domain expertise. It brings together a number of techniques, processes, and methodologies from these different fields, along with business vision and action. Data science is about bridging the different components that contribute to business optimization, and eliminating the silos that slow down business efficiency. It has its own unique core, too, including (for instance) the following topics:

- Advanced visualizations

- Analytics as a Service (AaaS) and API's

- Clustering and taxonomy creation for large data sets

- Correlation and R-squared for big data

- Eleven features any database, SQL, or NoSQL should have

- Fast feature selection

- Hadoop/Map-Reduce

- Internet topology

- Keyword correlations in big data
- Linear regression on an usual domain, hyperplane, sphere, or simplex
- Model-free confidence intervals
- Predictive power of a feature
- Statistical modeling without models
- The curse of big data
- What MapReduce can't do

Keep in mind that some employers are looking for Java or database developers with strong statistical knowledge. These professionals are very rare, so instead the employer sometimes tries to hire a data scientist, hoping he is strong in developing production code. You should ask upfront (during the phone interview, if possible) if the position to be filled is for a Java developer with statistics knowledge, or a statistician with strong Java skills. However, sometimes the hiring manager is unsure what he really wants, and you might be able to convince him to hire you without such expertise if you convey to him the added value your expertise does bring. It is easier for an employer to get a Java software engineer to learn statistics than the other way around.

Data Scientist Versus Statistician

Many statisticians think that data science is about analyzing data, but it is more than that. Data science also involves implementing algorithms that process data automatically, and to provide automated predictions and actions, such as the following:

- Analyzing NASA pictures to find new planets or asteroids
- Automated bidding systems
- Automated piloting (planes and cars)
- Book and friend recommendations on Amazon.com or Facebook
- Client-customized pricing system (in real time) for all hotel rooms
- Computational chemistry to simulate new molecules for cancer treatment
- Early detection of an epidemic
- Estimating (in real time) the value of all houses in the United States (Zillow.com)
- High-frequency trading
- Matching a Google Ad with a user and a web page to maximize chances of conversion
- Returning highly relevant results to any Google search

- Scoring all credit card transactions (fraud detection)
- Tax fraud detection and detection of terrorism
- Weather forecasts

All of these involve both statistical science and terabytes of data. Most people doing these types of projects do not call themselves statisticians. They call themselves data scientists.

Statisticians have been gathering data and performing linear regressions for several centuries. DAD performed by *statisticians* 300 years ago, 20 years ago, today, or in 2015 for that matter, has little to do with DAD performed by *data scientists* today. The key message here is that eventually, as more statisticians pick up on these new skills and more data scientists pick up on statistical science (sampling, experimental design, confidence intervals — not just the ones described in Chapter 5), the frontier between data scientist and statistician will blur. Indeed, I can see a new category of data scientist emerging: data scientists with strong statistical knowledge.

What also makes data scientists different from computer scientists is that they have a much stronger statistics background, especially in computational statistics, but sometimes also in experimental design, sampling, and Monte Carlo simulations.

Data Scientist Versus Business Analyst

Business analysts focus on database design (database modeling at a high level, including defining metrics, dashboard design, retrieving and producing executive reports, and designing alarm systems), ROI assessment on various business projects and expenditures, and budget issues. Some work on marketing or finance planning and optimization, and risk management. Many work on high-level project management, reporting directly to the company's executives.

Some of these tasks are performed by data scientists as well, particularly in smaller companies: metric creation and definition, high-level database design (which data should be collected and how), or computational marketing, even *growth hacking* (a word recently coined to describe the art of growing Internet traffic exponentially fast, which can involve engineering and analytic skills).

There is also room for data scientists to help the business analyst, for instance by helping automate the production of reports, and make data extraction much faster. You can teach a business analyst FTP and fundamental UNIX commands: ls -l, rm -i, head, tail, cat, cp, mv, sort, grep, uniq -c, and the pipe and redirect operators (|, >). Then you write and install a piece of code on the database server (the server accessed by the business analyst traditionally via a browser or tools such as Toad or Brio) to retrieve data. Then, all the business analyst has to do is:

1. Create an SQL query (even with visual tools) and save it as an SQL text file.

2. Upload it to the server and run the program (for instance a Python script, which reads the SQL file and executes it, retrieves the data, and stores the results in a CSV file).

3. Transfer the output (CSV file) to his machine for further analysis.

Such collaboration is win-win for the business analyst *and* the data scientist. In practice, it has helped business analysts extract data 100 times bigger than what they are used to, and 10 times faster.

In summary, data scientists are not business analysts, but they can greatly help them, including automating the business analyst's tasks. Also, a data scientist might find it easier get a job if she can bring the extra value and experience described here, especially in a company where there is a budget for one position only, and the employer is unsure whether hiring a business analyst (carrying overall analytic and data tasks) or a data scientist (who is business savvy and can perform some of the tasks traditionally assigned to business analysts). In general, business analysts are hired first, and if data and algorithms become too complex, a data scientist is brought in. If you create your own startup, you need to wear both hats: data scientist and business analyst.

Data Science Applications in 13 Real-World Scenarios

Now let's look at 13 examples of real-world scenarios where the modern data scientist can help. These examples will help you learn how to focus on a problem and its formulation, and how to carefully assess all of the potential issues — in short, how a data scientist would look at a problem and think strategically before starting to think about a solution. You will also see why some widely available techniques, such as standard regression, might not be the answer in all scenarios.

NOTE This chapter focuses on problems and how to assess them. Chapters 4 and 5 discuss solutions to such problems.

The *data scientist's* way of thinking is somewhat different from that of engineers, operations research professionals, and computer scientists. Although operations research has a strong analytic component, this field focuses on specific aspects of business optimization, such as inventory management and quality control. Operations research domains include defense, economics, engineering, and the military. It uses Markov models, Monte Carlo simulations, queuing theory, and stochastic process, and (for historical reasons) tools such as Matlab and Informatica.

CROSS-REFERENCE See Chapter 4 for a comparison of data scientists with business analysts, statisticians, and data engineers.

There are two basic types of data science problems:

1. **Internal data science problems**, such as bad data, reckless analytics, or using inappropriate techniques. Internal problems are not business problems; they are internal to the data science community. Therefore, the fix consists in training data scientists to do better work and follow best practices.

2. **Applied business problems** are real-world problems for which solutions are sought, such as fraud detection or identifying if a factor is a cause or a consequence. These may involve internal or external (third-party) data.

Scenario 1: DUI Arrests Decrease After End of State Monopoly on Liquor Sales

An article was recently published in the *MyNorthWest* newspaper about a new law that went into effect a year ago in the state of Washington that allows grocery stores to sell hard liquor. The question here is how to evaluate and interpret the reported decline in DUI arrests after the law went into effect.

As a data scientist, you would first need to develop a list of possible explanations for the decline (through discussions with the client or boss). Then you would design a plan to rule out some of them, or attach the correct weight to each of them, or simply conclude that the question is not answerable unless more data or more information is made available.

Following are 15 potential explanations for, and questions regarding, the reported paradox regarding the reported DUI arrest rates. You might even come up with additional reasons.

- There is a glitch in the data collection process (the data is wrong).
- The article was written by someone with a conflict of interest, promoting a specific point of view, or who is politically motivated. Or perhaps it is just a bold lie.
- There were fewer arrests because there were fewer policemen.
- The rates of other crimes also decreased during that timeframe as part of a general downward trend in crime rates. Without the new law, would the decline have been even more spectacular?
- There is a lack of statistical significance.
- Stricter penalties deter drunk drivers.
- There is more drinking by older people and, as they die, DUI arrests decline.
- The population of drinkers is decreasing even though the population in general is increasing, because the highest immigration rates are among Chinese and Indian populations, who drink much less than other population groups.

- Is the decrease in DUI arrests for Washington residents, or for non-residents as well?

- It should have no effect because, before the law, people could still buy alcohol (except hard liquor) in grocery stores in Washington.

- Prices (maybe because of increased taxes) have increased, creating a dent in alcohol consumption (even though alcohol and tobacco are known for their resistance to such price elasticity).

- People can now drive shorter distances to get their hard liquor, so arrests among hard liquor drinkers have decreased.

- Is the decline widespread among all drinkers, or only among hard liquor drinkers?

- People are driving less in general, both drinkers and non-drinkers, perhaps because gas prices have risen.

- A far better metric to assess the impact of the new law is the total consumption of alcohol (especially hard liquor) by Washington residents.

The data scientist must select the right methodology to assess the impact of the new law and figure out how to get the data needed to perform the assessment. In this case, the real cause is that hard liquor drinkers can now drive much shorter distances to get their hard liquor. For the state of Washington the question is, did the law reduce costs related to alcohol consumption (by increasing tax revenue from alcohol sales, laying off state-store employees, or creating modest or no increase in alcohol-related crime, and so on).

Scenario 2: Data Science and Intuition

Intuition and gut feeling are still what drive many decisions in executive circles. Yet, as demonstrated in this example, data science and statistical analysis are shown to be superior to intuition and keep you from forming wrong conclusions based on a gut feeling.

Twin data points are observations that are almost identical, and they tend to be the norm rather than the exception in many types of data sets. In any 2- or 3-dimensional data set with 300+ rows, if the data is quantitative and evenly distributed in a bounded space, you should expect to see a large proportion (>15 percent) of data points that have a close neighbor.

This applies to all data sets, but the discovery was first made by looking at a picture of stars in a galaxy. There are so many binary stars that you might intuitively assume that there is some mechanism that forces stars to cluster in pairs. However, if you look at pure probabilities, you would see that it is highly probable for 15 percent of all stars to belong to a binary star system without any external mechanism driving it.

For example, consider a galaxy containing 500 stars. Pure probability calculations on how many of these stars would be within binary systems reveal the following:

■ The probability of having at least 60 (12 percent) of the stars in a binary system is 85 percent.

■ The probability of having at least 80 (16 percent) of the stars in a binary system is 18 percent.

■ The probability of having at least 100 (20 percent) of the stars in a binary system is 0 percent (almost).

In reality, however, more than 80 percent of all stars are located within binary systems. This number is not supported by the probability statistics; thus, there is clearly some mechanism at work that forces stars to cluster in pairs.

This framework provides a good opportunity to test your analytic intuition. Look at a chart with twin observations, and visually assess whether the twin observations are natural (random) or not (too numerous or too few of them). It would also be a great exercise to write a piece of code (Python, Perl, or R) that performs these simulations (including the more complicated 3-D case) to double-check the theoretical results and compare R, Perl, and Python in terms of speed.

CROSS-REFERENCE Chapter 6, "Data Science Application Case Studies," contains additional tests you can use to assess your analytic intuition.

TECHNICAL NOTE

This note explains how the probabilities were computed. You may skip it if you are not a mathematician.

Say a night sky image featuring stars is 10 x 10 cm, and has about n=500 visible stars (data points), and a binary star is defined as a star having a neighboring star 1 millimeter away (or less) in the picture. If stars were distributed perfectly randomly, the expected number of stars in a binary star system would be 73 (on average) out of 500 stars. This number is far higher than most people would have thought. You can denote this proportion as p, thus p=14.5 percent, and n*p=73, the expected number of stars in a binary system, among these 500 stars.

You can compute the probability in question using the theory of stochastic processes — Poisson process in this case. The intensity L of the process is the number of points per square millimeter — that is L = 500/(100 mm x 100 mm) = 0.05 per square millimeter, if 500 points were distributed in a 100 x 100 mm area (a magnified picture of the night sky).

The probability p that a star has at least one neighbor within 1 mm is 1 - Proba(zero neighbor) = 1 - exp(-L*Pi*r^2), where r = 1 mm and Pi = 3.14. Here Pi*r^2 is the area of a circle of radius r = 1 mm. The exponential term comes from the fact that for a Poisson process, the number of points in a given set (circle, rectangle, and so on), has a Poisson distribution of mean L*Area. Thus p=0.145.

So being a binary star is a Bernoulli (1/0) variable of parameter p=0.145. *V* can denote the number of stars that are in a binary star system: *V* is the sum of *n* Bernoulli variables of parameter *p*, and thus has a Binomial distribution of parameters *n*, *p*. The standardized variable Z = (V - np)/SQRT{np(1-p)} is well approximated by a normal(0,1) distribution. This fact can be used to compute the preceding probabilities.

Alternative computation: The same results could have been obtained using Monte Carlo simulations, rather than using a theoretical model, to compute these probabilities. This would have involved the generation of a million simulated images (2-dimensional tables), and in each simulated image, counting the number of stars in a binary system. This task can be automated and performed in a few minutes, with modern computers, a good random number generator, and a smart algorithm.

It could be slow if you use a naive approach. You can do much better than O(n^2) in terms of computational complexity, to compute the n distances to the nearest stars. The idea is to store the data in a grid where granularity = 1 mm (that is, a 2-dim array with 100 x 100 = 10,000 cells). Thus for each star, you have to look only at the eight surrounding pixels to count the number of neighbors less than 1 mm away. The O(n^2) complexity has been reduced to O(n), at the expense of using 10,000 memory cells of 1 bit each (presence / absence of a star).

Note that I picked up the number 1,000,000 arbitrarily, but in practice it needs to be just big enough so that your estimates are stable enough, with additional simulations bringing few or no corrections. Selecting the right sample and sample size is a experimental-design problem, and using model-free confidence intervals facilitates this task and makes the results robust. This Monte Carlo simulation approach is favored by operations research professionals, as well as by some data scientists, computer scientists, and software engineers who love model-free statistical modeling. However, in this case the theoretical model is well known, simple if not elementary, and comes with a quick, simple answer. So unless you have to spend hours understanding how it works or to just discover its existence, go for the theoretical solution in this case

Caveat: In this example, stars are seen through a 2-D screen. But in reality, they lie in a 3-D space. Two stars might appear as neighbors because their X and Y coordinates are close to each other, but could be eons apart on the Z-axis. So to compute the real expected proportion of binary stars, you would have to simulate stars (points) in 3-D, then project them on a rectangle, and then count the binary stars. I'm not sure the theoretical model offers a simple solution in this case, but the Monte Carlo simulations are still straightforward. In practice, stars that are actually far away are not shiny enough to show up on the picture, so the 2-D model is indeed a good approximation of the real 3-D problem.

Also, in the theoretical model, some implicit independence assumptions are made regarding star locations (when mentioning the binomial model), but this is not the case in practice, because the 1 mm circles centered on each star sometimes overlap. The approximation is still good and is conservative — in the sense that the theoretical number, when corrected for overlap, will be even higher than 73.

Scenario 3: Data Glitch Turns Data Into Gibberish

There are many examples available of data screw-ups occurring during the import or export of data. It is usually the result of poor architecture, using the wrong tools, or blindly relying on them without performing data quality checks. How does a data scientist detect and fix this?

Microsoft Access sometimes cannot properly import or export data types. Automated and even forced type casting from a database table to text or CSV files (or the other way around) is poor, resulting in many errors. This occurs because the environment is not flexible enough to do smart type detection and casting. For example, have you ever dealt with a date that was recorded as an integer in one row and mmddyy (month, day, and year, as in 100516 for October 5, 2016) in the next row? Or perhaps you've had to deal with a comma inside a data field value that screws up your CSV file?

I've received many data files that had a data corruption rate above 5 percent. Sometimes two different types of values (advertiser keyword versus user query, or referral domain versus ad network domain) are stored in the same field. Sometimes the fields are not properly aligned. Sometimes it looks like the people who produced the data were not experts in regular expressions or used separators badly. Sometimes it's the software that messes things up.

Sometimes these screw-ups have undesirable side effects, such as one single artificial user ID in your database becoming a *garbage collector* for all users with no user ID, resulting in flaws when analyzing the data. At other times it's not a big deal.

Here are a few examples where messy data, messy formatting, and broken data integration resulted in serious errors, as well as how the problems were fixed.

- *Wells Fargo*: Tealeaf users' sessions were broken down into multiple sessions because each server had its own web log and the blending of all the web logs was not done properly. In this case, it was mostly an architecture design issue. Fortunately, the problem was discovered and fixed, and great insights were gained along the way.

- *eBay*: A data transfer removed special characters from French and German keywords, making reconciliation impossible. A temporary lookup table of foreign keywords was built, with correct and erroneous spellings, to fix the problem.

- *Click fraud detection*: The keyword field sometimes represented a user query (such as a Google query), and sometimes a pre-specified keyword category, depending on the type of ad network affiliate. Affiliates where the keyword was indeed a keyword category were erroneously heavily penalized because the keyword distribution was (by design, not by fraud) very poor. Adding a new field that specified the type of keyword fixed the problem.

As an exercise, I invite you to think more about these types of issues and answer the following questions. These are also interesting job interview questions.

- How do you address these issues?
- How do you automatically detect these screw-ups? How is it a quality assurance issue?
- Is it worse with big data? Is detecting or fixing it more difficult?
- How much bad data can we tolerate? One percent, or even less in problems such as fraud detection?
- What proportion of your time is wasted on fixing these issues?
- How can you design smart type casting?

Scenario 4: Regression in Unusual Spaces

This example illustrates the need to adapt old techniques, such as regression, before applying them to new problems. Some of these techniques are more than 100 years old, and have been the workhorses of statistical analysis. They were developed when data sets were small, and simple mathematical solutions could solve problems. This is no longer the case with the advent of big data and massive paralleled computing power.

Say you want to reverse-engineer the recipe for Coca-Cola. The response, Y, is how close the recipe is to the actual Coca-Cola recipe, based on a number of tastings performed by a number of different people (according to the experimental design). Indeed, it's quite similar to a clinical trial where a mix of atoms or chemical radicals (each combination producing a unique molecule) is tested to optimize a drug. The independent variables are binary, each one representing an ingredient, such as salt, water, corn syrup, and so on. The value is equal to 1 if the ingredient in question is present in the recipe, and 0 otherwise. It's quite different from standard linear or logistic regression.

> **TECHNICAL NOTE**
>
> The regression coefficient a_k ($k = 1,...,m$) must meet the following requirements:
>
> - Each k is positive (a_k is greater or equal to 0).
> - The sum of these coefficients is equal to 1.
>
> In short, you're doing a regression on the simplex domain where a_k represents the proportions of a mix. An interesting property of this regression is that the sum of the square of the a_k coefficients is equal to the square of the area of the $m-1$ dimensional face defined by $SUM(a_k) = 1$, and a_k is greater than or equal to zero. (This is just a generalization of Pythagoras's theorem.) It is a bit like a lasso, ridge, or logic (not logistic) regression, but it could also be solved using Markov Chain Monte Carlo (MCMC) in a Bayesian framework.

And what about solving a regression on a sphere? For instance:

- Identify the Canada Goose's migration flight paths based on bird sightings.
- Assess the trajectory and origin of a meteor that resulted in multiple aligned impact craters on a planet.
- Detect tectonic faults based on volcano locations (almost aligned, as in the Cascade Range, or in the mid-Atlantic, under the sea).
- Solve the regression of a plane by mapping a sphere onto the plane.

In this example, the intent is to create a competing product that tastes the same as Coca Cola, call it by a different name, and sell it for far less. If the taste is identical but the ingredients are different, then the Coca Cola manufacturer won't be able to successfully sue you for copying their recipe. I think Virgin almost managed to create a clone. And of course, Pepsi does not come close: the taste is so different, just like apples and oranges.

Finally, there are many different ways to solve this regression problem (or any data science problem. The solutions tend to be equivalent in terms of efficiency if you use the right parameters. For example, you could solve this problem with pure optimization/mathematics. Statisticians would argue that this approach would not allow you to build confidence intervals for the regression parameters, or test whether some are equal to zero. Alternately, a methodology of my own design computes confidence intervals without statistical models. The technique, known as the First Analyticbridge Theorem, is described in the more technical chapters of this book.

Scenario 5: Analytics Versus Seduction to Boost Sales

This example illustrates that even the best analytics are not very useful if you ignore other critical components that make a business successful. In short, analytics is not a panacea for all business problems.

The context here is about increasing conversion rates, such as converting website visitors into active users, or passive newsletter subscribers into business leads (a user who opens the newsletter and clicks on the links becomes a lead). Here the newsletter conversion problem is discussed, although this example can apply to many different settings.

To maximize the total number of leads, you need to use both seduction and analytics. Sales is a function of:

- Seduction
- Analytics
- Product
- Price

- Competition
- Reputation
- Marketing

NOTE How to assess the weight attached to each of these factors is beyond the scope of this chapter.

First, even measuring "seduction" or "analytics" is difficult. But you could use a 0-to-10 scale, 10 being the best, with seduction = 9 representing a company using significant efforts to seduce prospects, and analytics = 0 representing a company totally ignoring analytics.

In the context of newsletter optimization (to maximize lead quantity and volume), most companies set seduction to 1 and analytics to 4 or 5. Analytics is usually achieved through multivariate testing and mathematical segmentation and targeting of the user base. This approach originates from the way marketing people are trained — it is not, however, the best approach. Segmentation by ISP rather than by traditional user group is now critical. *Failing* to reach Gmail users is far worse than reaching Gmail users through a poor user segmentation (for example, where young and old users receive different messages, but not with efficient targeting).

Another critical mistake is to use the same keywords in the subject line over and over, which may work well at first, but eventually bores your subscribers to the point that they don't read your newsletter anymore (unless you've found a way to beat churn, maybe by hiring a growth hacker). The problem is compounded if your competitors use exactly the same keywords.

A rich variety of non-hype keywords works well with an analytic, highly educated, spam-averse audience. For example, a subject line such as *Weekly digest, July 29* (with a lowercase *d* in *digest*) works better than *25 Fantastic Articles From Top Big Data Gurus* (with an uppercase *F* in *From*). Sure, the latter will work well maybe two times, but eventually it stops working. In addition, the content of your newsletter must match the subject line; otherwise you will lose subscribers faster than you can acquire new ones.

This contrarian approach is based on Seduction 101 rather than Analytics 101 — that is, guessing what the users like to read today rather than designing content based on historical performance. Maybe it can be automated and turned into analytic rules — for example, by detecting how many times you can use hype, how long a great keyword such as "belly dancing analytics" will work, and so on. Overusing the tricks detected through analytics eventually kills seduction, as well as sales in the process. But for now, many online marketers still seem to ignore these rules. Seduction can provide a bigger lever than analytics (although they should be blended together), especially when building a business for the long term.

Scenario 6: About Hidden Data

In this scenario, your data is like Gruyere cheese. It has holes. Big holes. Sometimes the empty space occupies a bigger volume than the data itself — just like dark matter is more abundant than visible matter in the universe. This example is not about shallow or sparse data, but instead about data that you do not see, that you do not even know exists, yet contains better actionable nuggets than anything in your data warehouse.

Following are three cases of "Gruyere data," along with the remedy for each case.

Missing or Incomplete Data

This is the easiest problem to fix. Any talented data scientist can work around this issue using modern, unbiased imputation techniques. Most analytic software also includes mechanisms to handle missing data.

Censored Data

By censored, I mean censored from a statistical point of view. Here's an example that comes to mind: You want to estimate the proportion of all guns involved in a crime at least once during their lifetime. The data set that you use (gun or crime statistics) is censored, in the sense that a brand new gun has not killed someone today but might be used in a shooting next week. Also, some criminals get rid of their gun, and it might not be traceable after the crime.

How do you deal with this issue? Again, any talented data scientist will easily handle this problem using a statistical distribution (typically exponential) to measure time-to-crime, and estimate its mean based on censored data, using correct statistical techniques. Problem solved.

Hidden Data

Dealing with hidden data is a big issue. First, you don't even know it exists because it is invisible, at least from your vantage point. Domain expertise and statistical knowledge (rules of thumb more than technical knowledge) help you become aware of potential hidden data. Indeed, the data might not exist at all, in which case you have to assemble the data first.

Consider this example: Let's say Target is trying to optimize its revenue numbers. It analyzes its sales data to see when garden items sell best. It has no data about selling garden stuff in February — the company headquarters are in Minnesota, and anyone suggesting such an idea might be fired on the spot, or suspected of being on drugs. Yet in California, Target's competitors are all selling garden stuff in February, leaving next to nothing for Target, in terms of sales, when June comes around. Target, unaware of the cause, thinks there's not much money to be made on garden items in California.

How do you address this issue? Even though Target may lack data for garden sales in February, you could look at competitor data (for instance, scanning and analyzing the millions of pieces of junk mail sent every day) as a good first step in the right direction. But the real solution is to hire a *visionary data scientist*. Talented data scientists leverage data that everybody sees; *visionary data scientists* leverage data that nobody sees.

Scenario 7: High Crime Rates Caused by Gasoline Lead. Really?

Here is a typical example of a study you may read in respected news outlets, yet the analytics used to support the author's opinion are poor. Crime rates in big cities (where gasoline use is high) peaked about 20 years after lead was banned from gasoline, according to an econometric study by Rick Nevin. The 20-year time lag is the time elapsed between lead exposure at birth and turning into a 20-year-old criminal. At least that's the argument proposed by some well-known econometricians, based on crime-rate analysis over time in large cities. This is another example of a study done without proper experimental design.

So how would you design a better study? You could get a well-balanced sample of 10,000 people over a 30-year period across all cities of a certain size, split the sample into two subsets (criminals versus non-criminals), and check (using an odds ratio) whether criminals are more likely to have been exposed to lead at birth than non-criminals. In short, do the opposite of the original study and look at individuals rather than cities — that is, look at the micro rather than macro level — and perform a classic test of the hypothesis using standard sampling and proper design of experiment procedures.

Alternatively, if you really want to work on the original macro-level time series (assuming you have monthly granularity), then perform a *Granger causality test*, which takes into account all cross-correlation residuals after transforming the original time series into white noise (similar to spectral analysis of time series, or correlogram analysis). However, if you have thousands of metrics (and thus thousands of time series and multi-million correlations), you will eventually find a very high correlation that is purely accidental. This is known as the "curse" of big data, described in detail in the next chapter.

Correlation is not causation. Don't claim causation unless you can prove it. Many times, multiple inter-dependent factors contribute to a problem. Maybe the peak in crime occurred when baby boomers (a less law-abiding generation) reached the age of 20. This may be a more credible cause.

Scenario 8: Boeing Dreamliner Problems

The new Dreamliner plane from Boeing was grounded by the FAA for a few months shortly after its launch due to problems related to its batteries. The main problem was a new type of lithium-ion battery that had never been used in a plane before. This type of powerful battery easily overheats and catches fire, which resulted in a number of emergency landings over a short period of time.

The root cause was the lack of good experimental design by the vendor that designed the batteries. It was a quality control issue, and quality control relies heavily on analytics. The following questions support the fact that better quality control and experimental design could address problems like this one:

- Aren't these batteries (like pretty much any product that you can purchase, such as a car or laptop battery) going through extensive quality control testing, using sound statistical techniques to make sure that faulty batteries, or risk of failure over the lifetime of the product, is below an acceptable threshold?

- Could it be that the quality control tests were not performed according to best practices?

- Were the overheating simulations representative of real-world conditions as found in an airplane taking off?

- Did they not "stress" the battery for long enough?

- Are standards for quality control lower in Japan, which is where the battery was designed and produced?

- Were the statistical reports about the reliability of these batteries incorrect?

A possible solution is the use of better mechanisms to cool this type of battery, which had never been used in an airplane before but is found in all cell phones and was responsible for some spectacular cell phone fires in the past. Unlike in a cell phone or a laptop, it seems easy to cool (and even freeze) anything in a plane because the outside temperature is well below the freezing point.

Scenario 9: Seven Tricky Sentences for NLP

NLP means *Natural Language Processing*. The kind of problems that a data scientist faces when analyzing unstructured data, such as *raw* (uncategorized) *text*, is illustrated here. This type of analysis is known as *text mining*.

CROSS-REFERENCE Chapter 2 discusses how to create a structure (typically a taxonomy) on unstructured data.

Following are seven types of language patterns that are difficult to analyze with automated algorithms:

- "A land of milk and honey" becomes "A land of Milken Honey" (algorithm trained on *The Wall Street Journal* from the 1980s, where Michael Milken was mentioned much more than milk).

- "She threw up her dinner" versus "She threw up her hands."

- "I ate a tomato with salt" versus "I ate a tomato with my mother" or "I ate a tomato with a fork."

- Words ending with "ing" — for instance, "They were entertaining people."

- "He washed and dried the dishes," versus "He drank and smoked cigars" (in the latter case he did not drink the cigars).

- "The lamb was ready to eat" versus "Was the lamb hungry and wanting some grass?"

- Words with multiple meanings, such as "bay" to refer to a color, type of window, or body of water.

In these examples, as well as in sentiment analysis, the data scientist is trying to guess the user intention in order to correctly interpret the data and provide the right type of answer or decision. For instance, this could happen in the following situations:

- When analyzing Google search data, which relevant ads should you display based on the user query?

- When analyzing comments posted on a Facebook page about a product or company, how do you assess whether they are positive or negative?

- When analyzing Facebook posts, how do you decide if a post should be automatically deleted because it violates Facebook policies or some laws?

Using proxy metrics based on user profiles (if available), or web pages and e-mail where the content is found, can help resolve ambiguities, especially if the web pages are already categorized.

Scenario 10: Data Scientists Dictate What We Eat?

There are many factors that influence what the average American eats, but the biggest factor is the margin the grocery store makes on the products it sells. This explains why you can't get red currants or passion fruit anymore, but you can find plenty of high-energy drinks and foods rich in sugar. Of course, there's a feedback loop: Americans like sweet stuff, so many companies produce sweet food, and due to large-scale processing it's cheap, can be priced efficiently by grocery stores, and sells well.

Here's how a supermarket could increase revenue with better analytics. Behind all of this is data science, which helps answer the following questions:

- Which new products should be tested for customer interest and return on investement (ROI)? Red currant pie? Orange wine? French-style cherry pie? Wild boar meat? Purple cheese? Red eggs? Cheese shaped like a ball? (Although anything that is not shaped like a parallel-piped rectangle is suboptimal from a storage point of view, but that's another data science issue.)

- How do you determine success or failure for a new product? How do you test a new product (experimental-design issue)?

- Which products should be eliminated? (Passion fruit, passionfruit juice, and authentic Italian salamis are no longer sold in most grocery store in the United States.)

- How do you measure lift (increased revenue)? Do you factor in costs of marketing and other expenses?

- How do you price an item?

- How do you cross-sell?

- How do you optimize ROI on marketing campaigns?

- When and where do you sell each product (seasonal and local trends)?

- How do you improve inventory forecasting?

The last time I went to a grocery store, I wanted to buy full-fat unsweetened yogurt. It took me 10 minutes to find the only container left in the store (the brand was Dannon). I was ready to pay more to get that particular yogurt (a product that has been consumed worldwide by billions of people over several millennia) rather than the two alternatives: low fat, or plain but sweetened. (Ironically, the "low fat" version had 180 calories per serving, whereas the old-fashioned plain yogurt had 150. This is because they add corn starch to the low-fat product.)

Over time, I've seen the number of grocery product offerings shrink. More old products are eliminated than new products are introduced. Clearly the products eliminated are those with a smaller market, such as passion fruit. But could data science do a better job helping grocery retailers decide what goes on the shelves, when and where, in what proportions, and at what price?

The answer is yes. A good solution would be the use of more granular segmentation with lower variance in forecasted sales and revenue (per product) due to use of models with higher predictive power. In the case of the yogurt, while a broad spectrum of people try to avoid fat, there are plenty of thin people on the west and east coasts who don't mind eating plain yogurt. So it could make sense to sell plain yogurt in Seattle or Boston (maybe just a few containers with a high price tag, among dozens of cheaper low-fat brands) but not in Kansas City.

This would also create new opportunities for specialized grocery stores, like PCC Natural Markets in the northwest United States, selling precisely what other supermarkets have stopped selling (as long as it is sellable). In short, selling stuff that generates profit but that other supermarkets have written off.

This example also shows how communication skills are important for data scientists: to propose a new approach and convince senior management that there is a way to simultaneously optimize profit and bring long-term value to the customers. Of course, such an approach would be a long-term strategic investment, and the supermarket may not able to meet the financial numbers in the short term (which is something the CEO will need to address with shareholders).

Scenario 11: Increasing Amazon.com Sales with Better Relevancy

How could Amazon.com increase sales by redefining relevancy? Answer: By improving its search and relevancy engines to include item price as a main factor. The type of optimization and ROI boosting described here applies to all digital catalogs, although we are focusing on books in this discussion.

Search Engine

When you perform a keyword search on Amazon.com in the book section, it returns a search result page with, say, 10 suggested books matching your keywords. This task is performed by the search engine. The search engine displays the books in some type of order. The order is based either on price or keyword proximity.

Relevancy Engine

If you search for a specific book title, Amazon.com also displays other books that you might be interested in based on historical sales from other users. This task is performed by the relevancy engine.

TECHNICAL NOTE

The relevancy engine works like this: if m(A,B) users both purchased book A (the book you want to purchase) and another book B over the last 30 days, and if k(A) users purchased A, and k(B) users purchased B, then the association between A and B (that is, how closely these books are related from a cross-selling point of view) is defined as R(A,B) = m(A,B) / SQRT{k(A) * k(B)}. The order in which the suggested books are displayed is entirely determined by the function R(A,*).

Better Sorting Criteria

Expensive books generate very few sales, but each sale generates huge profit. Cheap books generate little money, but the sales volume more than compensates for the little profit per book. In short, if you show books that all have exactly the same relevancy score to the user, the book that you should show in the #1 position is the book with the optimum price with regard to total expected revenue. Figure 1-1 shows a hypothetical optimum book price of $21.

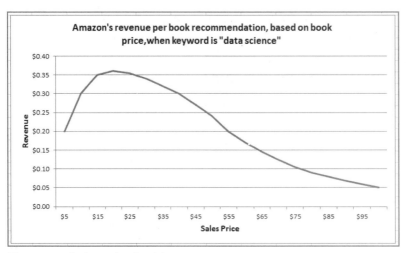

Figure 1-1: Optimum book pricing

This chart is based on simulated numbers, assuming that the chance for a sale is an exponentially decreasing function of the book price. That is:

$$P(sale \mid price) = a * exp(-b*price)$$

A more general model would be:

$$P(sale \mid price, relevancy\ score) = a * exp(-b*price) * f(relevancy\ score)$$

Another way to further increase revenue is to include user data in the formula. Some users have no problem purchasing an expensive book. Users who traditionally buy more expensive books should be shown more expensive books in their search results.

Putting It All Together

When a sale takes place, how do you know if it is because of showing rightly priced books at the top, or because of perfect relevancy? For instance, relevancy between "data science" and "big data" is good, but relevancy between "data science" and "cloud computing" is not as good. Does it make sense to suggest an expensive "cloud computing" book to a wealthy user interested in a "data science" book, or is it better to suggest a less expensive book related to "big data" if your goal is to maximize profit? It also depends on how you define revenue optimization: is it long term (then relevancy is more important) or short term? Usually it's a blend of short term and long term. As you can see, separating the influence of relevancy from the price factor is not easy.

The price factor is particularly useful when keyword or category relevancy is based on "small data," which is a specialized user query or a book with little volume. Also, detecting what causes a specific conversion or sale is a complex problem, known as *attribution*. In sophisticated settings, macro-economic (long-term, aggregate) indicators are used in the context of *marketing mix optimization*, and are blended with highly granular real-time attribution metrics. Price is also analyzed using *price elasticity models* and *efficiency curves.*

Another area of interest is customized pricing, where the price of a book is determined in real time, based on the user, sales history of the user (if available), the website where the book is sold (based on website demographics), and the book itself. Some studies suggest that a fixed price works best, as savvy users would try to purchase the same item multiple times until they are offered a price as low as possible (though they have no way to know when the minimum price is offered). Yet, selling at a higher price to users who don't mind purchasing expensive books (based on their sales history), and not recommending a book the user has already purchased, are low-hanging fruits for ROI improvement. However, such pricing strategies have been banned in some countries, and are controversial elsewhere. Using price customization, especially if secretly carried out without user consent and knowledge, via unethical data mining practices and privacy violations, could cost you the trust of your users, and eventually result in churn, lawsuits, and revenue drop. Eventually, users will notice that prices are customized.

Another way to maximize Amazon.com's profit would be to print books *on demand* rather than managing an inventory and having to forecast sales for each book and each month. Data science also helps determine where warehouses should be located to optimize delivery (in terms of speed and cost), as well as sales tax optimization to better compete with other booksellers.

Scenario 12: Detecting Fake Profiles or Likes on Facebook

Some websites sell fake Twitter followers ($10 for 1,000 followers), fake Facebook accounts, or even fake Yahoo! mail accounts to help spread spam or make the person or retailer appear more popular than it really is, supposedly to boost sales. They tell the buyer up front that these followers are fakes. They also sell Facebook Likes, though they claim that they are from "real" Facebook profiles.

The easiest way to automatically detect fake Likes is by looking at the number of relevant comments: if a Facebook (or any) post has 5,000 Likes and either no comments or 20 comments that are just variations of "this is a great post," then you can bet the Likes and comments are mass-produced by a robot or an army of zombies — they are fake.

Data science algorithms that rely on such metrics as well as on social graphs, velocity, and recency in account creation and postings, natural language processing, and Botnet/fraud detection rules, are used to handling this type of problem. Some fakes can be detected in real time, while some can be detected and eliminated later, such as after ad hoc analyses (reactive analytics performed by data analysts, after the fact) or automatically by end-of-day algorithms (prescriptive analytics).

Scenario 13: Analytics for Restaurants

Analytics can take various forms for small businesses, and restaurants in particular. Some of the problems these businesses need to solve include pricing optimization, inventory management, sales forecasting, access to competitor information and what your clients say about you (you need to regularly check restaurant reviews with some automated software), space optimization (how many tables you can squeeze in), wine and cheese selection, frequency in menu changes, hours and days when should you open and close, number of dishes that you offer, and how you keep your chef (including deciding on optimum salary.)

Possibly one of the easiest problems to solve is the table layout. The optimum solution consists of having your two-seat tables stacked against the wall, and your four-seat tables in the center of the room. Should these tables be round or square, parallel to the wall, or forming a 45-degree angle? It's easy to find a mathematical solution, or at least do some simulations to find out what works best. Square tables are better than round ones, and they allow you to easily combine them to accommodate larger parties. If you increase seating capacity by 20 percent, then your profit should also increase by 20 percent, assuming that you are always fully booked and profitable.

Data Science History, Pioneers, and Modern Trends

As data science has grown, other related professions have seen a decline, such as statistics and computer science. Publicly available data from Google (see `http://bit.ly/1aF8D5T`) shows the following:

- An increase in the number of data analysts since 2010
- A decline in the number of statisticians since 2005
- A decline in the number of computer scientists since 2005
- An explosion in the number of data scientists since 2012

You can find other public data on LinkedIn (number of applicants per job ad) or Indeed, but they tend to be job-market related.

Other similar data show that all traditional fields are declining: six sigma, data mining, statistics, and operations research. Big data started to emerge and grow exponentially around 2011, according to Google, and by 2013 was more popular than data mining or six sigma. Even though the rise of big data is dramatic, the explosion of searches for the keyword *analytics* is even more spectacular and started in 2006, according to the same source. It tapered off in 2012 at a level six times higher than *big data*.

Of course, many professionals (including me) who, in the year 2000, were doing statistics, operations research, computer science, six sigma, actuarial science, biostatistics, or some other narrowly defined analytic activity, have gained experience, leadership, broader knowledge, business acumen, and expertise spanning many fields. Thus they changed their job titles, but they all share something in common: analytics. At the same time, the growth of data and modern data architecture, such as MapReduce, hitting all disciplines has acted as a common denominator and cement for many related professions.

NOTE *Data scientist* is broader than *data miner*, and encompasses data integration, data gathering, data visualization (including dashboards), and data architecture. *Data scientist* also measures ROI on data science activities.

Statistics Will Experience a Renaissance

A lot has been said about the death of statistics, some of it by leading statisticians themselves. I believe statistical science will eventually come back, but it will be more applied, adapted to big data, and less model-driven. It will be integrated with computer science, predictive modeling, data mining, machine learning, some aspects of operations research and six sigma, and database architecture, under a big umbrella called data science, business analytics, decision science, data intelligence, analytics, or some other term yet to be created or reused. We are currently in the middle of this analytics revolution.

In particular, guys like me, although having a new job title — data scientist — still do statistics part-time, and even theoretical cutting edge statistics at times. In my case, I am reviving a quarter of a century-old but robust technique that was deemed too complicated in 1750 due to lack of computing power, and was abandoned. The lack of computing power in 1750 resulted in new, mathematically friendly techniques developed around 1800, with simple formulas such as least square regression. This framework has survived to this day and could be the cause of the current decline of traditional statisticians because robustness is more important than ever with big data, and computational complexity is no longer an issue when gigabytes of data can be processed in a few minutes on distributed systems (in the cloud with MapReduce). Also, most modern scientists, geographers, physicians, econometricians, operations research professionals, engineers, and so on have a decent, applied statistical knowledge. However, software engineers and computer scientists sometimes ignore or misuse statistical science, sometimes as badly as journalists, with bad consequences such as development of systems (for example, recommendation engines) with large numbers of undetected fake reviews and fraud. Eventually, statistical science will start pouring into these communities.

Some people say that most data analysts are statisticians. In my opinion, data analyst is a junior title, typically a person with a BS or BA degree. Statisticians have a more theoretical background, are trained to use models developed before the advent of big data, and have an MS or PhD degree. People spending their days writing SQL queries and reports are data analysts.

Part of the reason I moved away from being called a statistician is because of the American Statistical Association: it changed the meaning of the keyword *statistician*, as well as limited career prospects for future statisticians by making it almost narrowly and exclusively associated with the pharmaceutical industry, government (surveys, census, politics), and small data (from where most of its revenue derives). The Association has generally stayed outside the new statistical revolution that has come along with big data over the last 15 years. As a Belgian citizen, I can say the same about the Belgian Statistical Association. So this trend is not limited to the United States, and it is not limited to the (American) English language, but also includes the French and Dutch languages, among others.

Statisticians should be very familiar with computer science, big data, and software — 10 billion rows with 10,000 variables should not scare a true statistician. On the cloud (or even on a laptop as streaming data), this amount of data gets processed quickly. The first step is data reduction, but even if you must keep all observations and variables, it's still processable. A good computer scientist also produces confidence intervals: you don't need to be a statistician for that, just use the First Analyticbridge Theorem discussed later in this book. The distinction between computer scientist and statistician is getting thinner and fuzzier. No worries, though — the things you did not learn in school (in statistical classes), you can still learn online.

History and Pioneers

Now let's look at the history of data science and companies who were pioneers in analytics and data science. First, take a look at popular keywords used since the late 1980s, and one prediction for 2022:

- 1988: artificial intelligence. Also: computational statistics, data analysis, pattern recognition, and rule systems.

- 1995: web analytics. Also: machine learning, business intelligence, data mining, ROI, distributed architecture, data architecture, quant, decision science, knowledge management, and information science.

- 2003: business analytics. Also: text mining, unstructured data, semantic web, Natural Language Processing (NLP), Key Performance Indicator (KPI), predictive modeling, cloud computing, lift, yield, NoSQL, Business Intelligence (BI), real-time analytics, collaborative filtering, recommendation engines, and mobile analytics.

- 2012: data science. Also: big data, analytics, software as a service (SaaS), on-demand analytics, digital analytics, Hadoop, NewSQL, in-memory analytics, machine-to-machine, sensor data, healthcare analytics, utilities analytics, data governance, and in-column databases.

- 2022: data engineering. Also: analytics engineering, data management, data shaping, art of optimization, optimization science, optimization engineering, business optimization, and data intelligence.

Each of these milestones brings us to a more generic, global, comprehensive understanding of leveraging data. Google was one of the first significant contributors to the big data movement, starting around 1995. Google solved the database storage capacity limitations associated with traditional distributed systems/ Database Management System (DBMS) systems by introducing the Google file system, MapReduce. (Big tables were often discussed in industry conferences from 2003 to 2006.) Then came HBase and Hadoop Distributed File System (HDFS). In addition to Google, Yahoo!, and Facebook have also made significant contributions in the Hadoop and open source community that drives technology advancement.

Regarding the pioneering companies in the purely analytic sphere, consider the following 26 and their respective Wikipedia pages where you can learn a lot of interesting history. (Warning: Some of these web pages, as on any Wikipedia topic, contain commercial content promoted by people with conflicts of interest, insiders, or people with interests in the companies in question).

- Datawatch (http://en.wikipedia.org/wiki/Monarch)
- Excel (http://en.wikipedia.org/wiki/Microsoft_Excel)
- FICO (http://en.wikipedia.org/wiki/FICO)
- Greenplum (http://en.wikipedia.org/wiki/Greenplum)
- IMSL (http://en.wikipedia.org/wiki/IMSL_Numerical_Libraries)
- Informatica (http://en.wikipedia.org/wiki/Informatica)
- KNIME (http://en.wikipedia.org/wiki/KNIME)
- KXEN (http://en.wikipedia.org/wiki/KXEN_Inc.)
- Lavastorm (http://en.wikipedia.org/wiki/Lavastorm)
- MapReduce (http://en.wikipedia.org/wiki/MapReduce)
- Mathematica (http://en.wikipedia.org/wiki/Mathematica)
- Matlab (http://en.wikipedia.org/wiki/Matlab)
- Netezza (http://en.wikipedia.org/wiki/Netezza)
- NoSQL (http://en.wikipedia.org/wiki/NoSQL)
- Oracle (http://en.wikipedia.org/wiki/Oracle_Database)
- PMML (http://en.wikipedia.org/wiki/Predictive_Model_Markup_Language)
- R programming language (http://en.wikipedia.org/wiki/R_)
- RapidMiner (http://en.wikipedia.org/wiki/RapidMiner)
- S-PLUS (TIBCO) (http://en.wikipedia.org/wiki/S-PLUS)

- SAS (http://en.wikipedia.org/wiki/SAS_Institute)

- Splunk (http://en.wikipedia.org/wiki/Splunk)

- SPSS (http://en.wikipedia.org/wiki/SPSS)

- Statistica (http://en.wikipedia.org/wiki/STATISTICA)

- Sybase (http://en.wikipedia.org/wiki/Sybase)

- Tableau (http://en.wikipedia.org/wiki/Tableau_Software)

- Teradata (http://en.wikipedia.org/wiki/Teradata)

This list focuses on large analytics companies that have been around for some time. Countless others have sprung up in the last few years, especially around the MapReduce ecosystem.

CROSS-REFERENCE More information about the big data ecosystem is found in Chapter 2.

Modern Trends

In terms of new technology, much about what is going on today revolves around integrating analytics in big distributed databases. It is about having the data architect or engineer and the data scientist communicate with each other, moving away from the old dichotomy — data-to-analytics (the traditional data science approach) versus analytics-to-data (the more modern approached favored by data architects and database companies because it is faster). Analytics-to-data means performing the analytics inside or close to where the database or data environment resides, rather than downloading data locally and then processing it. This eliminates a lot of redundant downloads by multiple database users. Read the last section in this chapter for more details.

This, of course, boils down to building the right advanced analytics tools (not just the Extract, Transform, Load (ETL) aspects) in or close to where the database resides. When analytics is inside the database, it is sometimes called in-memory analytics. It is a stronger form of analytics-to-data in which analytics is integrated and embedded into the database architecture and takes place mostly in fast memory (RAM), sometimes using multiple servers. One of the issues is that modern database processing involves more complex programming languages, and right now most people are still using SQL. It is hard to change an old habit. So pioneering companies such as Pivotal have come up with a system called Fast SQL, where programmers accustomed to SQL don't need to learn a new more complicated language, and where the code is optimized to run under Hadoop (a distributed architecture).

Other modern trends include automated machine-to-machine communications in real time, such as in high-frequency trading strategies or massive bidding systems. An example of this is eBay updating keyword bids for 10 million keywords on Google pay-per-click campaigns, every day and in real time, based on keywords' past performance (when history is available) or analytic scoring for new keywords with no history. Some of these machine-to-machine communications are done via APIs or AaaS (on-demand analytics as a service). An API call is nothing more than an HTTP request (actually, an HTTPS request most of the time), with parameters (key/value pairs encoded in XML format) in the query string used to specify the type of services needed (such as keyword price and volume forecasts).

Also, what makes modern data different and unique is its variety (sometimes coming in unstructured format from Twitter tweets, well structured from mobile devices, or from sensors), its velocity, and its volume, which makes traditional statistical analyses not always suitable.

To summarize, these are the characteristics of the modern trends in data science:

- In-memory analytics
- MapReduce and Hadoop
- NoSQL, NewSQL, and graph databases
- Python and R
- Data integration: blending unstructured and structured data (such as data storage and security, privacy issues when collecting data, and data compliance)
- Visualization
- Analytics as a Service, abbreviated as AaaS
- Text categorization/tagging and taxonomies to facilitate extraction of insights from raw text and to put some structure on unstructured data

A final word about Perl: This great programming language, still popular five years ago, is a casualty of modern programming environments. It has been replaced by Python and its analytical and graphical libraries. Although very flexible, allowing you to code without concentrating on the code, Perl programs were very hard and costly to maintain. Perl did not survive in modern agile and lean environments. Some have said that Excel — the most popular analytic tool — would also die. I don't think so. Modern versions of Excel use the cloud, and retrieve data from the Internet and store it in cubes.

Recent Q&A Discussions

I recently had the following discussions with a number of data architects, in different communities — in particular with (but not limited to) the The Data Warehousing Institute (TDWI) group on LinkedIn. They show some of the challenges that still need to be addressed before this new analytics revolution is complete. Following are several questions asked by data architects and database administrators, and my answers. The discussion is about optimizing joins in SQL queries, or just moving away from SQL altogether. Several modern databases now offer many of the features discussed here, including hash table joins and fine-tuning of the query optimizer by end users. The discussion illustrates the conflicts between data scientists, data architects, and business analysts. It also touches on many innovative concepts.

Question: You say that one of the bottlenecks with SQL is users writing queries with (say) three joins, when these queries could be split into two queries each with two joins. Can you elaborate?

Answer: Typically, the way I write SQL code is to embed it into a programming language such as Python, and store all lookup tables that I need as hash tables in memory. So I rarely have to do a join, and when I do, it's just two tables at most.

In some (rare) cases in which lookup tables were too big to fit in memory, I used sampling methods and worked with subsets and aggregation rules. A typical example is when a field in your data set (web log files) is a user agent (browser, abbreviated as UA). You have more unique UAs than can fit in memory, but as long as you keep the 10 million most popular, and aggregate the 200 million rare UAs into a few million categories (based on UA string), you get good results in most applications.

Being an algorithm expert (not an SQL expert), it takes me a couple minutes to do an efficient four-table join via hash tables in Python (using my own script templates). Most of what I do is advanced analytics, not database aggregation: advanced algorithms, but simple to code in Python, such as hidden decision trees. Anyway, my point here is more about non-expert SQL users such as business analysts: is it easier or more effective to train them to write better SQL code including sophisticated joins, or to train them to learn Python and blend it with SQL code?

To be more specific, what I have in mind is a system where you have to download the lookup tables not very often (maybe once a week) and access the main (fact) table more frequently. If you must reupload the lookup tables very frequently, then the Python approach loses its efficiency, and you make your colleagues unhappy because of your frequent downloads that slow down the whole system.

Question: People like you (running Python or Perl scripts to access databases) are a Database Administrator's (DBA) worst nightmare. Don't you think you are a source of problems for DBAs?

Answer: Because I'm much better at Python and Perl than SQL, my Python or Perl code is bug-free, easy-to-read, easy-to-maintain, optimized, robust, and reusable. If I coded everything in SQL, it would be much less efficient. Most of what I do is algorithms and analytics (machine learning stuff), not querying databases. I only occasionally download lookup tables onto my local machine (saved as hash tables and stored as text files), since most don't change that much from week to week. When I need to update them, I just extract the new rows that have been added since my last update (based on timestamp). And I do some tests before running an intensive SQL script to get an idea of how much time and resources it will consume, and to see whether I can do better. I am an SQL user, just like any statistician or business analyst, not an SQL developer.

But I agree we need to find a balance to minimize data transfers and processes, possibly by having better analytic tools available where the data resides. At a minimum, we need the ability to easily deploy Python code there in non-production tables and systems, and be allocated a decent amount of disk space (maybe 200 GB) and memory (at least several GB).

Question: What are your coding preferences?

Answer: Some people feel more comfortable using a scripting language rather than SQL. SQL can be perceived as less flexible and prone to errors, producing wrong output without anyone noticing due to a bug in the joins.

You can write simple Perl code, which is easy to read and maintain. Perl enables you to focus on the algorithms rather than the code and syntax. Unfortunately, many Perl programmers write obscure code, which creates a bad reputation for Perl (code maintenance and portability). But this does not have to be the case.

You can break down a complex join into several smaller joins using multiple SQL statements and views. You would assume that the database engine would digest your not-so-efficient SQL code and turn it into something much more efficient. At least you can test this approach and see if it works as fast as one single complex query with many joins. Breaking down multiple joins into several simple statements allows business analysts to write simple SQL code, which is easy for fellow programmers to reuse or maintain.

It would be interesting to see some software that automatically corrects SQL syntax errors (not SQL logical errors). It would save lots of time for many non-expert SQL coders like me, as the same typos that typically occur over and over could be automatically fixed. In the meanwhile, you can use GUIs to produce decent SQL code, using tools provided by most database vendors or open source, such as Toad for Oracle.

Question: Why do you claim that these built-in SQL optimizers are usually black-box technology for end users? Do you think parameters can't be fine-tuned by the end user?

Answer: I always like to have a bit of control over what I do, though not necessarily a whole lot. For instance, I'm satisfied with the way Perl handles hash tables and memory allocation. I'd rather use the Perl black-box memory allocation/hash table management system than create it myself from scratch in C or, even worse, write a compiler. I'm just a bit worried with black-box optimization — I've seen the damage created by non-expert users who recklessly used black-box statistical software. I'd feel more comfortable if I had at least a bit of control, even as simple as sending an email to the DBA, having her look at my concern or issue, and having her help improve my queries, maybe fine-tuning the optimizer, if deemed necessary and beneficial for the organization and to other users.

Question: Don't you think your approach is 20 years old?

Answer: The results are more important than the approach, as long as the process is reproducible. If I can beat my competitors (or help my clients do so) with whatever tools I use, as one would say, "if it ain't broke, don't fix it." Sometimes I use APIs (for example, Google APIs), sometimes I use external data collected with a web crawler, sometimes Excel or cubes are good enough, and sometimes vision combined with analytic acumen and intuition (without using any data) works well. Sometimes I use statistical models, and other times a very modern architecture is needed. Many times, I use a combination of many of these.

CROSS-REFERENCE I have several examples of "light analytics" doing better than sophisticated architectures, including a few in the context of email marketing optimization and stock trading. These are discussed in Chapter 6.

Question: Why did you ask whether your data-to-analytic approach makes sense?

Answer: The reason I asked the question is because something has been bothering me, based on not-so-old observations (three to four years old) in which the practices that I mention are well entrenched in the analytic community (by analytic, I mean machine learning, statistics, and data mining, not ETL). It is also an attempt to see if it's possible to build a better bridge between two very different communities: data scientists and data architects. Database builders often (but not always) need the data scientist to bring insights and value out of organized data. And the data scientists often (but not always) need the data architect to build great, fast, efficient data processing systems so they can better focus on analytics.

Question: So you are essentially maintaining a cache system with regular, small updates to a local copy of the lookup tables. Two users like you doing the same thing would end up with two different copies after some time. How do you handle that?

Answer: You are correct that two users having two different copies (cache) of lookup tables causes problems. Although in my case, I tend to share my cache with other people, so it's not like five people working on five different versions of the lookup tables. Although I am a senior data scientist, I am also a designer/architect, but not a DB designer/architect, so I tend to have my own local architecture that I share with a team. Sometimes my architecture is stored in a local small DB and occasionally on the production databases, but many times as organized flat files or hash tables stored on local drives, or somewhere in the cloud outside the DB servers, though usually not very far if the data is big. Many times, my important "tables" are summarized extracts — either simple aggregates that are easy to produce with pure SQL, or sophisticated ones such as transaction scores (by client, day, merchant, or more granular) produced by algorithms too complex to be efficiently coded in SQL.

The benefit of my "caching" system is to minimize time-consuming data transfers that penalize everybody in the system. The drawback is that I need to maintain it, and essentially, I am replicating a process already in place in the database system itself.

Finally, for a statistician working on data that is almost correct (not the most recent version of the lookup table, but rather data stored in this "cache" system and updated rather infrequently), or working on samples, this is not an issue. Usually the collected data is an approximation of a signal we try to capture and measure — it is always messy. The same can be said about predictive models, the ROI extracted from a very decent data set (my "cache"), the exact original, most recent version of the data set, or a version where 5 percent of noise is artificially injected into it — it is pretty much the same in most circumstances.

Question: Can you comment on code maintenance and readability?

Answer: Consider the issue of code maintenance when someone writing obscure SQL leaves the company — or worse, when SQL is ported to a different environment (not SQL) — and it's a nightmare for the new programmers to understand the original code. If easy-to-read SQL (maybe with more statements, fewer elaborate high-dimensional joins) runs just as fast as one complex statement because of the internal user-transparent query optimizer, why not use the easy-to-read code instead? After all, the optimizer is supposed to make both approaches equivalent, right? In other words, if two pieces of code (one short and obscure; one longer and easy to read, maintain, and port) have the same efficiency because they are essentially turned into the same pseudocode by the optimizer, I would favor the longer version that takes less time to write, debug, maintain, and so on.

There might be a market for a product that turns ugly, obscure, yet efficient code into nice, easy-to-read SQL — an "SQL beautifier." It would be useful when migrating code to a different platform. Although this already exists to some extent, you can easily visualize any query or sets of queries in all DB systems with diagrams. The SQL beautifier would be in some ways similar to a program that translates Assembler into C++ — in short, a reverse compiler or interpreter.

Summary

This chapter began with a discussion of what data science *is not*, including how traditional degrees will have to adapt as business and government evolve. The changes necessary involve new ways of processing data, as well as new types of data, including big, unstructured, and high velocity streaming data, sometimes generated by sensors or transaction data.

Then a number of real-life scenarios were considered where data science can be used, and indeed help, in different ways. Finally, you considered the history of data science, including pioneering companies and modern trends.

Chapter 2 considers what makes data science a new discipline. It illustrates how big data is different from data seen even just 10 years ago, why standard statistical techniques fail when blindly applied to such data, and what the issues are and how they should be investigated and addressed.

Big Data Is Different

In Chapter 1, you considered what data science is and is not, and saw how data science is more than data analysis, computer science, or statistics. This chapter further explores data science as a new discipline.

The chapter begins by considering two of the most important issues associated with big data. Then it works through some real-life examples of big data techniques, and considers some of the communication issues involved in an effective big data team environment. Finally, it considers how statistics is and will be part of data science, and touches on the elements of the big data ecosystem.

Two Big Data Issues

There are two issues associated with big data that must be discussed and understood: the "curse" of big data and rapid data flow. These two issues are discussed in the following sections.

The Curse of Big Data

The "curse" of big data is the danger involved in recklessly applying and scaling data science techniques that have worked well for small, medium, and large data sets, but don't necessarily work well for big data. This problem is well illustrated by the flaws found in big data trading (for which solutions are proposed in this chapter).

In short, the curse of big data is that when you search for patterns in large data sets with billions or trillions of data points and thousands of metrics, you are bound to identify coincidences that have no predictive power. Even worse, the strongest patterns might

- Be caused entirely by chance (like winning the lottery)
- Be non-replicable
- Have no predictive power
- Include obscure weaker patterns that are ignored yet have strong predictive power

So the questions is, how do you discriminate between a real and an accidental signal in vast amounts of data? Let's focus on an example: identifying strong correlations or relationships between time series.

Example

If you have 1,000 metrics (time series), you can compute 499,500 = 1,000 * 999 / 2 correlations. If you include cross-correlations with time lags (for example, stock prices for IBM today with stock prices for Google two days ago), you deal with many millions of correlations. Out of all these correlations, a few will be extremely high just by chance, and if you use such a correlation for predictive modeling, you will lose. Keep in mind that analyzing cross-correlations on all metrics is one of the first steps statisticians take at the beginning of any project — it's part of the exploratory analysis step. However, a spectral analysis of normalized time series (instead of correlation analysis) provides a more robust mechanism to identify true relationships.

To further illustrate this issue, say that you have a k time series, each with n observations for something like price deltas (price increases or decreases) computed for k different stock symbols with various time lags over the same time period consisting of n days. You want to detect patterns such as "When the Google stock price goes up, the Facebook stock price goes down 1 day later." To detect such profitable patterns, you must compute cross-correlations over thousands of stocks with various time lags: one day and/or two days, or maybe one second and/or two seconds, depending on whether you do daily trading or extremely fast, intraday, high frequency trading.

Typically, you use a small number of observations (for example, n = 10 days or n = 10 milliseconds) because these patterns evaporate quickly. (When your competitors detect the patterns in question, those patterns stop becoming profitable.) In other words, you can assume that n = 10 or maybe n = 20. In other cases based on monthly data (environmental statistics and emergence of a new disease), maybe n = 48 for monthly data collected over a two-year time period. In some instances *n* might be much larger, but in that case the curse of big data is no longer a problem. The curse of big data is acute when *n* is smaller than 200 and k is moderately large, say k = 500. However, it is rare to find instances in which both *n* is large (>1,000) and *k* is large (>5,000).

Not all big data involves computing millions of cross-correlations. But the concept described here applies to transactional data in general, or data that is being scored after being binned into billions of (usually small) buckets. Also, big data ranges from 10 GB to petabytes, and involves more than 100 million observations — usually billions of observations per year, or sometimes billions per day or thousands per second. Note that in some cases, big data can be sparse or highly redundant and contain far less information than one might think. This is the case with social network data or streaming videos and, generally speaking, with any data set that can be compressed efficiently.

CROSS-REFERENCE Cross-correlation analysis is one of the first steps (part of the exploratory data analysis) in analyzing big data, along with the creation of a data dictionary. You can read more on data-processing steps in the following sections of this book:

- How to Build a Data Dictionary in Chapter 5
- Life Cycle of Data Science Projects in Chapter 5
- Definitions in Chapter 8

Now let's review a bit of mathematics to estimate the chance of being wrong when detecting a high correlation. You could do Monte Carlo simulations to compute the chance in question, but here you'll use plain old-fashioned statistical modeling.

Consider a new parameter, denoted as *m*, representing the number of paired (bivariate) independent time series selected out of the set of *k* time series at your disposal. You want to compute correlations for these *m* pairs of time series. Here's a theoretical question: assuming you have m independent paired time series, each consisting of *n* numbers generated via a random number generator (an observation being, for example, a simulated normalized stock price at a given time for two different stocks), what are the chances among the m correlation coefficients that at least one is higher than 0.80?

Under this design, the theoretical correlation coefficient (as opposed to the estimated correlation) is 0. To answer the question, assume (without loss of generality) that the time series (after a straightforward normalization) are Gaussian white noise. Then the estimated correlation coefficient, denoted as *r*, is (asymptotically — that is, approximately when *n* is not small) normal, with mean = 0 and variance = $1 / (n-1)$. The probability that r is larger than a given large number *a* (say, a = 0.80, meaning a strong correlation) is p = P(r>a), with P representing a normal distribution with mean = 0 and variance = 1/(n–1). The probability that among the m bivariate (paired) time series at least one has a correlation above a = 0.80 is thus equal to 1–[(1–p)^m] (1–p at power m).

Take the following for instance:

- If n = 20 and m = 10,000 (10,000 paired time series each with 20 observations), then the chance that your conclusion is wrong (that is, a = 0.80) is 90.93 percent.

- If n = 20 and m = 100,000 (still a relatively small value for m), then the chance that your conclusion is *very* wrong (that is, a = 0.90) is 98.17 percent.

Now, in practice it works as follows: You have *k* metrics or variables, each one providing a time series computed at *n* different time intervals. You compute all cross-correlations; that is, m = k*(k–1)/2. However, the assumption of independence between the m paired time series is now violated, thus concentrating correlations further away from a high value such as a = 0.90. Also, your data are not random numbers — it's not white noise. So the theoretical correlations are much higher than absolute 0, maybe approximately 0.15 when n = 20. Further, m will be much higher than, for example, 10,000 or 100,000 even when you have as few as k = 1,000 time series (for example, one time series for each stock price). These three factors (non-independence, theoretical r different from 0, and very large m) balance out and make the preceding computations quite accurate when applied to a typical big data problem. Note that the probabilities p=P(r>a) were computed using the online calculator *stattrek*. This online tool provides an immediate answer — you don't need to run a SAS, Python, or R program to get the number — you can compute that number from your iPad on a plane.

Conclusion

As this problem shows, it is crucial to have the right data scientist working on big data projects such as this one. You do not need to be highly technical, but you must think in a way similar to the preceding argumentation to identify possible causes of model failures before developing a statistical or computer science algorithm. Being a statistician helps, but you don't need to have advanced knowledge of statistics. Being a computer scientist also helps in scaling your algorithms and making them simple and efficient. Being an MBA analyst can help with understanding the problem that needs to be solved. Being all three of these at the same time is even better — and yes, such people do exist and are not that rare.

A real data scientist, faced with processing big data sets, would first know the intuitive fact that if you look at billions of patterns, some will be rare just by chance. The real data scientist will favor robust over standard metrics as outlined here, especially when looking at, comparing, and scoring billions of data bins. He will use simulations to assess whether a pattern is indeed as rare as initially thought, and will use metrics that compare whole distributions (adjusted for size) rather than metrics representing a narrow, single summary, such as mean or correlation, depending on the context.

Finally, fake data scientists can be identified by asking people if they agree with the following three statements. If they answer "yes" to any or all of them, they are not real data scientists:

- Algorithm complexity (the O notation) is more important than time spent in data transfers. (Wrong: With Hadoop and distributed clustered architectures, optimizing data transfer and in-memory usage is often more important than algorithmic complexity.)

- Statistics, computer science, and machine learning cannot be mastered by one person. (Wrong: A data scientist should have good knowledge and some domains of specialization in all these areas.)

- Business expertise is not important. A data set is a data set, no matter the business model. (Wrong: This is tunnel vision. Business models are now far more complex than in the past, and domain expertise is necessary. For example, if you develop a CAPTCHA system but are unaware that spammers have developed systems to bypass your captcha entirely, your captcha system has little if any value.)

TECHNICAL NOTE

Here is an example that illustrates the complex structure of correlations discussed in this section, and the fact that they are not independent of each other. Say you have three random variables X, Y, and Z, with corr(X,Y) = 0.70 and corr(X,Z) = 0.80. What is the minimum value for corr(Y,Z)? Can this correlation be negative?

The answer is 0.13, which is a positive number, as it must be. The proof is based on the fact that the correlation matrix is semi-definite positive and thus its determinant must be > 0 (see `http://bit.ly/1evFjBJ` for details).

When Data Flows Too Fast

A second big data challenge is figuring out what to do when data flows faster and in larger amounts than can be processed. Typically, this challenge presents itself in one of two ways: data that *cannot* be processed using current technology, and data that *can* be processed now but is still difficult to manage due to its size.

Handling Unprocessable Data

In some situations, no matter what processing and what algorithm are used, enormous amounts of data keep piling up so fast that you need to delete some of it (a bigger proportion every day) before you can even look at it.

An example of this is astronomical data used to detect new planets, new asteroids, and so on. The data keep coming faster and in larger amounts than can be processed on the cloud using massive parallelization. Maybe good sampling is a solution — carefully selecting which data to analyze — and which data to ignore before even looking at the data.

Another possibility is to develop better compression algorithms so that one day, when you have more computing power, you can analyze all of the data previously collected, compressed, and stored. Maybe in the year 2030, for example, you'll be able look at the hourly evolution of a far-away supernova that began in 2010 and continued over a period of 20 years but was undetected in 2010 because the data was parked on a sleeping server.

In general, solutions include sampling and/or compression in cases where it makes sense. Data scientists should get familiar with robust sampling techniques, unbalanced samples, and experimental design to design predictive models. Too frequently the approach being used is pure computer science (using the whole data set), due to lack of proper training. Sometimes it is argued that you cannot sample if you compute statistics, such as unique users in a month, for a website. This is because of the lack of statistical knowledge and the fact that an untrained analyst using samples to make such computations is likely to get his numbers wrong. For instance, he might sample 3 days out of 30 (including a Sunday with low traffic), then multiply by 10 to get a total count. The solution works for page views (assuming bias correction is addressed due to weekdays versus weekends), but it does not work for unique users. For unique users, the multiplier must be carefully estimated, and it will be well below 10 unless you only have one-time users.

Sampling has been used extensively on rather big data — for instance, by the census bureau. Compression can take two forms: text or image compression for data rarely accessed, or saving compact statistical summaries (tables) of old data rather than saving the entire data set.

CROSS-REFERENCE See the section Using Big Data Versus Sampling in Chapter 7 for more information on cases where sampling is not feasible.

Processable Yet Difficult Data

This type of situation is when data is coming in fast (sometimes in real time) and in big amounts, yet all of it *can* be processed with modern, fast, distributed,

MapReduce-powered algorithms or other techniques. The problem that presents itself is that the data are so vast, the velocity so high, and sometimes the data so unstructured that it can be processed only by crude algorithms, which typically result in bad side effects. Or at least that's what your CEO thinks. How do you handle this type of situation?

Let's focus on a few examples, particularly ones that relate to the CEO's perception of the problem, which is the most relevant to businesses. Consider the following data situations:

- Credit card transaction scoring in real time
- Spam detection
- Pricing/discount optimization in real time (retail)
- Antimissile technology (numerical optimization issue)
- High-frequency trading
- Systems relying on real-time 3-D streaming data (video and sound) such as autopilot (large planes flying on autopilot at low elevation in overcrowded urban skies)
- Facebook Likes, Twitter tweets, Yelp reviews, matching content with user (Google), and so on

Using crude algorithms on data sets such as these could result in the following:

- Too many false positives or false negatives and undetected fake reviews. For example, fake Tweets could result in stock market repercussions, or fake press releases about the White House being attacked could cause a nationwide panic, yet these fake Tweets may fail to be detected in real time by Twitter. This could be addressed with appropriate data governance policies, as well as by the website companies themselves. (http://www.vancouversun.com/technology/personal-tech/Yelp+sues+ North+Vancouver+reviewer+bogus+reviews/8958494/story.html.) Google is doing the same — punishing black hat search-engine optimization (SEO) and improving their algorithms at the same time.
- Billions of undetected fake Likes on Facebook, creating confusion for advertisers, and eventually a decline in ad spending. It also has a bad impact on users who eventually ignore the Likes, further reducing an already low click-through rate and lowering revenue. Facebook would have to come up with some new feature to replace the Likes, and the new feature would eventually be abused again, with the abuse not detected by machine learning algorithms or other means, perpetuating a cycle of microbubbles that must be permanently kept alive with new ideas to maintain revenue streams.

By crude algorithms, I mean Naive Bayes classifiers or algorithms that are too sensitive to outliers, such as huge decision trees or linear regressions on nonlinear (skewed) data. More sophisticated algorithms include a blending of multiple classifiers, or using resampling such as in bagged or boosted classifiers. Some of them are fast and easy to implement in MapReduce.

CROSS-REFERENCE See Chapter 5 for a discussion of hidden decision tress.

At issue is deciding which data can be dumped, which data is rarely accessed, and which fields can be ignored. (I've seen log files where the user agent takes 80 percent of the space. Why not use a lookup table of user agents to reduce data volume?) Also, MapReduce environments such as Hadoop become interesting when you start collecting a lot of unstructured data (for instance, text data) or blending data from multiple sources. Eventually you might be tempted to categorize and add a structure to your unstructured data using taxonomy creation algorithms such as the one discussed in this book, or by getting all text tagged when it is created or using metadata stored in file headers. Then the data is easier to retrofit and process in traditional databases. But the trend now is for vendors to develop solutions where analysts can use SQL to access low-level data buried under the Hadoop file management system, not the other way around.

Solution

In many cases, there is too much reliance on crowdsourcing and a reluctance to use sampling techniques, mainly because there are few experts who know how to get great samples out of big data. In some cases, you still need to come up with granular predictions (not summaries) — for instance, house prices for every house (Zillow) or weather forecasts for each ZIP code. Yet even in these cases, good sampling would help.

Many reviews, Likes, Tweets, or spam flags are made by users (sometimes Botnet operators, sometimes business competitors) with bad intentions of gaming the system on a large scale. Greed can also be part of the problem. Let's consider a hypothetical scenario: If fake Likes generate revenue for Social Network A and advertisers don't notice the fakes, Social Network A could feed the advertisers with more fake Likes because Social Network A thinks it doesn't have enough relevant traffic to serve *all* of its advertisers, so it wants to send good traffic to the bigger clients (with higher ad spend). When clients notice this is happening, Social Network A could either discontinue the practice or wait until it gets hit with a class action lawsuit — $90 million is peanuts for today's enormous social networks, and that's what Google and others settled for when they were hit with a class action lawsuit for delivering fake traffic.

Yet there is a solution that benefits everyone — users, and companies such as Google, Amazon.com, Netflix, Facebook, Twitter, and clients): better use of data science. This isn't about developing sophisticated, expensive statistical technology; it is about simply using the following:

- Better metrics

- Different weights (for example, put less emphasis on data resulting from crowdsourcing)

- Better linkage analysis, association rules to detect collusion, Botnets, and low frequency yet large-scale fraudsters

- Better and more frequently updated lookup tables (white lists of IP addresses)

All of this can be done without slowing down existing algorithms. Here's one example for social network data: instead of counting the number of Likes (not all Likes are created equal), you could do any of the following:

- Look at users that produce hundreds of Likes per day, as well as Likes arising from IP addresses that are flagged by Project Honeypot or Stop Forum Spam. But don't put all your trust in these two websites — they also, at least partially, rely on crowdsourcing (users reporting spam) and thus are subject to false positives and abuse.

- Identify situations such as 200 Likes that result in zero comments or 50 versions of the same "this is great" or "great post" comments — clearly you are dealing with a case of fake Likes. The advertiser should not be charged and the traffic source should be identified and discontinued.

- Look at buckets of traffic with a high proportion of low-quality users coming back too frequently with two Likes a day, with red flags such as no referral domain or tons of obscure domains, IP address frequently not resolving to a domain, traffic coming from a sub-affiliate, and so on.

- Use metrics such as unique users that are much more robust (more difficult to fake) than page views (but you still need to detect fake users).

- Use a simple, robust, fast, data-driven (rather than model-driven) algorithm, such as hidden decision trees, to score Likes and comments. You can even compute confidence intervals for scores without any statistical modeling.

- Create or improve ad relevancy algorithms with simple taxonomy concepts. This applies to many applications where relevancy is critical, not just ad delivery. It also means better algorithms to detect influential people (in one example, you had to be a member of PeerIndex to get a good score), to better detect plagiarism, to better detect friends, to better score job applicants, to improve attribution systems (advertising mix optimization, including long-term components in statistical models), and the list goes on and on.

The problem of detecting Facebook Likes is part of a more general class of business techniques that includes scoring Internet traffic such as clicks, keywords, members, page impressions, and so on. The purpose is twofold: detecting fraud (fake users, fake clicks, duplicate users), and assigning a quality score (a proxy for conversion rate or value) to each element (click, keyword, user) being measured.

CROSS-REFERENCE You will find more information on fraud detection in Chapter 6.

Of course, in the case of Facebook advertising, savvy advertisers use other metrics to measure return on investment (ROI) on ad spend. They use "customer lifetime" value and/or engagement on their own websites. For example, Starwood Hotels presented at a global conference saying the company is measuring an "engagement index" that includes how its fans are sharing the hotel content (virality and fan acquisition), patronage of the hotel, and engagement rate on their website. As the industry is getting more mature (advertisers, publishers, and users), the black market selling Facebook Likes will get smaller and smaller, but bad guys will still find new ways to exploit new features introduced by Facebook or any publisher, as they've always done.

CROSS-REFERENCE The section Attribution Modeling in Chapter 6 provides information on a "macro-economic" way to measure ROI on ad spend. This macro-economic approach is much cheaper in terms of data storage, tracking, and processing, because you only look at big aggregates.

Note that traffic scoring is especially useful when bidding in real time, or when purchasing large numbers of new keywords for which no historical conversion data is available (eBay is doing this every day). Better algorithms and data governance (creating standards as the IAB, *Internet Advertising Bureau*, did with click and user metrics) will help to eradicate these problems, for instance by defining what counts as a Like and which Likes should be discarded.

When Data Insights Flow Too Fast

When you can, you should analyze data (usually in real time with automated algorithms) and extract insights faster than they can be delivered to and digested by the end users (executives and decision makers). But you need to do something with those insights *before* passing them along to the end users — it's bad when the decision makers get flooded with tons of unprioritized reports.

The solution is to prioritize reports or alerts (in a dashboard system), determine who receives what, provide good visualizations, and allow users to unsubscribe from automated reports sent by e-mail. It is also good policy to provide only summaries and light graphs in an e-mail message, along with a link to the full report; some CEOs complain about their e-mail inboxes being regularly full due to multiple large daily reports.

CROSS-REFERENCE See Chapter 4 for information on visualization tools.

Sometimes this type of situation arises from machines talking to machines; for example, eBay automatically pricing millions of bid keywords every day and automatically feeding those prices to Google AdWords via the Google API. Too many engineers receive detailed reports every day about this activity, when a summary would be good enough.

Examples of Big Data Techniques

Let's now look at some of the techniques and tools that data scientists use to handle data in light of these two big data issues. For details on how a data science project is executed, including the different steps, see the section Life Cycle of Data Science Projects in Chapter 5.

Big Data Problem Epitomizing the Challenges of Data Science

The example problem discussed here is about building better search tools. This is the kind of problem from which big data and data science originate.

Have you ever done a Google search for *mining data*? It returns the same results as for *data mining*. Yet these are two different keywords: *mining data* usually means data about mining (as in coal, gold, and so on). If you search for *data about mining* you get the same results.

Yet Google has one of the best search algorithms out there. Imagine an e-store selling products: it allows users to search for products via a catalog powered with search capabilities, but returning irrelevant results 20 percent of the time. What a loss of money! Indeed, if you were an investor looking on Amazon. com to purchase a report on mining data, all you would find are books on data mining and you wouldn't buy anything, which could lead to a substantial loss for Amazon.com. Repeat this millions of times a year, and the opportunity cost is billions of dollars.

Following is a discussion of a workable solution for this type of problem and an explanation in simple terms that can help any business and analytic team to easily fix such a problem.

Any search query entered by a user is processed using the following steps:

1. The user query is cleaned: typos are removed.

2. It is then stemmed: plural is replaced by singular, verbs (ing form) are replaced by nouns (thus mining becomes mine), and so on.

3. Stop words are removed: the, or, and, of, from, about, it, with, and so on. For instance, *IT jobs* becomes *jobs*, and *data about mining* becomes *data mining* and (because of step 2) *data mine*.

4. The query is normalized: the tokens are rearranged in alphabetical order (*mine data* becomes *data mine*).

5. Algorithms are used to determine if the query contains the name of a city, book, song, product, or movie, using lookup tables.

6. Other algorithms are used to detect whether two tokens must be attached. For example, *San Francisco* is one token, not two, even though it looks like two.

7. Synonyms are detected. For example, perhaps *automobile* can be replaced by *car* to reduce the size of the index.

8. An algorithm is used to detect user intention (sometimes based on a user profile) for queries spanning multiple categories.

If you search for IT jobs, you get all jobs. In my case, when I search for "IT jobs," the search results include all jobs in Issaquah, Washington, where I live. Google correctly identified that I live in Issaquah (via my IP address), but wrongly assumed that I am interested in local jobs, and forgot that I'm only interested in IT jobs. The first job ad I clicked was for an insurance agent.

EXERCISE

Question: Should removing stop words be step 1 rather than step 3?

Answer: Have you thought about the fact that *mine* and *yours* could also be stop words? So in a bad implementation, *data mining* would become *data mine* after stemming, then *data*, which could trigger search results associated with one of the most popular *data* keywords: *data entry*. In practice, you remove stop words before stemming. So step 3 should indeed become step 1.

If you use *exact match* in your Google search, you get results slightly better for "IT jobs," "mining data," and "data about mining." So Google seems to have a solution. I believe the real fix is to make exact match the default option, rather than *broad match*. How many people know about exact match? Probably less than 1 percent. Anyway, as stated, it's more a business than a technical issue.

I can imagine Google benefiting from showing poor results (setting the default option to broad match). Indeed, it makes users more likely to click the Google ads, and thus boost Google revenue. But for Amazon.com, it does not make sense. Maybe Amazon.com's search box is powered by Google. If that's the case, then Amazon.com should configure the default search setting as exact match, not broad match. But I tried exact match on "data about mining" and it did not improve the search results on Amazon.com. (In fact, it made it even worse.)

Clearly, Amazon.com has a more severe problem, both from technical and business points of view. I think the problem is worse on Amazon.com than Google because Amazon.com has a much smaller inventory of search results pages from which to choose, because Amazon.com's inventory is mostly products, such as books, whereas Google's inventory is the entire Internet.

Clustering and Taxonomy Creation for Massive Data Sets

This section discusses potential algorithms that can perform clustering extremely fast on big data sets, as well as the graphical representation of such complex clustering structures. By "extremely fast" I mean a computational complexity on the order of O(n) and sometimes even faster, such as O(n/log n). This is much faster than good hierarchical agglomerative clustering (see http://en.wikipedia .org/wiki/Hierarchical _ clustering), which is typically O (n^2 log n). For big data, this means several million or even possibly a billion observations.

Clustering algorithms are slow, and matrices used in clustering algorithms take a lot of in-memory space (the square of the number of observations — in this case it would be more than a quadrillion elements). No memory is big enough to store such matrices. Yet these matrices are extremely sparse. In this section, we address these issues: speed improvement, memory reduction, and memory optimization with MapReduce. Clustering is one of the most fundamental machine learning, statistical, and big data techniques. Its output is called a *taxonomy* in the context of unstructured text data.

This technology has been used to produce keywords representing "user intent." Blending keywords representing the same intent (for instance, buying car insurance in California) into the same cluster allows advertisers to purchase these pre-computed clusters rather than individual keywords. The advantage to them is getting better targeting by focusing on intent, and a bigger reach by making sure all potential keywords of interest are included in the clusters in question.

Potential Applications

Creating a keyword taxonomy categorizes the entire universe of cleaned (standardized) valuable English keywords. This is about 10 million keywords made up of one, two, or three *tokens* — approximately 300 times the number of keywords found in an English dictionary. The purpose might be to categorize all bid keywords that could be purchased by eBay and Amazon.com on Google (for pay-per-click ad campaigns) to better price them. The application of this is discussed here in terms of the following:

- Clustering millions of documents (for example, books on Amazon.com)
- Clustering web pages, or even the entire Internet, which consist of approximately 100 million top websites and billions of web pages
- Determining when it makes sense to perform such massive clustering, and how MapReduce can help

NOTE In case you are not familiar with this terminology, a *token* is a term in a user query. The keyword *car insurance Alabama* has three tokens. *N-grams* are different combinations of these tokens — for instance, *insurance Alabama car* and *Alabama insurance car.*

Part 1: Building a Keyword Taxonomy

The solution described here involves two steps: preprocessing and clustering.

Step 1: Preprocessing

You gather tons of keywords over the Internet with a web crawler (crawling Wikipedia or DMOZ directories) and compute the frequencies for each keyword and for each keyword pair. A *keyword pair* is two keywords found on the same web page or close to each other on the same web page. A keyword might be something like *California insurance*; a keyword usually contains more than one token, but rarely more than three. Using all the frequencies you can, create a table (typically containing millions of keywords, even after keyword cleaning) like the following one where each entry is a pair of keywords and three numbers.

A = California insurance

B = home insurance

x = 543

y = 998

z = 11

where:

- x is the number of occurrences of keyword A in all the web pages that you crawled.
- y is the number of occurrences of keyword B in all the web pages that you crawled.
- z is the number of occurrences where A and B form a pair (for example, they are found on the same page).

This "keyword pair" table can indeed be easily and efficiently built using MapReduce. Note that the vast majority of keywords A and B do not form a keyword pair; in other words, $z = 0$. So by ignoring these null entries, your "keyword pair" table is still manageable and might contain as few as 100 million entries.

> **NOTE** Step 1 constitutes the final step of a number of interesting applications. For instance, it is used in search engine technology to identify or recommend keywords related to other keywords. An example of such an application is presented in Chapter 5 in the section Source Code for Keyword Correlation API. Interestingly, a few years ago a similar app was licensed to search engines by Ask for $500,000 per year.

Step 2: Clustering

To create a taxonomy, you want to put the identified keywords into similar clusters. One way to do this is to compute a dissimilarity $d(A,B)$ between two keywords A, B. For instance, $d(A, B) = z / SQRT(x * y)$, although other choices are possible. Note that the denominator prevents extremely popular keywords (for example, "free") from being close to all the keywords and from dominating the entire keyword relationship structure. Indeed, it favors better keyword bonds, such as *lemon* with *law* or *pie*, rather than *lemon* with *free*.

The higher $d(A, B)$ is, the closer keywords A and B are to each other. Now the challenge is to perform some kind of clustering — for example, hierarchical — on the "keyword pair" table using any kind of dissimilarity. Part 2 presents the solution and a potential alternative solution for your consideration.

Part 2: Using a Fast Clustering Algorithm

Although the following algorithm is described in the context of keyword clustering, it is straightforward to adapt it to other contexts. Assume that you have $n = 10,000,000$ unique keywords and $m = 100,000,000$ keyword pairs {A, B}, where $d(A,B)>0$. That is, you have an average of $r=10$ related keywords attached to each keyword.

The algorithm incrementally proceeds in several (five or six) rounds, as follows:

- **Initialization (Round 0): the small data (or seeding) step**. Select 10,000 seed keywords and create, for example, 100 categories and create a hash table $hash where key is one of the 10,000 seed keywords, and value is a list of categories to which the keyword is assigned.

```
$hash{"cheap car insurance"} = {"automotive","finance"}
```

The choice of the initial 10,000 seed keywords is very important. Until more research is done on this subject, I suggest picking the top 10,000 keywords in terms of number of associations — that is, keywords A with many Bs where d(A,B)>0. This will speed up the convergence of the algorithm.

▪ **Round 1: The big data step**. Browse the table of m keyword pairs, from beginning to end. When you find a pair {A, B} where, for example, $hash{A} exists and $hash{B} does not, do the following:

  ▪ $hash{B} = $hash{A}

  ▪ $weight{B} = d(A,B)

When you find a pair {A, B} where both A and B are already in $hash, do this:

  ▪ If $d(A,B) > $weight(B) then { $hash{B} = $hash{A}; $weight{B} = $d(A, B) } ; # B gets re-categorized to A's category.

  ▪ If $d(A,B) > $weight(A) then { $hash{A} = $hash{B}; $weight{A} = $d(A, B) } ; # A gets re-categorized to B's category.

▪ **Round 2**: Repeat Round 1. ($hash and $weight are kept in memory and keep growing at each subsequent round.)

▪ **Round 3**: Repeat Round 1.

▪ **Round 4**: Repeat Round 1.

▪ **Round 5**: Repeat Round 1.

The computational complexity is q * m=O(n), with q being the number of rounds. This is n=10,000,000 times faster than good clustering algorithms. However, all these hash-table accesses will slow it a bit to O(n log n), as $hash and $weight grow bigger at each subsequent round.

Would presorting the big table of m pairs help (sorting by d(A, B))? It would allow you to drastically reduce the number of hash-table accesses by eliminating the need for the recategorizations, but sorting is an $O(n \log n)$ process, so you would not gain anything. Note that sorting can be efficiently performed with MapReduce. The reduce step, in this case, consists of merging a bunch of small, sorted tables.

This clustering algorithm seems (at first glance) easy to implement using MapReduce. However, because the big table has only 100,000,000 entries, it might fit in RAM.

You can improve computational complexity by keeping the most important m/log n entries (based on volume and d(A,B)) in the big table and deleting the remaining entries. In practice, deleting 65 percent of the big table (the very long tail only, but not the long tail from a keyword distribution point of view) will have little impact on the performance — you will have a large bucket of uncategorized keywords, but in terms of volume, these keywords might represent less than 0.1 percent.

Alternative Algorithm

Alternatively, you could use Tarjan's strongly connected components algorithm to perform the clustering. To proceed, you first bin the distances: d(A, B) is set to 1 if it is above some pre-specified threshold; otherwise it is set to 0. This is a graph theory algorithm, where each keyword represents a node, and each pair of keywords where d(A, B) = 1 represents an edge. The computational complexity of the algorithm is O(n+m), where *n* is the number of keywords and *m* is the number of pairs (edges). To take advantage of this algorithm, you might want to store the big "keyword pair" table in a graph database (a type of NoSQL database).

Other Considerations

Visualization: How do you represent these keywords, with their cluster structure determined by d(A, B), in a nice graph? Ten million keywords would fit in a 3,000 x 3,000-pixel image. If you are interested in graphical representations, see the Fruchterman and Reingold algorithm that is extensively used to display cluster structures. Note that its computational complexity is $O(n^3)$, so you need to significantly improve it for this keyword clustering application — including the graphical representation. The graphical representation could be a raster image with millions of pixels, like a heat map where color represents category, and when you point to a pixel, a keyword value shows up (rather than a vector image with dozens of nodes). Neighboring pixels would represent strongly related keywords.

    Need: Do you really need this clustering algorithm? Most of the time you are trying to answer a simpler question (for example, which keywords are related to keyword A), or you already have a taxonomy and want to extend or improve it. In this case, full clustering is not necessary. But it's nice to know that efficient, simple algorithms exist, if you need them.

    Type of science: Is this stuff statistical science, computer science, or data science?

    Data sets: My own big table of keyword pairs, including the d(A, B) values, is available for you to download, as described in the next section. In addition, DMOZ data (one million categorized URLs) can be downloaded for free at `https://ak.quantcast.com/quantcast-top-million.zip` and is a good starting point to extract millions of keywords and categories, either from the data set itself or by crawling all the URLs and related links using distributed architecture. Quantcast also offers a free list of the top one million domain names. Finally, a good source of keyword data is query logs from search engines. These query logs are particularly useful for the preprocessing discussed in Step 1.

Excel with 100 Million Rows

Like most data scientists, I've used Excel a lot in my career, and it definitely has some powerful features. Probably the greatest one is its ability to help design, test, and update models in real time — just change the value of a few core parameters, and all your cells (thousands of them) and all your charts are updated at once.

> **NOTE** To see an example of an interactive spreadsheet where all cells and charts get updated with just one click, download the spreadsheet at `http://www.analyticbridge.com/profiles/blogs/three-classes-of-metrics-centrality-volatility-and-bumpiness`.

Other nice features includes Excel's ability to connect to databases or Microsoft APIs via the Internet (for example, to the Bing API), extract useful information, and summarize it in cubes and pivot tables. Although cubes and pivot tables have a strong feel of being an old-fashioned, SQL relational database environment, they are still useful in many contexts.

The main drawback is Excel's slowness. It is slow in ways that are unexpected. If you sort 500,000 observations in one column it's actually quite fast. But say that you simultaneously sort two columns: A and B, where B is the log of A values. So B contains a formula in each row. This dramatically slows down the sort. It is much faster to sort A alone and leave B as is. The formulas in B will correctly update all the values, quickly and automatically.

As a general rule, any operation that involves recomputing, for example, 200,000+ rows across multiple cells linked via dependence relationships, is done slowly in these cases:

- One of the columns includes functions such as VLOOKUP at each cell.
- SORT or other sublinear processes are required (sublinear means processes that are O(n log n) or worse).

There's an easy and efficient (but ugly) way around this, and it seems a bit odd that it's not a built-in feature of Excel and transparent to the user:

- Replace VLOOKUP formulas with hard-coded values, perform the update on hard-coded values, and then put back the formulas.
- Perform SORT only on the minimum number of columns where necessary, and then update cells in columns involving formulas.

It is also odd that VLOOKUP is so slow in the first place. I use it all the time to join, for example, a three-million-row dataset with a 200,000-entry lookup table in Perl, and it's fast. In Excel, the dataset and the lookup table would be stored in two separate worksheets within the same spreadsheet, and it would take days (if it was even possible) to perform this "join." (It isn't possible.) It may be that Excel indirectly performs a full join, thus exponentially slowing down the operation. But few people ever do a full join on large datasets. This is an area in which significant improvements could be made.

Finally, leveraging the cloud would be a way to further speed computations and process data sets far bigger than one million rows. Microsoft could allow the user to export the data to some cloud in a transparent way, in one click (for example, just click an Export to Cloud button). Then you would simulate the time-consuming operations on the local Excel version on your desktop, which amounts to using a local Excel spreadsheet as a virtual spreadsheet. When done, you click Retrieve from Cloud and get an updated spreadsheet. The Retrieve from Cloud would do the following:

1. Send your Excel formulas to the cloud via the Internet.

2. Apply your formula to the cloud version of your data, leveraging MapReduce as needed.

3. Get the processed data back to your local spreadsheet on your desktop.

Another painfully slow process is when you need to apply a formula to a whole column with 500,000 cells. Fortunately, there is a trick. Say you want to store the product of A and B in column C. You would do the following:

1. Select the whole Column C.

2. Enter the formula: =A1*B1.

3. Press the Ctrl key and Enter key together.

I wish it were easier than that, something like ==A1*A1 (formula with double equal to indicate that the formula applies to the entire column, not just one cell). This is another example of how Excel is not user friendly.

Many times, there are some obscure ways to efficiently do something. You will see another example in the section Regression With Excel in Chapter 5, which can teach you how to write a formula that returns multiple cells — in particular with LINEST, which returns the regression coefficients associated with a linear regression. Yes, you can do it in basic Excel without an add-in.

If you are interested in creating a column with one million values (for example, to test the speed of some Excel computations), here's how to proceed (this would be a good job interview question):

1. Start with 200 cells.

2. Duplicate these cells; now you have 400.

3. Duplicate these cells; now you have 800.

Another 10 iterations of this process, and you'll be at 800,000 cells. It's much faster than the naive approach (drag down with the mouse), and if your initial 200 numbers consist of the formula =RAND(), at the end you'll end up with one million pseudo-random numbers, though of poor quality.

Finally, languages such as Perl, Python, R, C, Sort, Grep, and others can be used to do data summarization before feeding stuff to Excel. But if Excel came with the features just discussed, much more could be done within it.

How to Upgrade Excel to Work With Big Data

You should use the PowerPivot add-in from Microsoft to work with large datasets. If you have Excel 2010, you can get and install it from `powerpivot.com`. If you have Office 2013, PowerPivot is included with the Office Professional Plus edition. (It is disabled by default, so you need to enable it.) If you want to do predictive analyses in Excel, you should look at Predixion Insight (`www.predixionsoftware.com`). It was developed by the same group of people who did data mining add-ins at Microsoft. The Developer edition of Predixion Insight is free. Predixion Insight has nice integration with PowerPivot.

The latest version of PowerPivot has extended external data connectors such as OData, Azure marketplace, and so on. PowerPivot is like having a proof-of-concept version of the SQL Server analysis server inside of Excel.

Also, 1010data (`www.1010data.com`) has developed the Trillion Row Spreadsheet, which enables companies to use a spreadsheet interface to perform data discovery and analyze trillions of rows of data, all through a cloud-based GUI. In addition to basic spreadsheet calculations, the Trillion Row Spreadsheet enables you to run advanced statistical analyses and create machine learning algorithms, all using the familiar spreadsheet paradigm. Best of all, this is done without the need to write MapReduce code.

Another solution is to use the Google spreadsheet plus BigQuery. See `https://developers.google.com/apps-script/articles/bigquery_tutorial` for a tutorial.

What MapReduce Can't Do

Let's now consider a large class of big data problems where MapReduce can't be used — at least not in a straightforward way — and a rather simple, analytic, statistical solution.

MapReduce is a technique that splits big data sets into many smaller ones, processes each small data set separately (but simultaneously) on different servers or computers, and then gathers and aggregates the results of all the subprocesses to produce the final answer. Such a distributed architecture allows you to process big data sets 1,000 times faster than traditional (nondistributed) designs if you use 1,000 servers and split the main process into 1,000 subprocesses.

MapReduce works very well in contexts where variables or observations are processed one by one. For instance, you analyze 1 terabyte of text data, and you want to compute the frequencies of all keywords found in your data. You can divide the 1 terabyte into 1,000 data sets, each 1 gigabyte. Now you produce 1,000 keyword frequency tables (one for each subset) and aggregate them to produce a final table.

However, when you need to process variables or data sets jointly, (meaning 2×2 or 3×3), MapReduce offers no benefit over nondistributed architectures. You must come up with a more sophisticated solution.

The Problem

Say that your data set consists of *n* observations and *k* variables. For instance, the k variables represent k different stock symbols or indexes (say that k = 10,000) and the n observations represent stock price signals (up/down) measured at n different times. You want to find high correlations (ideally with time lags to make a profit) — for example, if Google is up today, Facebook is up tomorrow.

You have to compute k * (k–1) / 2 correlations to solve this problem, despite the fact that you have only k = 10,000 stock symbols. You cannot split your 10,000 stock symbols into 1,000 clusters, each containing 10 stock symbols, and then use MapReduce. The vast majority of the correlations that you have to compute will involve a stock symbol in one cluster and another one in another cluster (because you have far more correlations to compute than you have clusters). These cross-cluster computations make MapReduce useless in this case. The same issue arises if you replace the word *correlation* with any other function, say *f*, and compute on two variables rather than one. This is why I claim that we are dealing here with a large class of problems where MapReduce can't help.

Three Solutions

Three possible solutions to this problem are sampling, binning, and classical data reduction.

Solution 1: Sampling

Instead of computing all cross-correlations, just compute a fraction of them. Select *m* random pairs of variables — for example, m = 0.001 * k * (k-1)/2 — and compute correlations for these m pairs only. A smart strategy consists of starting with a small fraction of all possible pairs and increasing the number of pairs until the highest (most significant) correlations barely grow anymore. Or you may use a simulated-annealing approach to decide which variables to keep and which ones to add to form new pairs after computing correlations on, for example 1,000 randomly selected seed pairs of variables.

CROSS-REFERENCE In the section Automated Fast Feature Selection with Combinatorial Optimization in Chapter 6, you will find a discussion on a semi-combinatorial strategy to handle not only 2x2 combinations (as in this correlation issue), but 3x3, 4x4, and so on to find high-quality multivariate vectors (in terms of predictive power) in the context of statistical scoring or fraud detection.

Solution 2: Binning

If you can bin your variables in a way that makes sense, and if n is small (for example, 5 or less), then you can precompute all potential correlations and save them in a lookup table. In our example, variables are already binned: we are dealing with signals (up or down) rather than actual, continuous metrics such as price deltas. With n=5, there are at most 512 potential paired time series. An example of such a pair is {(up, up, down, up, down), (up, up, up, down, down)} where the first five values correspond to a particular stock and the last five values to another stock. It is thus easy to precompute all 512 correlations. You still have to browse all k * (l–1) / 2 pairs of stocks to solve your problem, but now it's much faster because for each pair you get the correlation from the lookup table — no computation required, only accessing a value in a hash table or an array with 512 cells.

Note that with binary variables, the mathematical formula for correlation simplifies significantly, and using the simplified formula on all pairs might be faster than using lookup tables to access 512 precomputed correlations. However, the principle works regardless of whether you compute a correlation or a more complicated function f.

Solution 3: Classical Data Reduction

Traditional reduction techniques can also be used, such as forward or backward step-wise techniques where (in turn) you add or remove one variable at a time (or maybe two). The variable added is chosen to maximize the resulting entropy. Entropy can be measured in various ways. In a nutshell, if you have two data subsets from the same large data set such as these:

- Set A with 100 variables, which is 1.23 GB when compressed.
- Set B with 500 variables, including the 100 variables from set A, which is 1.25 GB when compressed

then you can say that the extra 400 variables (for example, stock symbols) in set B don't bring any extra predictive power and can be ignored. In other words, the lift obtained with the set B is so small that it's probably smaller than the noise inherent to these stock price signals.

> **NOTE** An interesting solution consists of using a combination of these three strategies. Also make sure that the high correlations found are not an artifact caused by the "curse of big data" discussed previously.

Conclusion: When to Use MapReduce

Data that comes sequentially as transactional data or log data — anything where you don't need computations involving large-scale point interactions between a large number of far-away points (for instance, weather patterns that are global but feed on local patterns would not work) — is a good candidate for MapReduce. Scoring algorithms, in particular, are good candidates. Processing massive amounts of unstructured text data, collaborative filtering, web crawlers, and search engines are other good examples.

It's more difficult to use MapReduce in situations involving processing n^2 points (or n^3), where n is one billion and where you truly need to do all n^2 computations. This n^2 issue also appeared in the section *"Clustering and Taxonomy Creation for Massive Data Sets"* earlier in this chapter, but the data structure used there somehow managed to get rid of the n^2 matrix. It was possible because that big data was sparse, making MapReduce still useful despite the unfriendly nature of the problem at first glance, from a parallel computation perspective. The same can be said about Google's page-rank algorithm, which requires inverting the n^2 matrix, where n = number of web pages on the Internet (n > 100 billion). It can be done with MapReduce thanks to smart algorithms.

Communication Issues

The example discussed in the previous section, Big Data Problem Epitomizing the Challenges of Data Science, illustrates that the issue sometimes is not technical difficulty, but rather corporate silos, poor communication, and teams that do not collaborate optimally.

There are a few issues that make this search engine problem (matching search results with a user query) difficult to fix. The problem is easy for decision makers, CTOs, or CEOs to notice, understand, and then assess the opportunity cost (just run 200 high value random search queries, and see how many return irrelevant results), yet the communication between the analytics teams and business people is faulty: there is a short somewhere.

There might be multiple analytics teams working as silos — computer scientists, statisticians, engineers — sometimes aggressively defending their own turfs and having conflicting opinions. What the decision makers eventually hear is a lot of noise and a lot of technicalities, and they don't know how to begin addressing the problem, how complex the issue is, how much it will cost to fix it, and who should fix it.

The people involved in steps 1 through 8 of the earlier example are all on different teams, or are people working independently. The decision makers don't even know *who* to talk to about the problem. Sometimes the use of data science terminology with non–data scientists can exacerbate the problem. For example, data scientists use terms such as *n-grams* to discuss Step 4, and mention *computational complexity* as the bottleneck preventing Step 4 from being improved. They will tell decision makers that a query involving three tokens has 6 n-grams, another involving four tokens has 24 n-grams, another with six tokens has 720 n-grams, and if they need to consider all combinations of tokens in the keyword index, the index will explode! Then maybe the decision maker says, "OK, let's buy tons of servers and a clustered architecture (Hadoop)."

But when scientists claim that the keyword index will explode, they are wrong. They are wrong because they think like scientists, not like business people. In practice, how many queries have more than four tokens? Very few. And for queries with three or four tokens, very few n-grams have decent traffic. The vast majority can be replaced by the dominant n-gram (in terms of traffic). For instance, people sometimes search for *car insurance* but rarely for *insurance car*. So having only one entry for these two queries makes sense. But for *data mining* and *mining data*, it makes sense to keep two separate entries. So instead of a table exploding in size by a factor 1,000, in reality we see a size increase of approximately 50 percent, which is perfectly manageable. When users search for *mining data*, the algorithm should first check to see if there is one entry for this specific n-gram (there should be one), and if not, proceed to rearrange tokens in alphabetical order — that is, look for *data mining* in the keyword index.

TIP The keyword index should contain keywords no more than four tokens long.

Another fix concerns Step 2. Sometimes, for some words like *mining* or *booking*, you cannot stem (replace them with *mine* or *book*). You need to have a lookup table of the top 10,000 words ending with "ing" that cannot be stemmed.

The same applies to Step 3: Have a lookup table of the top 10,000 combinations involving a stop word, where the stop word cannot be removed. For example, *IT job* would be in the lookup table attached to the stop word *it*.

TIP As a rule of thumb, don't remove stop words in queries consisting of only two tokens.

One of the challenges of effective communications is how to create an optimal team structure. But perhaps most important is to have high-level professionals that work across multiple teams, a bit like a management consultant. This person should get the big picture of the problem, be somewhat technical *and* business oriented (maybe an MBA with strong analytics skills), and bridge the gaps between multiple data science groups or people.

CROSS-REFERENCE The typical process of a data science project is explained in the section Life Cycle of Data Science Projects in Chapter 5.

This example issue and solution are exactly why the data science position was created: to bridge the gap between statisticians, business people, computer scientists, and engineers, and frequently to deal with big data problems as in this example. Note that to develop a solution like the one presented in this section, the data scientist must have solid domain expertise — in this case, in search technology.

This problem epitomizes what data science is all about and its challenges. A case study like this one is typical, and the problem is not just related to search engines. It's not solved just by hiring the right statistician or data miner. Indeed if you read the solution, you don't need to hire anyone; maybe you need to fire some people instead. But it's definitely a people/organization issue.

Data Science: The End of Statistics?

This section starts with examples in which traditional statistics are misused and lead to wrong conclusions, especially when applied to modern data, which is typically less structured, bigger, and requires merging data sets that are not fully compatible from various sources. Then you see how modern statistics can help make data science better.

The Eight Worst Predictive Modeling Techniques

Most of the following techniques have evolved over time (in the last 10 years) to the point where most of their drawbacks have been eliminated, making the updated tool far different from and better than its original version. Typically, these bad techniques are still widely used.

1. **Linear regression** relies on the normal, heteroscedasticity, and other assumptions and does not capture highly nonlinear, chaotic patterns. It is prone to overfitting, parameters are difficult to interpret, and it is very unstable when independent variables are highly correlated. Fixes include reducing variables, applying a transformation to your variables, and using constrained regression (for example, ridge or lasso regression).

2. **Traditional decision trees** are large decision trees that are unstable, impossible to interpret, and prone to overfitting. Fixes could include combining multiple small decision trees instead of using one large decision tree.

3. **Linear discriminant analysis** is used for supervised clustering. It is a bad technique because it assumes that clusters do not overlap and are well separated by hyperplanes. In practice, this is never the case. Use density estimation techniques instead.

4. **K-means clustering** tends to produce circular clusters and does not work well with data points that are not a mixture of Gaussian distributions.

5. **Neural networks** are difficult to interpret, unstable, and subject to overfitting.

6. **Maximum likelihood estimation** requires your data to fit with a pre-specified probabilistic distribution. It is not data driven, and in many cases the pre-specified Gaussian distribution is a terrible fit for your data.

7. **Density estimation in high dimensions** is subject to dimensionality. One fix is to use nonparametric kernel density estimators with adaptive bandwidths.

8. **Naive Bayes** are used, for example, in fraud and spam detection and for scoring. They assume that variables are independent, but if they are not it will fail miserably. In the context of fraud detection or spam detection, variables (sometimes called rules) are highly correlated. One fix is to group the variables into independent clusters of variables where each cluster contains variables that are highly correlated. Then apply naive Bayes to the clusters or use data reduction techniques. Bad text mining techniques (for example, basic "word" rules in spam detection) combined with naive Bayes produces absolutely terrible results with many false positives and false negatives.

TIP Always remember to use sound cross-validation techniques when testing models.

The reasons why such poor models are still widely used include the following:

- Many university curricula use outdated textbooks; thus many students are not exposed to better data science techniques.

- People use black-box statistical software, not knowing the limitations, the drawbacks, or how to correctly fine-tune the parameters and optimize the various knobs, or not understanding what the software actually produces.

- Governments force regulated industries (pharmaceutical and banking — see Basel III regulations for banks) to use 30-year-old SAS procedures for statistical compliance. For instance, better scoring methods for credit scoring, even if available in SAS, are not allowed and are arbitrarily rejected by authorities. The same goes for clinical-trial analyses submitted to the FDA, in which SAS is the mandatory software to be used for compliance, allowing the FDA to replicate analyses and results from pharmaceutical companies.

- Modern data sets are considerably more complex than and different from the data sets used when these techniques were initially developed. In short, these techniques have not been developed for modern data sets.

- There's no perfect statistical technique that would apply to all data sets, but there are many poor techniques.

In addition, poor cross-validation allows bad models to make the cut by over-estimating the true lift to be expected in future data, the true accuracy, or the true ROI outside the training set. Good cross-validations consist of the following:

- Splitting your training set into multiple subsets (test and control subsets)

- Including different types of clients and more recent data in the control sets than in your test sets

- Checking the quality of forecasted values on control sets

- Computing confidence intervals for individual errors (error defined, for example, as *true value minus forecasted value*) to make sure that the error is small enough and not too volatile (that it has a small variance across all control sets)

Marrying Computer Science, Statistics, and Domain Expertise

Let's now use a real-life problem to illustrate how to blend statistics, computer science, and domain expertise to offer a data science solution applied to a modern big data problem.

Consider an article written by scientists about how to predict ad clicks based on user queries and the ad's text. The article, available at `https://static.google-usercontent.com/external_content/untrusted_dlcp/research.google.com/en/us/pubs/archive/41159.pdf`, was written by a team of scientists and focuses on the large number of metrics in the model (billions of features), the use of logistic regression (a statistical technique), and optimization techniques (numerical analysis gradient methods) to solve the logistic regression (find the optimum regression coefficients). As you would expect, they discuss at length how the feature space is sparse and how to take advantage of sparsity to design an efficient algorithm.

All this sounds great, and it is certainly a textbook example of a correct, good, interesting application of machine learning. Indeed this is computer science. I have two criticisms, however, and pretty much in all "pure science" stuff that I have read, the criticism is identical. It involves using a nuclear weapon to kill a fly and not realizing it, and not showing the lift over a basic methodology designed by domain experts — in this case, experts with deep expertise simultaneously in ad technology, business management, and statistics. Although Google is doing better than many companies with its algorithms, it could do even better with less effort by focusing less on science and more on domain expertise. This is precisely the gap that data science is trying to bridge.

Following is an example of the ad prediction-technique developed by Google.

What Are You Trying to Accomplish?

That's the first question all data scientists should ask. Here, maybe Google is trying to maximize the number of clicks delivered to advertisers to boost its revenue. Maybe the research paper is to be used by Google internally. Or maybe the purpose is to help advertisers, who always want more clicks — as long as they are converting to sales.

If the paper is for Google's internal use, there should be a discussion about the fact that boosting click-through-rate (CTR) to increase Google's revenue works only in the short term. Overboosting CTR (by the publisher, in this case Google) eventually results in lower ROI for many advertisers, as I have experienced countless times. There should at least be a discussion about long-term goals (boosting conversions) along with short-term goals (boosting CTR). Both are necessary and cannot be considered separately in any business optimization problem.

If the paper is for advertisers, it misses the point: most advertisers (those interested in real traffic by real humans) are interested in conversions. It's easy for advertisers to change the wording in their ads and add keywords to their campaigns to generate tons of clicks — and negative ROI. The exception is advertisers who are publishers and bill their advertising clients downstream using a per-impression model (where a click from Google is an impression for their clients) — in short, click arbitrageurs.

NOTE The example discussed here is probably one of the most extreme cases you could encounter. But the key concept is that the statistical approach should not be underestimated. In many circles, the solution is a system with billions of rules that can cover everything possible and process entire big data sets. The point is that there are less costly alternatives.

Do You Need a Nuclear Weapon to Kill a Fly?

Using billions of features, most of them almost never triggered, makes no sense. How do you handle co-dependencies among these features, and what statistical significance do you get from 99.9 percent of the features that are triggered no more than three times in 500 billion observations (clicks)? Sure, you could do some feature blending and clustering — a rather expensive technique, computationally speaking — but this issue of feature aggregation was not even discussed in the paper.

Also, the vast majority of these features are probably automatically created through a feature generation algorithm. This is by far the most intriguing component of the system, but it is not discussed in the paper. It's a combinatorial optimization problem, looking at all relationships (ratios, products, log transformations, and other mappings, such as IP category) among a set of base metrics such as log-file fields to discover features with predictive power. Some features are also created in bulk by analysts looking at data. This set of billions of features could be missing two or three core (but nonobvious) features that would make the algorithm far superior. The paper does not mention any of the features used in Google's algorithm.

You can solve this ad-click-prediction problem with just a couple of features (a feature is a variable) carefully selected by a domain expert. Here are the ones that are unlikely to be created by an automated feature generation algorithm, but are recommended features to predict ad clicks:

- Keyword category: Match the keyword category to the category assigned to a text ad. This means that you have an algorithm to assign categories to a user query and a text ad. You have another algorithm to standardize user queries and to discriminate, for example, between mining data (data about mining) and data mining. It also means that you have a list of 500 categories, 100,000 subcategories, and three million sub-subcategories, enough to cover 99.99 percent of all commercial user queries (where advertisers are bidding). Note that a keyword can have two or three terms, as in *car insurance Alabama* and two categories such as *insurance* and *regional*.

- Special keywords: Create or acquire a list of special keywords found in a text ad (for example, *2013*, *new*, *free*, *best*).

- Rare sub-category: Identify text ads and user queries that share the same rare sub-subcategory. This will increases the odds of the user clicking.

- Advertiser type: Check for a high CTR (which is from clicks that do not convert). A high CTR indicates it is a false advertiser, because real advertisers usually have low CTRs.

- Number of ad views: Identify how many times a user has viewed the ad (First, second, or third time?). Good ads work well initially, but if you never change your text ad, it stops performing and CTR goes down.

- Popular events: Identify ads and user queries related to the same popular event.

- Trustworthy domain name: Prepare or acquire a list of domain names that are trustworthy and respected. You need to have an algorithm that scores domains, broken down by category.

- Special characters: Prepare a list of special characters and uppercase letters present in the ad.

Of course, the best solution is to blend features with the top features detected by an automated, machine learning algorithm and analysts.

Where Smart Statistics Help

After noticing the high sparsity of the feature space, I developed hidden decision trees to solve this type of problem. Do you need logistic regression with a gradient algorithm? Do you need an exact solution when the data is messy? I bet you can do great predictions using only 20 carefully selected features, and that's where the data scientist can also help by applying statistical knowledge to create a system that runs 1,000 times faster, using many fewer computer resources, and providing similar or better results. You don't need to use standard techniques such as robust logistic regression. I've been working with model-free statistics for a long time with great satisfaction, and yes, I also computed model-free confidence intervals, which are discussed in Chapter 5.

Another area in which statistics can help — if you like working with billions of features — is in identifying features with predictive power. Most of the billion features used by Google have no predictive power; in fact, predictive power is never discussed in the paper previously discussed. Sometimes two features have no individual predictive power, but when combined they do. For example, country (US versus UK) and time of day have far greater predictive power when combined. Statistical science can help define predictive power and assess when it is significant.

Finally, if you have billions of features, you can find features that seem to have predictive power but actually don't. Worse is the fact that these spurious features might overshadow the ones that truly have predictive power, making your system prone to systemic errors, and resulting in chaotic predictions. This is an issue that should be addressed using ad hoc statistical analyses, not the kind of stats currently taught in university curricula.

NOTE The reason for this problem (and the fix) is explained in detail in an article on the curse of big data, available at http://www.analyticbridge.com/profiles/blogs/the-curse-of-big-data.

The Big Data Ecosystem

A book about big data would not be complete without at least a brief mention of the components of the big data ecosystem. The big data ecosystem consists of the following products and services (for which some examples are also listed):

- Hardware providers.
- Cloud providers, including public, private, and hybrid clouds. Examples include EMC, Cloudera, and Amazon Web Services. Security companies are included in this category to protect your data.
- Data integration vendors.
- MapReduce/Hadoop environment.

- Database vendors for NoSQL, NewSQL graph, in-memory analytics, and databases. Examples include Teradata and Pivotal.

- Business Intelligence and dashboards, such as BIRT.

- Visualization tools such as Tableau and TIBCO.

- Data science and analytics tools, including SAS, StatSoft, Revolution Analytics, R, and Python data analysis libraries.

These products and services can be either open source or enterprise solutions. For more information on big data ecosystems and related subjects, see the following:

- `http://www.bigdatanews.com/profiles/blogs/big-data-ecosystem`

- `http://www.bigdatanews.com/profiles/blogs/42-big-data-startup`

- `http://www.bigdatanews.com/profiles/blogs/`
  `big-data-vendor-revenue-and-market-forecast-2012-2017`

Summary

This chapter continued the discussion of what makes data science a new discipline, by illustrating how big data is different from data seen even just 10 years ago, showing why standard statistical techniques fail when blindly applied to such data, and identifying the pertinent issues with both misuse and lack of use of statistics, and how this should be investigated and addressed.

The "curse" of big data and fast-flowing data were considered, and then real-life examples of big data techniques were presented and evaluated. Communication issues in big data environments were discussed, followed by the issue of how and why statistics will come back in the context of big data. Finally, you considered a summary of elements of the big data ecosystem.

Chapter 3, "Becoming a Data Scientist," discusses what a data scientist is, the different paths you can take as a data scientist, and how to acquire the right training to get hired as a data scientist.

Becoming a Data Scientist

Because big data and data science are here to stay, this chapter explores key features of data scientists, types of data scientists, and how to become a data scientist, including training programs available and the different types of data scientist career paths.

Key Features of Data Scientists

There are a few key features of data scientists you may have already noticed. These key features are discussed in this section, along with the type of expertise they should have or acquire, and why horizontal knowledge is important. Finally, statistics are presented on the demographics of data scientists.

Data Scientist Roles

Data scientists are not statisticians, nor data analysts, nor computer scientists, nor software engineers, nor business analysts. They have some knowledge in each of these areas but also some outside of these areas.

One of the reasons why the gap between statisticians and data scientists grew over the last 15 years is that academic statisticians, who publish theoretical articles (sometimes not based on data analysis) and train statisticians, are... not statisticians anymore. Also, many statisticians think that data science is about analyzing data, but it is more than that. It also involves implementing algorithms that process data automatically to provide automated predictions and actions, for example:

- Automated bidding systems
- Estimating (in real time) the value of all houses in the United States (Zillow.com)
- High-frequency trading
- Matching a Google ad with a user and a web page to maximize chances of conversion
- Returning highly relevant results from any Google search
- Book and friend recommendations on Amazon.com or Facebook
- Tax fraud detection and detection of terrorism
- Scoring all credit card transactions (fraud detection)
- Computational chemistry to simulate new molecules for cancer treatment
- Early detection of an epidemic
- Analyzing NASA pictures to find new planets or asteroids
- Weather forecasts
- Automated piloting (planes and cars)
- Client-customized pricing system (in real time) for all hotel rooms

All this involves both statistical science and terabytes of data. People doing this stuff do not call themselves statisticians, in general. They call themselves data scientists. Over time, as statisticians catch up with big data and modern applications, the gap between data science and statistics will shrink.

Also, data scientists are not statisticians because statisticians know a lot of things that are not needed in the data scientist's job: generalized inverse matrixes, eigenvalues, stochastic differential equations, and so on. When data scientists indeed use techniques that rely on this type of mathematics, it is usually via high-level tools (software), where these mathematics are used as black boxes — just like a software engineer who does not code in assembly language anymore. Conversely, data scientists need new statistical knowledge, typically data-driven, model-free, robust techniques that apply to modern, large, fast-flowing, sometimes unstructured data. This also includes structuring unstructured data and becoming an expert in taxonomies, NLP (natural language processing, also known as text mining) and tag management systems.

Data scientists are not computer scientists either — first, because they don't need the entire theoretical knowledge computer scientists have, and second, because they need to have a much better understanding of random processes, experimental design, and sampling, typically areas in which statisticians are expert. Yet data scientists need to be familiar with computational complexity, algorithm design, distributed architecture, and programming (R, SQL, NoSQL, Python, Java, and C++). Independent data scientists can use Perl instead of Python, though Python has become the standard scripting language. Data scientists developing production code and working in teams need to be familiar with software development life cycle and lean architectures.

Data scientists also need to be domain experts in one or two applied domains (for instance, the author of this book is an expert in both digital analytics and fraud detection), have success stories to share (with metrics used to quantify success), have strong business acumen, and be able to assess the ROI that data science solutions bring to their clients or their boss. Many of these skills can be acquired in a short time period if you already have several years of industry experience and training in a lateral domain (operations research, applied statistics working on large data sets, computer science, engineering, or an MBA with a strong analytic component).

Thus, data scientists also need to be good communicators to understand, and many times guess, what problems their client, boss, or executive management is trying to solve. Translating high-level English into simple, efficient, scalable, replicable, robust, flexible, platform-independent solutions is critical.

Finally, the term *analyst* is used for a more junior role, for people who typically analyze data but do not create systems or architectures to automatically analyze, process data, and perform automated actions based on automatically detected patterns or insights.

To summarize, data science = Some (computer science) + Some (statistical science) + Some (business management) + Some (software engineering) + Domain expertise + New (statistical science), where

- Some () means the entire field is not part of data science.
- New () means new stuff from the field in question is needed.

Horizontal Versus Vertical Data Scientist

Vertical data scientists have deep technical knowledge in some narrow field. For instance, they might be any of the following:

- Computer scientists familiar with computational complexity of all sorting algorithms
- Statisticians who know everything about eigenvalues, singular value decomposition and its numerical stability, and asymptotic convergence of maximum pseudo-likelihood estimators
- Software engineers with years of experience writing Python code (including graphic libraries) applied to API development and web crawling technology

- Database specialists with strong data modeling, data warehousing, graph database, Hadoop, and NoSQL expertise

- Predictive modelers with expertise in Bayesian networks, SAS, and SVM

The key here is that by "vertical data scientist" I mean those with a more narrow range of technical skills, such as expertise in all sorts of Lasso-related regressions but with limited knowledge of time series, much less of any computer science. However, deep domain expertise is absolutely necessary to succeed as a data scientist. In some fields, such as stock market arbitrage, online advertising arbitrage, or clinical trials, a lack of understanding of very complex business models, ecosystems, cycles and bubbles, or complex regulations is a guarantee of failure. In fraud detection, you need to keep up with what new tricks criminals throw at you (see the section on fraud detection in Chapter 6 for details).

Vertical data scientists are the by-product of a university system that trains a person to become a computer scientist, a statistician, an operations researcher, or an MBA — but not all the four at the same time.

In contrast, *horizontal data scientists* are a blend of business analysts, statisticians, computer scientists, and domain experts. They combine vision with technical knowledge. They might not be experts in eigenvalues, generalized linear models, and other semi-obsolete statistical techniques, but they know about more modern, data-driven techniques applicable to unstructured, streaming, and big data, such as the simple and applied first Analyticbridge theorem to build confidence intervals. They can design robust, efficient, simple, replicable, and scalable code and algorithms.

So by "horizontal data scientist," I mean that you need cross-discipline knowledge, including some of computer science, statistics, databases, machine learning, Python, and, of course, domain expertise. This is technical knowledge that a typical statistician usually lacks.

Horizontal data scientists also have the following characteristics:

- They have some familiarity with Six Sigma concepts (80/20 rule in particular), even if they don't know the terminology. In essence, speed is more important than perfection for these analytic practitioners.

- They have experience in producing success stories out of large, complicated, messy data sets, including measuring the success.

- They have experience in identifying the real problem to be solved, the data sets (external and internal) needed, the database structures needed, and the metrics needed, rather than being passive consumers of data sets produced or gathered by third parties lacking the skills to collect or create the right data.

- They know rules of thumb and pitfalls to avoid, more than theoretical concepts. However, they have a bit more than just basic knowledge of computational complexity, good sampling and design of experiment, robust statistics and cross-validation, modern database design, and programming languages (R, scripting languages, MapReduce concepts, and SQL).

▪ They have advanced Excel and visualization skills.

▪ They can help produce useful dashboards (the ones that people use on a daily basis to make decisions) or alternative tools to communicate insights found in data (orally, by e-mail, or automatically and sometimes in real-time machine-to-machine mode).

▪ They think outside the box. For instance, when they create a recommendation engine, they know that it will be gamed by spammers and competing users; thus they put an efficient mechanism in place to detect fake reviews.

▪ They are innovators who create truly useful stuff. Ironically, this can scare away potential employers, who, despite claims to the contrary and for obvious reasons, prefer the good soldier to the disruptive creator.

Another part of the data scientist's job is to participate in the database design and data gathering process, and to identify metrics and external data sources useful to maximize value discovery. This includes the ability to distinguish between the deeply buried signal and huge amounts of noise present in any typical big data set. For more details, read the section The Curse of Big Data in Chapter 2 which describes correlogram matching versus correlation comparisons to detect true signal when comparing millions of time series. Also see the section on predictive power in Chapter 6, which discusses a new type of entropy used to identify features that capture signal over those that are "signal-blind."

Data scientists also need to be experts in robust cross-validation, confidence intervals, and variance reduction techniques to improve accuracy or at least measure and quantify uncertainty. Even numerical analysis can be useful, especially for those involved in data science research. This and the importance of business expertise become clearer in the section on stock trading in Chapter 6.

Finally, there are three main types of analytics that data scientists deal with: descriptive, predictive, and prescriptive. Each type brings business value to the organization in a different way. I would also add "automated analytics" and "root cause analyses" to this list, although they overlap with predictive and prescriptive analytics in some ways.

The broad yet deep knowledge required of a true horizontal data scientist is one of the reasons why recruiters can't find them (so they find and recruit mostly vertical data scientists). Companies are not yet familiar with identifying horizontal data scientists—the true money makers and ROI generators among analytics professionals. The reasons are twofold:

▪ Untrained recruiters quickly notice that horizontal data scientists lack some of the traditional knowledge that a true computer scientist, statistician, or MBA must have—eliminating horizontal data scientists from the pool of applicants. You need a recruiter familiar with software engineers, business analysts, statisticians, and computer scientists, who can identify qualities not summarized by typical résumé keywords and identify which skills are critical and which ones that can be overlooked to detect these pure gems.

- Horizontal data scientists, faced with the prospects of a few job opportunities, and having the real knowledge to generate significant ROI, end up creating their own startups, working independently, and sometimes competing directly against the companies that are in need of real (supposedly rare) data scientists. After having failed more than once to get a job interview with Microsoft, eBay, Amazon.com, or Google, they never apply again, further reducing the pool of qualified talent.

EXERCISE

Can you name a few horizontal data scientists? D.J. Patil, previously a chief data scientist at LinkedIn, is an example of a horizontal data scientist. See if you can research and find a few others.

Types of Data Scientists

There are several different types of data scientists, including fake, self-made, amateur, and extreme. The following sections discuss each of these types of data scientists and include examples of amateur and extreme data science.

Fake Data Scientist

Fake data science and what a fake data scientist is has been previously discussed—a professional with narrow expertise, possibly because she is at the beginning of her career and should not be called a data scientist. In the previous section, vertical real scientists were considered not to be real data scientists. Likewise, a statistician with R and SQL programming skills, who never processed a 10-million-row data set, is a statistician, not a data scientist. A few books have been written with titles that emphasizes data science, while being nothing more than re-labeled statistic books.

Self-Made Data Scientist

A self-made data scientist is someone without the formal training (a degree in data science) but with all the knowledge and expertise to qualify as a data scientist. Currently, most data scientists are self-made because few programs exist that produce real data scientists. However, over time they will become a minority and even disappear. The author of this book is a self-made data scientist, formally educated in computational statistics at the PhD level. Just like business executives existed long before MBA programs were created, data scientists must exist before official programs are created. Some of them are the professionals who are:

- Putting together the foundations of data science
- Helping businesses define their data science needs and strategies
- Helping universities create and tailor programs
- Launching startup to solve data science problems
- Developing software and services (Data Science or Analytics as a Service)
- Creating independent training, certifications, or an apprenticeship in data science (including privately funded data science research)

Amateur Data Scientist

Another kind of data scientist worth mentioning is the *amateur data scientist*. The amateur data scientist is the equivalent of the amateur astronomer: well equipped, she has the right tools (such as R, a copy of SAS, or RapidMiner), has access to large data sets, is educated, and has real expertise. She earns money by participating in data science competitions, such as those published on Kaggle, CrowdANALYTIX, and Data Science Central, or by doing freelancing.

Example of Amateur Data Science

With so much data available for free everywhere, and so many open tools, a new kind of analytics practitioner is emerging: the amateur data scientist. Just like the amateur astronomer, the amateur data scientist will significantly contribute to the art and science, and will eventually solve mysteries. Could someone like the Boston Marathon bomber be found because of thousands of amateurs analyzing publicly available data (images, videos, tweets, and so on) with open source tools? After all, amateur astronomers have been detecting exo-planets and much more.

Also, just like the amateur astronomer needs only one expensive tool (a good telescope with data recording capabilities), the amateur data scientist needs only one expensive tool (a good laptop and possibly subscription, to some cloud storage/computing services).

Amateur data scientists might earn money from winning Kaggle contests, working on problems such as identifying a Botnet, explaining the stock market flash crash, defeating Google page ranking algorithms, helping find new complex molecules to fight cancer (analytical chemistry), and predicting solar flares and their intensity. Interested in becoming an amateur data scientist? The next section gives you a first project to get started.

Example of an Amateur Data Science Project

Question: Do large meteors cause multiple small craters or a big one? If meteors usually break up into multiple fragments, or approach the solar system already broken down into several pieces, they might be less dangerous than if they hit with a single, huge punch. That's the idea; although I'm not sure if this assumption is correct. Even if the opposite is true, it is still worth asking the question about frequency of binary impact craters.

Eventually, knowing that meteorites arrive in pieces rather than intact could change government policies and priorities, and maybe allow us to stop spending money on projects to detect and blow up meteors (or the other way around).

So how would you go about estimating the chance that a large meteor (hitting Earth) creates multiple small impacts, and how many impacts on average? An idea consists in looking at moon craters and checking how many of them are aligned. Yet what causes meteors to explode before hitting (and thus create multiple craters) is Earth's thick atmosphere. Thus the moon would not provide good data. Yet Earth's crust is so geologically active that all crater traces disappear after a few million years. Maybe Venus would be a good source of data? No, even worse than Earth. Maybe Mars? No, it's just like the moon. Maybe some moons from Jupiter or Saturn would be great candidates.

After a data source is identified and the questions answered, deeper questions can be asked, such as, *When you see a binary crater (two craters, same meteor), what is the average distance between the two craters?* This can also help better assess population risks and how many billion dollars NASA should spend on meteor tracking programs.

In any case, as a starter, I did a bit of research and found data at `http://www.stecf.org/~ralbrech/amico/intabs/koeberlc.html`, along with a map showing impact craters on Earth.

Visually, with the naked eye, it looks like multiple impacts (for example, binary craters) and crater alignment is the norm, not the exception. But the brain can be lousy at detecting probabilities. So a statistical analysis is needed. Note that the first step consists of processing the image to detect craters and extract coordinates, using some software or writing your own code. But this is still something a good amateur data scientist could do; you can find the right tools on the Internet.

Extreme Data Scientist

Another interesting type of data scientist is the *extreme data scientist*: Just like extreme mountain climbing or extreme programming, extreme data science means developing powerful, robust predictive solutions without any statistical models.

Example of Extreme Data Science

Extreme data science is a way of doing data science to deliver high value quickly. It can best be compared to extreme mountain climbing, where individuals manage to climb challenging peaks in uncharted territory, in a minimum amount of time, with a small team and small budget, sometimes successfully using controversial climbing routes or techniques. For instance, Reinhold Messner climbing Mount Everest in winter, alone, in three days, with no oxygen and no Sherpa — yes, he really did it!

Extreme data science borrows from lean six sigma, agile development and analytics, extreme programming, and in many cases advanced statistical analyses on big data performed without statistical models, yet providing superior ROI. (Part of it is due to saving money that would otherwise have been spent on a large team of expensive statisticians.)

Just like extreme mountain climbing, it is not for the faint-hearted: few statisticians can design sound predictive techniques and confidence intervals without mathematical modeling and heavy artillery such as general linear models.

The only data scientists who can succeed with extreme data science are those with good intuition, good judgment, and vision. They combine deep analytics and advanced statistical knowledge with consistently correct gut feelings and the ability to quickly drill down to the essence of any problem. They can offer a better solution to business problems, in one month of work, than a team of "regular," model-oriented data scientists working six months on the same project. Better also means, simpler, more scalable, and more robust. These data scientists tend to be polyvalent. Sometimes their success comes from extensive automation of semi-mundane tasks.

One of the problems today is that many so-called data scientists do extreme data science without knowing it. But they don't have the ability to successfully do it, and the results are miserable as they introduce biases and errors at every step when designing and implementing algorithms. Job interview questions don't test the ability to work as an extreme data scientist. Result? If you had 50 respected professional mountain climbers, climbing Everest in winter with no Sherpa, no oxygen, and little money, 48 would fail (not reach the summit). However, 25 would achieve a few milestones (5 almost succeeding), 5 would die, 10 would refuse to do it, 8 would fail miserably, and 2 would win. Expect the same with extreme data science.

But those who win will do better than anyone equipped with dozens of Sherpas, several million dollars, and all the bells and whistles. Note that because (by design) the extreme data scientists work on small teams, they must be polyvalent — just like Reinhold Messner in his extreme mountain climbing expeditions, where he is a mountain climber, a medical doctor, a cameraman, a meteorologist, and so on, all at once.

Data Scientist Demographics

The information discussed in this section is based on web traffic statistics and demographics for the most popular data science websites, based on Quantcast.com data, as well as on internal traffic statistics and other sources.

The United States leads in the number of visitors to data science websites. Typically, visitors from India are the second most frequent, yet are approximately four to five times less frequent than those from the United States. U.S. visitors tend to be in more senior and management roles, whereas visitors from India are more junior, entry-level analysts, with fewer executives. A few places that have experienced recent growth in data science professionals include Ireland, Singapore, and London.

Good sources of such data include:

- Quantcast.com. Data about gender, income, education level, and race is produced using demographic information gathered by ZIP codes. ZIP code data is derived from IP addresses.

- User information from ISPs (Internet service providers). Several big ISPs sell information about user accounts, broken down by IP address, to Quantcast. Then the Quantcast data science engine performs statistical inferences based on this sample ISP data.

- Surveys or other sources — for example, when you install some toolbar on your browser, allowing your web browsing activity to be monitored to produce summary statistics. (This methodology is subject to big biases, as people installing toolbars are different from those who don't.) This was Alexa.com's favorite way to produce the traffic statistics a while back.

Data science websites attract highly educated, wealthy males, predominantly with Asian origin, living mostly in the United States.

Training for Data Science

A few universities and other organizations have started to offer data science degrees, training, and certificates. The following sections discuss a sampling of these.

University Programs

Following is a list of some of the U.S. universities offering data science and scientist programs. Included are descriptions of their programs as listed on their websites.

- **University of Washington (Seattle, WA)**: Develop the computer science, mathematics, and analytical skills needed to enter the field of data science. Use data science techniques to analyze and extract meaning from extremely large data sets, or big data. Become familiar with relational and nonrelational databases. Apply statistics, machine learning, text retrieval, and natural language processing to analyze data and interpret results. Learn to apply data science in fields such as marketing, business intelligence, scientific research, and more. (http://www.pce.uw.edu/certificates/data-science.html)

- **Northwestern University (Evanston, IL)**: As businesses seek to maximize the value of vast new stores of available data, Northwestern University's Master of Science degree in predictive analytics program prepares students to meet the growing demand in virtually every industry for data-driven leadership and problem solving. Advanced data analysis, predictive modeling, computer-based data mining, and marketing, web, text, and risk analytics are just some of the areas of study offered in the program. (http://www.scs.northwestern.edu/info/predictive-analytics.php)

- **UC Berkeley (Berkeley, CA)**: The University of California at Berkeley School of Information offers the only professional Master of Information and Data Science (MIDS) degree delivered fully online. This exciting program offers the following:

  - A multidisciplinary curriculum that prepares you to solve real-world problems using complex and unstructured data.

  - A web-based learning environment that blends live, face-to-face classes with interactive, online course work designed and delivered by UC Berkeley faculty.

  - A project-based approach to learning that integrates the latest tools and methods for identifying patterns, gaining insights from data, and effectively communicating those findings.

  - Full access to the I School community including personalized technical and academic support.

  - The chance to build connections in the Bay Area—the heart of the data science revolution—and through the UC Berkeley alumni network. (http://requestinfo.datascience.berkeley.edu/index.html)

- **CUNY (New York, NY)**: The Online Master's degree in data analytics (M.S.) prepares graduates to make sense of real-world phenomena and everyday activities by synthesizing and mining big data with the intention of uncovering patterns, relationships, and trends. Big data has emerged as the driving force behind critical business decisions. Advances in the ability to collect, store, and process different kinds of data from traditionally unconnected sources enables you to answer complex, data-driven questions in ways that have never been possible before. (http://sps.cuny.edu/programs/ms _ dataanalytics)

- **New York University (New York, NY)**: Its initiative is university-wide because data science has already started to revolutionize most areas of intellectual endeavor found at NYU and in the world. This revolution is just beginning. Data science is becoming a necessary tool to answer some of the big scientific questions and technological challenges of our times: How does the brain work? How can we build intelligent machines? How do we better find cures for diseases?

  Data science overlaps multiple traditional disciplines at NYU such as mathematics (pure and applied), statistics, computer science, and an increasingly large number of application domains. It also stands to impact a wide range of spheres—from healthcare to business to government—in which NYU's schools and departments are engaged. (http://datascience.nyu.edu/)

- **Columbia University (New York, NY)**: The Institute for Data Sciences and Engineering at Columbia University strives to be the single world-leading institution in research and education in the theory and practice of the emerging field of data science broadly defined. Equally important in this mission is supporting and encouraging entrepreneurial ventures emerging from the research the Institute conducts. To accomplish this goal, the Institute seeks to forge closer relationships between faculty already at the University, to hire new faculty, to attract interdisciplinary graduate students interested in problems relating to big data, and to build strong and mutually beneficial relationships with industry partners. The Institute seeks to attract external funding from both federal and industrial sources to support its research and educational mission. (http://idse.columbia.edu/)

- **Stanford University (Palo Alto, CA)**: With the rise of user-web interaction and networking, as well as technological advances in processing power and storage capability, the demand for effective and sophisticated knowledge discovery techniques has grown exponentially. Businesses need to transform large quantities of information into intelligence that can be used to make smart business decisions.

  With the Mining Massive Data Sets graduate certificate, you will master efficient, powerful techniques and algorithms for extracting information from large datasets such as the web, social-network graphs, and large document repositories. Take your career to the next level with skills that will give your company the power to gain a competitive advantage.

  The Data Mining and Applications graduate certificate introduces many of the important new ideas in data mining and machine learning, explains them in a statistical framework and describes some of

their applications to business, science, and technology. (http://scpd
.stanford.edu/public/category/courseCategoryCertificateProfile.do?
method=load&certificateId=10555807)

(http://scpd.stanford.edu/public/category/courseCategoryCertificateProfile
.do?method=load&certificateId=1209602)

- **North Carolina State University (Raleigh, NC)**: If you have a mind
  for mathematics and statistical programming, and a passion for working with data to solve challenging problems, this is your program. The
  MSA is uniquely designed to equip individuals like you for the task of
  deriving and effectively communicating actionable insights from a vast
  quantity and variety of data—in 10 months. (http://analytics.ncsu
  .edu/?page _ id=1799)

Many other institutions have strong analytics programs, including Carnegie
Mellon, Harvard, MIT, Georgia Tech, and Wharton (Customer Analytics Initiative).
For a map of academic data science programs, visit the following websites:

- http://www.analyticbridge.com/group/analyticscourses/forum/topics/
  data-science-university-programs

- http://whatsthebigdata.com/2012/08/09/
  graduate-programs-in-big-data-and-data-science/

A typical academic program at universities such as the ones listed here features the following courses:

- Introduction to Data (data types, data movement, terminology, and so on)
- Storage and Concurrency Preliminaries
- Files and File-Based Data Systems
- Relational Database Management Systems
- Hadoop Introduction
- NoSQL — MapReduce Versus Parallel RDBMS
- Search and Text Analysis
- Entity Resolution
- Inferential Statistics
- Gaussian Distributions, Other Distributions, and The Central Limit Theorem
- Testing and Experimental Design
- Bayesian Versus Classical Statistics
- Probabilistic Interpretation of Linear Regression and Maximum Likelihood
- Graph Algorithms
- Raw Data to Inference Model
- Motivation and Applications of Machine Learning

- Supervised Learning
- Linear and Non-Linear Learning Models
- Classification, Clustering, and Dimensionality Reduction
- Advanced Non-Linear Models
- Collaborative Filtering and Recommendation
- Models That are Robust
- Data Sciences with Text and Language
- Data Sciences with Location
- Social Network Analysis

Corporate and Association Training Programs

A few other types of organizations — both private companies and professional organizations — offer certifications or training. Here are a few of them:

- INFORMS (Operations Research Society): Analytics certificate
- Digital Analytics Association: certificate
- TDWI (The Data Warehousing Institute): Courses; focus is on database architecture
- American Statistical Association: Chartered statistician certificate
- Data Science Central: Data science apprenticeship
- International Institute for Analytics: More like a think tank. Founded by the famous Tom Davenport (visiting Harvard Professor and one of the fathers of data science).
- Statistics.com: Statistics courses

Fees range from below $100 for a certification with no exam, to a few thousand dollars for a full program.

It is also possible to get data science training at many professional conferences that focus on analytics, big data, or data science, such as the following:

- Predictive Analytics World
- GoPivotal Data Science
- SAS data mining and analytics
- ACM — Association for Computing Machinery
- IEEE — Institute of Electrical and Electronics Engineers analytics/big data/data science
- IE Group — Innovation Enterprise Group
- Text Analytics News

- IQPC — International Quality and Productivity Center
- Whitehall Media

Vendors such as EMC, SAS, and Teradata also offer valuable training. Websites such as Kaggle.com enable you to participate in data science competitions and get access to real data, and sometimes the award winner is hired by a company such as Facebook or Netflix.

Free Training Programs

You can get some data science training without having to mortgage your house. Here are a couple of the top free training sites and programs.

Coursera.com

Coursera.com offers online training at no cost. The instructors are respected university professors from around the globe, so the material can sometimes feel a bit academic. Here are a few of the offerings, at the time of this writing:

- Machine Learning (Stanford University)
- Data Structures and Algorithms (Peking University)
- Web Intelligence and Big Data (Indian Institute of Technology)
- Introduction to Data Science (University of Washington)
- Maps and Geospatial Revolution (Penn State)
- Introduction to Databases (Stanford University, self-study)
- Computing for Data Analysis (Johns Hopkins University)
- Initiation à la Programmation (EPFL, Switzerland, in French)
- Statistics One (Princeton University)

Data Science Central

The data science apprenticeship offered at `https://www.datasciencecentral` `.com` is online, on demand, self-service, and free. The curriculum contains the following components:

- Training basics
- Tutorials
- Data sets
- Real-life projects
- Sample source code

The apprenticeship covers the following basic subjects:

- How to download Python, Perl, Java, and R, get sample programs, get started with writing an efficient web crawler, and get started with Linux, Cygwin, and Excel (including logistic regression)

- Hadoop, Map Reduce, NoSQL, their limitations, and more modern technologies

- How to find data sets or download large data sets for free on the web

- How to analyze data, from understanding business requirements to maintaining an automated (machine talking to machine) web/database application in production mode: a 12-step process

- How to develop your first "Analytics as a Service" application and scale it

- Big data algorithms, and how to make them more efficient and more robust (application in computational optimization: how to efficiently test trillions of trillions of multivariate vectors to design good scores)

- Basics about statistics, Monte Carlo, cross-validation, robustness, sampling, and design of experiments

- Start-up ideas for analytic people

- Basics of Perl, Python, real-time analytics, distributed architecture, and general programming practices

- Data visualization, dashboards, and how to communicate like a management consultant

- Tips for future consultants

- Tips for future entrepreneurs

- Rules of thumb, best practices, craftsmanship secrets, and why data science is also an art

- Additional online resources

- Lift and other metrics to measure success, metrics selection, use of external data, making data silos communicate via fuzzy merging, and statistical techniques

Special tutorials are included focusing on various data science topics such as big data, statistics, visualization, machine learning, and computer science. Several sample data sets are also provided for use in connection with the tutorials.

Students complete several real-life projects using what they learn in the apprenticeship. Examples of projects that are completed during the apprenticeship include the following:

- Hacking and reverse-engineering projects.

- Web crawling to browse Facebook or Twitter webpages, then extract and analyze harvested content to estimate the proportion of inactive or duplicate accounts on Facebook, or to categorize tweets.

- Taxonomy creation or improving an existing taxonomy.

- Optimal pricing for bid keywords on Google.

- Web app creation to provide (in real time) better-than-average trading signals.

- Identification of low-frequency and Botnet fraud cases in a sea of data.

- Internship in computational marketing with a data science start-up.

- Automated plagiarism detection.

- Use web crawlers to assess whether Google Search favors its own products and services, such as Google Analytics, over competitors.

Sample source code is provided with the apprenticeship, along with links to external code such as Perl, Python, R, and C++, and occasionally XML, JavaScript, and other languages. Even "code" to perform logistic regression and predictive modeling with Excel is included, as is a system to develop automated news feeds.

Data Scientist Career Paths

This section discusses career paths for individuals interested in entrepreneurial initiatives. Resources for professionals interested in working for small or large employers and organizations are found in Chapter 8, "Data Science Resources."

The Independent Consultant

One career option for the data scientist is to become an independent consultant, either full-time or part-time to complement traditional income (salary) with consulting revenue. Consultants typically have years of experience and deep domain expertise, use software and programming languages, and have developed sales and presentation skills. They know how to provide value, how to measure lift, and how to plan a consulting project. The first step is to write a proposal. Consultants can spend as much as 50 percent of their time chasing clients and doing marketing, especially if they charge well above $100/hour.

Finding Clients

Attending conferences, staying in touch with former bosses and colleagues, and building a strong network on LinkedIn (with recommendations and endorsements and a few thousand relevant connections) are critical and can take several months to build. To grow your online network, post relevant, noncommercial articles or contribute to forums (answer questions) on niche websites:

- Analyticbridge.com
- BigDataNews.com

- DataScienceCentral.com
- LinkedIn groups
- Google+ big data groups
- Quora.com

For instance, the LinkedIn group "Advanced Business Analytics, Data Mining and Predictive Modeling" has more than 100,000 members. It is the leading data science group, growing by 3,000 members per month, with many subgroups such as big data, visualization, operations research, analytic executives, training, and so on. (See `www.linkedin.com/groups/Advanced-Business-Analytics-Data-Mining-35222`.)

You can earn money and fame (and new clients) by participating in Kaggle contests (or in our own contests — for instance, see `http://bit.ly/1arClAn`), or being listed as a consultant on Kaggle. Its "best" consultants bill at $300 per hour (see `http://bit.ly/12Qqqnm`). However, you compete with thousands of other data scientists from all over the world, the projects tend to be rather small (a few thousand dollars each), and Kaggle takes a big commission on your earnings.

Managing Your Finances

I started without a business plan (15 years later, I still don't have one), no lawyer, no office (still don't have one), no employees, with my wife taking care of our Internet connection and accounting. Now we have a bookkeeper (40 hours per month) and an accountant; they cost about $10,000 per year, but they help with invoicing and collecting money. They are well worth their wages, which represent less than 1 percent of our gross revenue.

You can indeed start with little expense. All entrepreneurs are risk takers, and a little bit of risk means better rewards in the future, as the money saved on expensive services can help you finance your business and propel its growth. When we incorporated as an LLC in 2000, we used a service called MyCorporation.com (it still exists), which charged us only a few hundred dollars and took care of everything. To this date, we still have no lawyer, though we subscribed to some kind of legal insurance that costs $50/month. And our business model, by design, is not likely to create expensive lawsuits: we stay away from what could cause lawsuits. The same applies to training: you can learn a lot for free on the Internet, or from this book, or by attending free classes at Coursera.com.

One big expense is marketing and advertising. One way to minimize marketing costs is to create your own community and grow a large list of people interested in your services, to in essence "own" your market. Posting relevant discussions on LinkedIn groups and creating your own LinkedIn groups is a way to start growing your network. Indeed, when we started growing our community, we eventually became so large—the leading community for data scientists—that we just stopped there, and we now make money by accepting advertising and sending sponsored eBlasts and messages, blended with high-value, fresh noncommercial content, to our subscribers. This also shows that being a digital publisher is a viable option for data scientists interested in a nontraditional career path.

A final node about working with employees: You might work remotely with people in Romania or India, pay a fraction of the cost of an employee in Europe or the United States, not be subject to employee laws, and experience a win-win relationship. Indeed, as your consultancy grows but the number of hours you can spend any month is fixed, one way to scale is to take on more projects but outsource some work, maybe the more mundane tasks, abroad. Another way to grow is to automate many tasks such as report production, analyses, data cleaning, and exploratory analysis. If you can run a script that in one night, will work on five projects when you sleep, and produce the same amount of work as five consultants, now you have found a way to multiply your revenue by three to five times. You can then slash your fee structure by 50 percent and still make more money than your competitors.

Salary Surveys

Many websites provide information about salaries; though usually it applies to salaried employees rather than consultants. Job ads on LinkedIn typically show a salary range. Indeed.com and PayScale.com are also good resources. Glassdoor .com lists actual salaries as reported by employees. Data Science Central regularly publishes salary surveys, including for consultants, at `http://bit.ly/19vAOn1`.

Kaggle is known to charge $300/hour for data science projects, but typically the rate in the United States is between $60/hour and $250/hour based on project complexity and the level of expertise required. The field of statistical litigation tends to command higher rates, but you need to be a well-known data scientist to land a gig.

Here are a few hourly rates advertised by statistical consultants, published on statistics.com in 2013:

- Michael Chernick: $150
- Joseph Hilbe: $200
- Robert A. LaBudde: $150
- Bryan Manly: $130

  - James Rutledge: $200
  - Tom Ryan: $125
  - Randall E. Schumacker: $200

Sample Proposals

The starting point in any $3,000 project and above is a proposal, which outlines the scope of the project, the analyses to be performed, the data sources, deliverables and timelines, and fees. Here are two sample proposals.

Sample Proposal #1

This project was about click fraud detection. Take note of the following information:

  - How much and how I charge (I'm based in Issaquah, WA)
  - How I split the project into multiple phases
  - How to present deliverables and optional analysis, as well as milestones

The proposal included the following work items.

1. Proof of Concept (5 days of work)

   - Process test data set: 7 or 14 most recent days of click data; includes fields such as user KW (keyword), referral ID (or better, referral domain), feed ID, affiliate ID, CPC (cost-per-click), session ID (if available), UA (user agent), time, advertiser ID or landing page, and IP address (fields TBD)
   - Identification of fraud cases or invalid clicks in test data set via my base scoring system
   - Comparing my scores with your internal scores or metrics
   - Explain discrepancies: false positives/false negatives in both methodologies. Do I bring a lift?
   - Cost: $4,000

2. Creation of Rule System

   - Creation of four rules per week, for four weeks; focus on most urgent/powerful rules first
   - Work with your production team to make sure implementation is correct (QA tests)
   - Cost: $200/rule

3. Creation of Scoring System

    - From day one, have your team add a flag vector associated with each click in production code and databases:

        - The flag vector is computed on the fly for each click and/or updated every hour or day.

        - The click score will be a simple function of the flag vector.

        - Discuss elements of database architecture, including look up tables.

    - The flag vector stores for each click:

        - Which rules are triggered

        - The value (if not binary) associated with each rule

        - Whether the rule is active

    - Build score based on flag vector: that is, assign weights to each rule and flag vector.

    - Group rules by rule clusters and further refine the system (optional, extra cost).

    - Cost: $5,000 (mostly spent on creating the scoring system)

4. Maintenance

    - Machine learning: Test the system again after three months to discover new rules, fine-tune rule parameters, or learn how to automatically update/discover new rules.

    - Assess frequency of look up tables (for example, bad domain table) updates (every three months).

    - Train data analyst to perform ad-hoc analyses to detect fraud cases/ false positives.

    - Perform cluster analysis to assign a label to each fraud segment (optional; will provide a reason code for each bad click if implemented).

    - Impression files: Should we build new rules based on impression data (for example, clicks with 0 impressions)?

    - Make sure scores are consistent over time across all affiliates.

    - Dashboard/high-level summary/reporting capabilities.

    - Integration with financial engine.

    - Integrate conversion data if available, and detect bogus conversions.

    - Cost: TBD

The data mining methodology will mostly rely on robust, efficient, simple, hidden decision tree methods that are easy to implement in Perl or Python.

Sample Proposal #2

This project was about web analytics, keyword bidding, sophisticated A/B testing, and keyword scoring. The proposal included the following components:

1. Purpose: The purpose of this project is to predict the chance of converting (for keywords with little or no historical data), in pay-per-click programs. Using text mining techniques, a rule engine, and predictive modeling (logistics regression, decision trees, Naive Bayes classifiers, or hybrid models), a keyword score will be built for each client. Also, a simple parametric keyword bidding algorithm will be implemented. The bidding algorithm will rely on keyword scores.

2. Methodology: The scores will initially be based on a training set of 250,000 keywords from one client. For each bid keyword/match type/source (search or content), the following fields will be provided: clicks, conversions, conversion type, and revenue per conversion (if available), collected over the last eight weeks.

   The bidding algorithm will use a hybrid formula, with strong weight on conversion rate for keywords with reliable conversion rates, and strong weight on score for keywords with no historical data. If the client already uses a bidding algorithm based on conversion rate, we will simply use the client's algorithm, substituting the conversion rate with an appropriate function of the score for keywords with little history. The score is used as a proxy for conversion rate.

   If the client does not use a bidding algorithm, we will provide a parametric bidding algorithm depending on a parameter a (possibly multivariate), with a randomly chosen value for each keyword, to eventually detect the optimum a. For instance, a simplified version of the algorithm could be: Multiply bid by a if predicted ROI (for a given keyword) is higher than some threshold, a being a random number between 0.85 and 1.25. In this type of multivariate testing, the control case corresponds to $a=1$.

   The predicted ROI is a simple function of the current bid, the score (which in turn is a predictor of the conversion rate, by design) and the revenue per conversion.

3. Deliverables and Timeline:
   - Step 1: 250,000 keywords scored (include cross-validation). Algorithm and source code provided to score new keywords. Formula or table provided to compute predicted conversion rate as a function of the score. Four weeks of work, $4,000. Monthly updates to adjust the scores (machine learning): $500/month.

■ Step 2: Implementation of bidding algorithm with client: Four weeks of work, $4,000.

■ Payment: For each step, 50 percent upfront; 50 percent after completion.

CRM Tools

You need Customer Relationship Management (CRM) software that tracks leads (potential clients) and logs all your interactions with them (including contact information, typically more than one contact per company). Log entries look like this:

■ My partner met with VP of engineering at the INFORMS meeting on June 5, 2013, and discussed reverse clustering. This prospect is a hot lead, very interested.

■ I sent a follow-up e-mail on June 8.

■ Phone call with IT director scheduled on July 23.

■ Need to request sample data in connection with its project xyz.

■ Discussed performing a proof of concept on simulated data. Waiting for data.

Another useful tool is FreshBooks.com, which is an online bookkeeping system that allows you to send invoices (and track if they were opened) and is great at measuring money flows per month. I used it as a financial CRM tool, and some of the reports from its dashboard are useful for budgeting purposes and to have a big picture about your finances.

Finally, processing credit cards and having a credit card authorization form can prove useful.

NOTE The section Managing Your Finances in this chapter is also applicable to the entrepreneur career path.

The Entrepreneur

Entrepreneurship is more complex than managing a consultancy, as you want to scale, aim at higher revenues, and have an exit strategy. Raising venture capital (VC) money was popular in the late '90s but has become both more difficult and less necessary. The time you will spend chasing funding is substantial, like a six-month full-time job with no guarantee of success. We did it in 2006, raising $6 million to create a company that would score all Internet clicks, keywords, or impressions, in order to detect fake clicks and bad publishers, and also to help advertisers determine a bidding price for Google keywords with little or no history (the long tail). It lasted a few years and was fun. The one mistake we made was having a bunch of investors who, at one point, started to fight against each other.

VC money is less necessary now because you can launch a new company with little expense, especially if you purposely choose a business model that can easily be scaled and deployed using a lean approach. For instance, our Data Science Central platform relies on Ning.com. We don't have engineers, web developers, sys admins, and security gurus—all these functions are outsourced to Ning. We did not buy any servers: we are co-hosted on Ning for less than $200/month. The drawback is that you have more competitors as such barriers evaporate.

If you really need money for small projects associated with your business, crowdfunding could be a solution. We tried to raise money to pay a professor to write our training material for our data science apprenticeship but were not able to sign up on the crowd funding platforms. If we do raise money through crowd funding, we will actually do it entirely ourselves without using brokers, by advertising our offer in our mailing list.

Another issue with raising money is that you will have to share your original idea with investors and their agents (analysts doing due diligence on your intellectual property—IP). Your intellectual property might end up being stolen in the process. One way to make your IP theft-proof is to make it highly public so that it is not patentable. I call this an *open source patent*. If you do so (and it definitely fits with the idea of having a lean business with little cost), you need to make sure to control your market; otherwise, competitors with better funding will market your same product better than you can do it. If you own your market—that is, you own the best, largest opt-in mailing list of potential clients—anyone who wants to advertise the product in question must do it through you. It is then easy for you to turn down competitors. Owning your market is also a big component of a lean business because it reduces your marketing costs to almost zero.

Finally, you can use cheap services such as MyCorporation.com to incorporate (also a great lean business principle) and not have a business plan (another lean business idea), as long as you are highly focused yet with a clear vision, and don't get distracted by all sorts of new ideas and side projects. If you are a creator, associate yourself with a pragmatic partner. And think bottom line every day.

My Story: Data Science Publisher

In my case, as a data scientist, I generate leads for marketers. A good-quality lead is worth $40. The cost associated with producing a lead is $10. It requires data science to efficiently generate a large number of highly relevant leads (by detecting and purchasing the right traffic, optimizing organic growth, and using other analytic techniques). If I can't generate at least 10,000 leads a year, nobody will buy due to low volume. If my leads don't convert to actual revenue and produce ROI for the client, nobody will buy.

Also, because of data science, I can sell leads for a lower price than competitors—much less than $40. For instance, our newsletter open rate went from 8 percent to 24 percent, significantly boosting revenue and lowering costs. We also reduced churn to a point where we actually grow, all this because of data science. Among the techniques used to achieve these results are:

- Improving user, client, and content segmentation
- Outsourcing and efficiently recruiting abroad
- Using automation
- Using multiple vendor testing in parallel (A/B testing)
- Using competitive intelligence
- Using true computational marketing
- Optimizing delivery rate from an engineering point of view
- Eliminating inactive members
- Detecting and blocking spammers
- Optimizing an extremely diversified mix of newsletter metrics (keywords in subject line, HTML code, content blend, ratio of commercial versus organic content, keyword variance to avoid burnout, first sentence in each message, levers associated with retweets, word-of-mouth and going viral, and so on) to increase total clicks, leads, and conversions delivered to clients. Also, you need to predict sales and revenues—another data science exercise.

Startup Ideas for Data Scientists

For those interested in becoming a data science entrepreneur, here are a few ideas. Hopefully they will also spark other ideas for you.

R in Your Browser

Create a platform allowing users to enter R commands on Chrome or Firefox in a browser-embedded console. Wondering how easy it would be to run R from a browser on your iPad? I'm not sure how you would import data files, but I suppose R offers the possibility to open a file located on a web or FTP server, rather than a local file stored on your desktop. Or does it? Also, it would be cool to have Python in a browser.

See the example at `http://www.datasciencecentral.com/profiles/blogs/r-in-your-browser`.

A New Type of Weapons-Grade Secure E-mail

This could be a great opportunity for mathematicians and data scientists: creating a startup that offers encrypted e-mail that no government or entity could ever decrypt, and offering safe solutions to corporations who don't want their secrets stolen by competitors, criminals, or the government.

Here's an example of an e-mail platform:

- It is offered as a web app, for text-only messages limited to 100 KB. You copy and paste your text on some web form hosted on some web server (referred to as A). You also create a password for retrieval, maybe using a different app that creates long, random, secure passwords. When you click Submit, the text is encrypted and made accessible on some other web server (referred to as B). A shortened URL displays on your screen; that's where you or the recipient can read the encrypted text.

- You call (or fax) the recipient, possibly from and to a public phone, provide him with the shortened URL and password necessary to retrieve, and decrypt the message.

- The recipient visits the shortened URL, enters the password, and can read the unencrypted message online (on server B). The encrypted text is deleted after the recipient has read it, or 48 hours after the encrypted message was created, whichever comes first.

TECHNICAL NOTE

The encryption algorithm which adds semi-random text to your message prior to encryption, has an encrypted timestamp, and won't work if no semi-random text is added first. It is such that (i) the message cannot be decrypted after 48 hours (if the encrypted version is intercepted) because a self-destruction mechanism is embedded into the encrypted message and the executable file itself, and (ii) if you encrypt the same message twice (even an empty message or one consisting of just one character), the two encrypted versions will be very different (of random length and at least 1 KB in size) to make reverse engineering next to impossible.

- Maybe the executable file that does perform the encryption would change every three to four days for increased security and to make sure a previously encrypted message can no longer be decrypted. (You would have the old version and new version simultaneously available on B for just 48 hours.)

- The executable file (on A) tests if it sits on the right IP address before doing any encryption, to prevent it from being run on, for example, a government server. This feature is encrypted within the executable code. The same feature is incorporated into the executable file used to decrypt the message, on B.

- A crime detection system is embedded in the encryption algorithm to prevent criminals from using the system by detecting and refusing to encrypt messages that seem suspicious (child pornography, terrorism, fraud, hate speech, and so on).

- The platform is monetized via paid advertising, by advertisers and anti-virus software.

- The URL associated with B can be anywhere, change all the time, or be based on the password provided by the user and located outside the United States.

- The URL associated with A must be more static. This is a weakness because it can be taken down by the government. However, a workaround consists of using several specific keywords for this app, such as *ArmuredMail*, so that if A is down, a new website based on the same keywords will emerge elsewhere, allowing for uninterrupted service. (The user would have to do a Google search for *ArmuredMail* to find one website—a mirror of A—that works.)

- Finally, no unencrypted text is stored anywhere.

Indeed, the government could create such an app and disguise it as a private enterprise: it would in this case be a honeypot app. Some people worry that the government is tracking everyone and that you could get in trouble (your Internet connection shut down and bank account frozen) because you posted stuff that the government algorithms deem extremely dangerous, maybe a comment about pressure cookers. At the same time, I believe the threat is somewhat exaggerated.

Anyone interested in building this encryption app? Note that no system is perfectly safe. If there's an invisible camera behind you, filming everything you do on your computer, then my system offers no protection for you—though it would still be safe for the recipient, unless he also has a camera tracking all his computer activity. But the link between you and the recipient (the fact that both of you are connected) would be invisible to any third party. And increased security can be achieved if you use the web app from an anonymous computer—maybe from a public computer in some hotel lobby.

Averaging Text, Not Numbers

Averaging numbers is easy, but what about averaging text? I ask the question because the Oxford dictionary recently added a new term: big data.

So how do you define big data? Do you pick up a few experts (how do you select them?) and ask them to create the definition? What about asking thousands of practitioners (crowdsourcing) and somehow average their responses? How would you proceed to automatically average their opinions, possibly after clustering their responses into a small number of groups? It looks like this would require

- Using taxonomies.

- Standardizing, cleaning, and stemming all keywords, very smartly (using stop lists and exception lists — for instance, *booking* is not the same as *book*).

- Using n-grams, but carefully. (Some keywords permutations are not equivalent—use a list of these exceptions. For example, *data mining* is not the same as *mining data*.)

- Matching cleaned/normalized keyword sequences found in the responses, with taxonomy entries, to assign categories to the response, to further simplify the text averaging process.

- Maybe a rule set associated with the taxonomy, such as average(entry A, entry C)=xyz.

- A synonym dictionary.

On a different note, have you ever heard of software that automatically summarizes text? This would be a fantastic tool!

Typed Passwords Replaced by Biometrics

What if the traditional login/password to your favorite websites was replaced by a web app asking you to talk for one second, to get your picture taken from your laptop camera, or to check your fingerprint on your laptop touch screen? Your one-second voice message or the image of your fingerprint could then be encoded using a combination of several metrics and stored in a database for further login validation.

The idea is to replace the traditional login/password (not a secure way to connect to a website) with more secure technology, which would apply everywhere on any computer, laptop, cell phone, or device where this ID checking app would be installed.

Also, the old-fashioned login/password system could still coexist as an option. The aim of the new system would be to allow anyone to log on with just one click, from any location/device on any website, without having to remember a bunch of (often) weak passwords. This methodology requires large bandwidth and considerable computer resources.

Web App to Run Polls and Display Real-Time Results

It should handle ten questions, each with multiple choices, and display the results in real time on a world map, using colors. Geolocation of each respondent is detected in real time based on an IP address. The color displayed (for each respondent) would represent the answer to a question. For instance, male=red, female=yellow, and other=green. I used to work with Vizu; the poll service was available as a web widget, offering all these features for free, but it's now gone. It would be great if this type of poll/survey tool could handle 2,000 actual responses, and if you could zoom in on the map.

Inbox Delivery and Management System for Bulk E-mail

Here's a new idea for Google to make money and cover the costs of processing or filtering billions of messages per day. This is a solution to eliminate spam as well, without as many false positives as currently. The solution would be for Google to create its own newsletter management system. Or at least, Google would work with major providers (VerticalResponse, Constant Contact, iContact, MailChimp, and so on) to allow their clients (the companies sending billions of messages each day, such as LinkedIn) to pay a fee based on volume. The fee would help the sender to not end up in a Gmail spam box, as long as it complies with Google policies. Even better: let Google offer this newsletter management service directly to clients who want to reach Gmail more effectively, under Google's controls and conditions.

I believe Google is now in a position to offer this service because more than 50 percent of new personal e-mail accounts currently created are Gmail, and they last much longer than any corporate e-mail accounts. (You don't lose your Gmail account when you lose your job.) Google could reasonably charge $100 per 20,000 messages sent to Gmail accounts: the potential revenue is huge.

If Google would offer this service internally (rather than through a third party such as Constant Contact), it would make more money and have more control, and the task of eliminating spam would be easier and less costly.

Currently, because Google offers none of these services, you will have to face the following issues:

- A big component in Gmail antispam technology is collaborative filtering algorithms. Your newsletter quickly ends up in the spam box, a few milliseconds after the delivery process has started, if too many users complain about it, do not open it, or don't click.

- Thus fraudsters can create tons of fake Gmail accounts to boost the "open" and "click" rates so that their spam goes through, leveraging collaborative filtering to their advantage.

- Fraudsters can also use tons of fake Gmail accounts to fraudulently and massively flag e-mail received from real companies or competitors as fraud.

Newsletters are delivered too quickly: 100,000 messages are typically delivered in five minutes by newsletter management companies. If Gmail were delivering these newsletters via its own system (say, Gmail Contact), then it could deliver more slowly, and thus do a better job at controlling spam without creating tons of false positives.

In the meanwhile, a solution for companies regularly sending newsletters to a large number of subscribers is to do the following:

- Create a special segment for all Gmail accounts, and use that segment more sparingly. In our case, it turns out that our Gmail segment is the best one (among all our segments) in terms of low churn, open rate, and click rate—if we do not use it too frequently and reserve it for our best messages.

- Ask your newsletter management vendor to use a dedicated IP address to send messages.

- Every three months, remove all subscribers who never open or even those who never clicked. (Although you will lose good subscribers with e-mail clients having images turned off.)

- Create SPF (Sender Policy Framework) records.

Pricing Optimization for Medical Procedures

Problem:

The cost of healthcare in the United States is extremely high and volatile. Even standard procedures have high price volatility. If you ask how much your hospital will charge for what is typically a $5,000 or more procedure by explicitly asking how much it charged for the last five patients, it will have no answer (as if it doesn't keep financial records).

Would you buy a car if the car dealer has no idea how much it will charge you, until two months after the purchase? If you did, and then you hear your neighbor got exactly the same car from a different dealer for one-half the price, what would you do? Any other type of business would quickly go bankrupt if using such business practices.

Causes:

- Despite hiring the brightest people (surgeons and doctors) hospitals lack basic analytic talent for budgeting, pricing, and forecasting. They can't create a statistical financial model that includes revenues (insurance payments and so on) and expenses (clients not paying, labor, drug costs, equipment, lawsuits, and so on).

- Costs are driven in part by patients and hospitals being too risk-averse (fear of litigation) and asking for unnecessary tests. Yet few patients ever mentioned that their budget is, say, $2,000 for XYZ procedure, and that he won't pay more and will cancel or find another provider that can meet that budget, if necessary.

- Volatility is expected in prices but must be controlled. If I provide consulting services to a client, the client (like any patient) has a finite budget, and I (like hospitals) have constraints and issues. (I need to purchase good quality software; the data might be much messier than expected, and so on.)

Solution:

An Internet start-up offering prices for 20 top medical procedures, across 5,000 hospitals and 20 patient segments. Prices would come from patients filling a web form or sharing their invoice details, and partners such as cost-efficient hospitals willing to attract new patients. Statistical inferences would be made to estimate all these 20×20×500=200,000 prices (and their volatility) every month based on maybe as little as 8,000 data points. The statistical engine would be similar to Zillow (estimating the value of all houses based on a limited volume of sales data), but it would also have a patient review component (like Yelp), together with fake review detection.

Revenue would be coming from hospital partners, from selling data to agencies, from advertising to pharmaceutical companies, and from membership fees (premium members having access to more granular data).

Checks Sent by E-mail

Checks sent by e-mail, rather than snail mail—the idea works as follows:

- You (the payer) want to send a check to, for example, John, the payee.
- You log on to this new start-up website, add your bank information (with account name, account number, and routing number) and a picture of your signature (the first time you use the service), and then for each check, you provide the dollar amount, payment reason, the payee's name, and his e-mail address.
- The payee receives an e-mail notification and is requested to visit a URL to process his check.
- He prints his check from the URL in question (operated by the start-up), just like you would print a boarding pass.
- The payee goes to his bank to cash his check.

Note that this start-up could charge the payee 20 cents per check (it's less than 50 percent of the cost of a stamp) and have a higher successful delivery rate than snail mail, which is easy to beat.

The analytic part of this business model is in the security component to prevent fraud from happening. To a lesser extent, there are also analytics involved to guarantee that e-mail is delivered to the payee at least 99.99 percent of the time. Information must travel safely through the Internet, and in particular, the e-mail sent to payees must contain encrypted information in the URL used to print the check.

PayPal already offers this type of functionality (online payments), but not the check printing feature. For some people or some businesses, a physical check is still necessary. I believe checks will eventually disappear, so I'm not sure if such a start-up would have a bright future.

Anonymous Digital Currency for Bartering

Several digital currencies already exist and are currently being used (think about PayPal and Bitcoin), but as far as I know, they are not anonymous.

An anonymous digital currency would be available as encrypted numbers that can be used only once; it would not be tied to any paper currency or e-mail address. Initially, it could be used between partners interested in bartering. (For example, I purchase advertising on your website in exchange for you helping me with web design—no U.S. dollars exchanged). The big advantages are:

- It is not a leveraged currency — no risk of "bank run," inflation, and so on.
- Transactions paid via this currency would not be subject to any tax.

What are the challenges about designing this type of currency? The biggest ones are:

- Getting many people to trust and use it.
- Difficult to trade it in for dollars.
- The entity managing this currency must make money in some way. How? Can it be done by charging a small fee for all transactions? The transaction fee would be much smaller than the tax penalty if the transaction were made in a non-anonymous currency (digital or not).
- Security: Being an antifraud expert, I know how to make it very secure. I also know how to make it totally anonymous.

Detect Scams Before They Go Live

Based on tweets and blog posts, identify new scams before they become widespread.

- Search for keywords such as *scam, scammed, theft, rip-off, fraud*, and so on.
- Assign a date stamp, location, and category to each posting of interest.
- Identify and discard bogus postings that report fake fraud stories.
- Score each post for scam severity and trustworthiness.
- Create a taxonomy to categorize each posting.
- Create a world map, updated hourly, with scam alerts. For each scam, indicate a category, an intensity, and a recency measurement.

Is such a public system already in place? Sure, the FBI must have one, but it's not shared with the public. Also, such a scam alert system is quite similar to systems based on crowd sourcing to detect diseases spreading around the world. The spreading mechanism in both cases is similar: scam/disease agents use viruses to spread and contaminate. In the case of scams, computer viruses infect computers using Botnets and turn them into spam machines (zombies) to send scam e-mail to millions of recipients.

Amusement Park Mobile App

Will analytics help amusement parks survive the 21st century? My recent experience at Disneyland in California makes me think that a lot of simple things can be done to improve revenue and user experience. Here are a few starting points:

- Optimize lines. Maybe charge an extra $1 per minute for customers who need more than five minutes to purchase their tickets.

- Offer online tickets and other solutions (not requiring human interactions) to avoid the multiple checkpoint bottlenecks.

- Make tickets more difficult to counterfeit; assess and fight fraud due to fake tickets. (These tickets seem relatively easy to forge.)

- Increase prices and find optimum prices. (Obviously, it must be higher than current prices due to the extremely large and dense crowds visiting these parks, creating huge waiting lines and other hazards everywhere—from the few restaurants and bathrooms to the attractions.)

- Make waiting time for each attraction available on cell phones to optimize user experience. (Allow users to choose attractions based on waiting times. I've seen attractions where fun lasts 5 minutes but waiting time is 2 hours, creating additional problems, such as people who need to go to the bathroom after a 90-minute wait.)

- More restaurants, and at least one upscale restaurant.

- Create more attractions where you join on demand, something like a gondola or Ferris Wheel where you can enter when the gondola or Ferris Wheel is in action. (In short, attractions that don't need to get stopped every five minutes to get everybody out and get new people in, but attractions where people are continuously entering and exiting. This, of course, reduces waiting times.)

- Recommend to users the best days to visit to avoid huge crowds based on historical trends (and change ticket prices accordingly—cheaper on "low days").

Software to Optimize Hotel Room Prices in Real Time

When you book five nights in a hotel, usually each night (for the same room) will have a different price. The price is based on a number of factors, including these:

- Season
- Day of the week
- Competitor prices
- Inventory available

I am wondering which other metrics are included in the pricing models. For instance, do they include weather forecasts, special events, price elasticity? Is the price user-specific (for example, based on IP addresses) or based on how the purchase is made (online, over the phone, using an American Express card versus a Visa card), how long in advance the purchase is made, and so on?

For instance, a purchase performed long in advance results in lower prices, but it is because inventory is high. So you might be fine by just using inventory available.

Finally, how often are these pricing models updated, and how is model performance assessed? Is the price changing in real time?

Web App to Predict Risk of a Tax Audit

What are your chances of being audited? And how can data science help answer this question, for each of us individually?

Some factors increase the chance of an audit, including

- High income
- Being self-employed versus being a partner in an LLC
- Filing early
- Having earnings both from W2s and self-employment
- Business losses four years in a row
- Proportion of your total deductions in travel and restaurant categories >40%
- Large donations
- High home office deductions

Companies such as Deloitte and KPMG probably compute tax audit risks quite accurately (including the penalties in case of an audit) for their large clients because they have access to large internal databases of audited and non-audited clients.

But for you and me, how could data science help predict our risk of an audit? Is there data publicly available to build a predictive model? A good start-up idea would be to create a website to help you compute your risk of tax audit. Its risk scoring engine would be based on the following three pieces:

- Users can anonymously answer questions about their tax return and previous audits (if any), or submit an anonymized version of their tax returns
- User data is gathered and analyzed to give a real-time answer to users checking their audit risk
- As more people use the system, the better the predictions, the smaller the confidence intervals for estimated audit probabilities

Indeed, this would amount to reverse-engineering the IRS algorithms.

Which metrics should be used to assess tax audit risk? And how accurate can the prediction be? Could such a system attain 99.5 percent accuracy — that is, wrong predictions for only 0.5 percent of taxpayers? Right now, if you tell someone "You won't be audited this year," you are correct 98 percent of the time. More interesting, what level of accuracy can be achieved for higher-risk taxpayers?

Finally, if your model predicts both the risk of audit and the penalty if audited, then you can make smarter decisions and decide which risks you can take and what to avoid. This is pure decision science to recoup dollars from the IRS, not via exploiting tax law loopholes (dangerous), but via honest, fair, and smart analytics—outsmarting the IRS data science algorithms rather than outsmarting tax laws.

Summary

This chapter explored how to become a data scientist, from university degrees currently available, certificate training programs, and the online apprenticeship provided by Data Science Central.

Different types of data science career paths were also discussed, including entrepreneur, consultant, individual contributor, and leader. A few ideas for data science start-ups were also provided, in case you want to become an entrepreneur.

The next chapter describes selected data science techniques in detail without introducing unnecessary mathematics. It includes information on visualization, statistical techniques, and metrics relevant to big data and new types of data.

Data Science Craftsmanship, Part I

This is the most technical chapter of the book. Metric selection is discussed in some detail before moving on to new visualization techniques to represent complex spatial processes evolving over time. It then digs deeper into the technical aspects of a range of topics.

This chapter presents some interesting techniques developed recently to handle modern business data. It is more technical than previous chapters, yet it's easy to read for someone with limited statistical, mathematical, or computer science knowledge. The selection of topics for this chapter was based on the number of analytics practitioners that found related articles useful when they were first published at Data Science Central. This chapter is as broad as possible, covering many different techniques and concepts.

Advanced statistics, in particular cross-validation, robust statistics, and experimental design, are all part of data science. Likewise, computational complexity is part of data science when it applies to algorithms used to process modern large, unstructured, streaming data sets. Therefore, many computer science and statistical techniques are discussed at a high level in this chapter.

> **NOTE** Material that is traditionally found in statistical textbooks (such as the general linear model), as well as run-of-the mill, old computer science concepts (such as sorting algorithms) are not presented in this book. You can check out Chapter 8, "Data Science Resources" for an introduction to those subjects.

New Types of Metrics

Identifying powerful metrics—that is, metrics with good predictive power—is a fundamental role of the data scientist. The following sections present a number of metrics used in optimizing digital marketing campaigns and in fraud detection. Predictive power is defined in Chapter 6 in the section Predictive Power of a Feature, Cross-Validations. Metrics used to measure business outcomes in a business model are called KPIs (key performance indicators). A metric used to predict a trend is called a leading indicator.

Some metrics that are not KPIs still need to be identified and tracked. For instance, if you run e-mail campaigns to boost membership, two KPIs are the number of new members per month (based on number of e-mails sent), and churn. But you still need to track open rates, even open rates broken down by ISP, segments, and message sent, as these metrics, while clearly not KPIs, are critical to understand variations in new members and improve new members stats/reduce churn. For instance, analyzing open rates will show you that sending an e-mail on a Saturday night is much less efficient than on a Wednesday morning; or that no one with a Gmail e-mail address ever opens your message—a problem that is relatively easy to fix, but must be detected first. You can't fix it if you can't detect it; you can't detect it if you don't track open rates by ISP.

Big data and fast, clustered computers have made it possible to track and compute more sophisticated metrics, test thousands of metrics at once (to identify best predictors), and work with complex compound metrics: metrics that are a function of other metrics, such as *type of IP address*. These compound metrics are sometimes simple transformations (like a logarithmic transformation), sometimes complex combination and ratios of multiple base metrics, and sometimes derived from based metrics using complex clustering algorithms, such as the previous example: *type of IP address* (which will be discussed later in this chapter in the section Internet Topology Mapping).

Compound metrics are to base metrics what molecules are to atoms. Just like as few as seven atoms (oxygen, hydrogen, helium, carbon, sodium, chlorine, and sulfur) can produce trillions of trillions of trillions of molecules and chemical compounds (a challenge for analytical and computational chemists designing molecules to cure cancer), the same combinatorial explosion takes place as you move from base to compound metrics. Base metrics are raw fields found in data sets.

The following list of metrics (mostly compound metrics) is by no means comprehensive. You can use it as a starting point to think about how to create new metrics.

Metrics to Optimize Digital Marketing Campaigns

If you run an online newsletter, here are a number of metrics you need to track:

- Open rate: Proportion of subscribers opening your newsletter. Anything below 10 percent is poor, unless your e-CPM is low.

- Number of opens: Some users will open your message multiple times.

- Users opening more than two times: These people are potential leads or competitors. If few users open more than once, your content is not interesting, or maybe there is only one clickable link in your newsletter.

- Click rate: Average number of clicks per open. If less than 0.5, your subject line might be great, but the content (body) irrelevant.

- Open rate broken down per client (Yahoo! Mail, Gmail, Hotmail, and so on): If your open rate for Hotmail users is low, you should consider eliminating Hotmail users from your mailing list because they can corrupt your entire list.

- Open rate and click rate broken down per user segment.

- Trends: Does open rate, click rate, and such per segment go up or down over time? Identify best performing segments. Send different newsletters to different segments.

- Unsubscribe and churn rate: What subject line or content increases the unsubscribe or complaint rate?

- Spam complaints: these should be kept to less than one per thousand messages sent. Identify segments and clients (for example, Hotmail) generating high complaint rates, and remove them.

- Geography: Are you growing in India but shrinking in the United States? Is your open rate better in Nigeria? That's not a good sign, even if your overall trend looks good.

- Language: Do you have many Hispanic subscribers? If yes, can you send a newsletter in Spanish to these people? Can you identify Spanish speakers? (You can if you ask a question about language on sign-up.)

- Open rate by day of week and time: Identify best times to send your newsletter.

- User segmentation: Ask many questions to new subscribers; for example, about their interests. Make these questions optional. This will allow you to better target your subscribers.

- Growth acceleration: Are you reaching a saturation point? If yes, you need to find new sources of subscribers or reduce your frequency of e-mail blasts (possibly finding fewer but better or more relevant advertisers to optimize e-CPM).

- Low open rates: Are images causing low open rates? Are redirects (used to track clicks) causing low open rates? Some URL shorteners such as bit. ly, although useful, can result in low open rates or people not clicking links due to risk of computer infection.

- Keyword tracking: Have you tracked keywords that work well or poorly in the subject line to drive your open rate up?

- From field: Have you tried changing your *From* field to see what works best? A/B testing could help you get better results.

- Size of message: If too large, this could cause performance issues.

- Format: Text or HTML? Do some A/B testing to find optimum format.

You should note that *e-CPM* is the revenue generated per thousand impressions. It is your most important metric, together with churn.

Metrics for Fraud Detection

Many data scientists work on fraud detection projects. Since 1995, metrics dealing with fraud detection have been refined so that new powerful metrics are now used. The emphasis in this discussion of modern fraud detection metrics is on web log data. The metrics are presented here as rules. More than one rule must be triggered to fire an alarm if you use these metrics to build an alarm system. You may use a system such as hidden decision trees to assign a specific weight to each rule.

- Extreme events: Monte Carlo simulations to detect extreme events. For example, a large cluster of non-proxy IP addresses that have exactly eight clicks per day, day after day. What is the chance of this happening naturally?

- Blacklists and whitelists: Determine if an IP address or referral domain belongs to a particular type of blacklist or whitelist. For example, classify the space of IP addresses into major clusters, such as static IP, anonymous proxy, corporate proxy (white-listed), edu proxy (high risk), highly recycled IP (higher risk), and so on.

- Referral domain statistics: Gather statistics on time to load with variance (based on three measurements), page size with variance (based on three measurements), or text strings found on web page (either in HTML or JavaScript code). For example, create a list of suspicious terms (*Viagra*, *online casino*, and so on) or create a list of suspicious JavaScript tags or codes but use a whitelist of referral domains (for example, top publishers) to eliminate false positives.

- Analyze domain name patterns: For example, a cluster of domain names, with exactly identical fraud scores, are all of the form xxx-and-yyy.com, and their web pages all have the same size (1 char).

- Association analysis: For example, buckets of traffic with a huge proportion (> 30 percent) of very short (< 15 seconds) sessions that have two or more unknown referrals (that is, referrals other than Facebook, Google, Yahoo!, or a top 500 domain). Aggregate all these mysterious referrals across these sessions; chances are that they are all part of a same Botnet scheme (used, for example, for click fraud).

- Mismatch in credit card fields: For example, phone number in one country, e-mail or IP address from a proxy domain owned by someone located in another country, physical address yet in another location, name (for example, Amy) and e-mail address (for example, joy431232@hotmail.com) look different, and a Google search on the e-mail address reveals previous scams operated from same account, or nothing at all.

- Gibberish: For example, a referral web page or search keyword attached to a paid click contains gibberish or text strings made of letters that are close on the keyboard, such as *fgdfrffrft*.

- E-mail address anomalies: For example, an e-mail address contains digits other than area code, year (for example, 73), or ZIP code (except if from someone in India or China).

- Transaction time: For example, if the time to the first transaction after sign-up is short.

- Abnormal purchase pattern: For example, on a Sunday at 2 a.m., a customer buys the most expensive product on your e-store, from an IP outside the United States, on a B2B e-store targeted to U.S. clients.

- Repetitive small purchases: For example, when multiple $9.99 purchases are made across multiple merchants with the same merchant category, with one or two transactions per cardholder.

The key point here is that fraud detection metrics keep getting more complicated and diversified, as criminals constantly try to gain a competitive advantage by reverse-engineering fraud detection algorithms. There will always be jobs for data scientists working on fraud detection. Fraud detection also includes metrics to fight non-criminals—for instance, marketers who want to game search engines to get their websites listed first on Google, as well as plagiarists and spammers.

Choosing Proper Analytics Tools

As a data scientist, you will often use existing tools rather than reinventing the wheel. So before diving deeper into the technical stuff, it's important that you identify and choose the right tools for your job. Following are some important questions you need to ask and criteria to keep in mind when looking for a vendor for analytics software, visualization tools, real-time products, and programming languages.

Analytics Software

Here are a few good criteria and questions to consider that will help you select appropriate analytics software. Those I've found to be very important are indicated with an asterisk.

- Is it a new product or company, or well established?
- Is it open source or, if not, is a free trial available?
- Can it work with big data?*
- Price*
- Compatible with other products
- Easy to use and GUI offered*
- Can work in batch or programmable mode*
- Offers an API
- Capable of fetching data on the Internet or from a database (SQL supported)
- Nice graphic capabilities (to visualize decision trees, for instance)*
- Speed of computations and efficiency in the way memory is used*
- Good technical support, training, or documentation available*
- Local company
- Offers comprehensive set of modern procedures
- Offers add-ons or modules at an extra charge (this could be important as your needs grow)*
- Platform-independent*
- Technique-specialized (for example, time series, spatial data, scoring technology) versus generalist
- Field-specialized (for example, web log data, healthcare data, and finance)
- Compatible with your client (for example, SAS because your clients use SAS)*
- Used by practitioners in the same analytic domain (quant, econometrics, Six Sigma, operations research, computer science, and so on)
- Handles missing data, data cleaning, auditing functionality, and cross-validation
- Supports programming languages such as C++, Python, Java, and Perl rather than internal, ad hoc languages (despite the fact that an ad hoc language might be more efficient)*
- Learning curve is not too steep*
- Easy to upgrade*

- Able to work on the cloud, or to use MapReduce and NoSQL features
- Real-time features (can be integrated in a real-time system, such as auction bidding)

In some cases, three products might be needed: one for visualization, one with a large number of functions (neural networks, decision trees, constrained logistic regression, time series, and simplex), and one that will become your "work horse" to produce the bulk of heavy-duty analytics.

Related questions you should ask include:

- When do you decide to upgrade or purchase an additional module to an existing product, for example, SAS/GRAPH or SAS/ACCESS, to use on top of SAS Base?
- Who is responsible in your organization to make a final decision on the choice of analytics software? End users? Statisticians? Business people? The CTO?

Visualization Tools

Ask yourself the following questions to help you select the proper visualization tools for each of your projects:

- How do you define and measure the quality of a chart?
- Which tools allow you to produce interactive graphs or maps?
- Which tools do you recommend for big data visualization?
- Which visualization tools can be accessed via an API, in batch mode (for instance, to update earthquake maps every 5 minutes, or stock prices every second)?
- What do you think of Excel? And Python or Perl graph libraries? And R?
- Are there any tools that allow you to easily produce videos about your data (for example, to show how fraud cases or diseases spread over time)?
- In Excel you can update your data, and then your model and charts get updated right away. Are there any alternatives to Excel, offering the same features, but having much better data modeling capabilities?
- How do you produce nice graph structures—for example, to visually display Facebook connections?
- What is a heat map? When does it make sense to use it?
- How do you draw force-directed graphs?
- Is the tool a good choice for raster images, vector images, graphs, decision trees, fractals, time series, stock prices, maps, spatial data, and so on?
- How can you integrate R with other graphical packages?

- How do you represent five dimensions (for example, time, volume, category, price, and location) in a simple two-dimensional graph? Or is it better to represent fewer dimensions if your goal is to communicate a message to executives?

- Why are the visualization tools used by mathematicians and operations research practitioners (for example, Matlab) different from the tools used by data scientists? Is it because of the type of data, or just historical reasons?

Real-Time Products

These questions will help you get a good handle on the use and selection of real-time products:

- In addition to transaction scoring (credit card transactions and online ad delivery systems), what other applications need true real time?

- What types of applications work better with near real time, rather than true real time?

- How do you boost performance of true real-time scoring? For example, by having preloaded, permanent, in-memory, small, lookup tables (updated hourly) or other mechanisms? Explain.

- How do you handle server load at peak times because it can be 10 times higher than, for example, at 2 a.m.? And at 2 a.m., do you use idle servers to run hourly or daily algorithms to refine or adjust real-time scores?

- Are real-time algorithms selected and integrated into production by data scientists, mostly based on their ability to be easily deployed in a distributed environment?

- How do you solve difficult problems such as 3-D streaming video processing in real time from a moving observation point (to automatically fly a large plane at low elevations in crowded skies)?

- Do you think end users (for example, decision makers) should have access to dashboards updated in true real time, or is it better to offer five-minute delayed statistics to end users? In which application is real time better for end users?

- Is real time limited only to machine generated data?

- What is machine generated data? What about a real-time trading system that is based on recent or even extremely recent tweets or Facebook posts? Do you call this real time, big data, machine data, machine talking to machines, and so on?

- What is the benefit of true real time over five-minute-delayed signals? Does the benefit (increased accuracy) outweigh the extra cost? (On Wall Street, usually the answer is yes. But what about with keyword bidding algorithms—is a delayed reaction okay?)

- Are there any rules regarding optimum latency (when not implementing true real time) depending on the type of application? For instance, for Internet traffic monitoring, 15 minutes is good because it covers most user sessions.

- What kinds of programming environments are well suited for big data in real time? (SQL is not, C++ is better, what about Hadoop? What technology do you use?)

- What kind of applications are well suited for real-time big data?

- What type of metrics are heavily or easily used in real time (for example, time to last transaction)?

- To deliver clicks evenly and catch fraud right away, do you think that the only solution for Google is to monitor clicks (on paid ads) in true real time?

- Do you think Facebook uses true real time for ad targeting? How can it improve its very low impression-to-click ratio? Why is this ratio so low despite the fact that it knows so many things about its users? Could technology help?

- What is the future of real time over the next 10 years? What will become real time? What will stay hourly for end-of-day systems?

- Are all real-time systems actually hybrid, relying also on hourly and daily or even yearly (with seasonality) components to boost accuracy? How are real-time predictions performed for sparse highly granular data, such as predicting the yield of any advertising keyword in real time for any advertiser? (Answer: Group sparse data into bigger buckets; make forecasts for the entire bucket.)

Programming Languages

Python and R have become very popular: They're open source, so you can just download them from the web, get sample scripts, and start coding. Python offers analytics libraries, known as *Pandas*. R is also very popular. Java, Perl, and C++ have lost some popularity, though there are still people coding in C (in finance) because it's fast and lots of libraries are available for analytics as well as for visualization and database access. Perl is great and very flexible, especially if you are an independent creative data scientist and like to code without having to worry about the syntax, code versioning, team work, or how your code will be integrated by your client. Perl also comes with the Graph library.

Of course, you also need to know SQL. Hadoop has become the standard for MapReduce programming. SAS is widespread in some environments, especially government and clinical trials. I sometimes use R for advanced graphing (including videos) because it works well with palettes and other graphic features. R used to be limited by the memory available in your machine, although there are solutions that leverage the cloud (RHadoop).

Visualization

This section is not a review of visualization tools or principles. Such a review is beyond the scope of this book and would constitute a book by itself. Readers can check the Books section in Chapter 8 for references. You can also get more information on how to choose a visualization tool at `http://bit.ly/1cGlFA5`.

This section teaches you how to produce advanced charts in R and how to produce videos about data, or data videos—information. It also includes code to produce any kind of color pattern you want, because of the *rgb* (red/green/blue) R function embedded in an R *plot* command. By creating videos rather than pictures, you automatically add more dimension to your visuals—most frequently but not always, that dimension is time, as in time series. So this section is a tutorial on producing data videos with R. Finally, you can upload your data videos on YouTube. R is chosen for this discussion because it is very easy to use, and it is one of the most popular tools used by data scientists today.

Producing Data Videos with R

Following is a step-by-step process for producing your video. The first three sections explain how to do it. Then the subsequent sections provide additional detail you may find helpful.

Videos are important because they allow you to present spatial information that changes over time (spatial-temporal data), or display one additional dimension to what is otherwise a static image. They're also used to see the convergence (or lack thereof) and speed of convergence of data science algorithms. Song-Chun Zhu is one of the pioneers in producing "data videos" (see `http://www.stat .ucla.edu/~sczhu/publication.html`).

Another useful aspect of videos is the ability to show rotating 3-D charts so that the user can see the chart from all angles and find patterns that traditional 2-D projections (static images) don't show (unless you look at dozens of projections). The basic principles are:

- Deciding which metric will be used as your time variable (let's call it "time")
- How fast frames are moving
- How granular time is (you decide)
- Producing the data frames (one for each time—that's where R, Python, or Perl is used)
- Displaying the frames (easy with R) and/or getting them embedded into a video file (open source ActivePresenter is used here)

Two important points are how the data should be visualized and who should make this decision—the data scientist, the business analyst, or the business user.

The business user typically decides, but the data scientist should also propose new visualizations to the business user (depending on the type of data being analyzed and the KPIs used in the company), and let the business user eventually decide, based on how much value he can extract from a visualization and how much time it takes to extract that value.

Visualizations communicating business value linked to KPIs, solving a costly issue, or showing a big revenue opportunity, and that can be understood in 30 seconds or less, are the best. The worst graphs have one or more of the following features: (1) they're cluttered, (2) the data is rescaled, (3) unimportant data masks or hides valuable information, and (4) they display metrics that are not comparable.

Produce the Data You Want to Visualize

Using Python, R, Perl, Excel, SAS, or any other tool, produce a text file called `rfile.txt`, with four columns:

- k: frame number
- x: x-coordinate
- y: y-coordinate
- z: color associated with (x,y)

Or, if you want to exactly replicate my experiment, you can download my `rfile.txt` (sample data to visualize) at http://www.datashaping.com/first.r.txt.

Run the Following R Script

Note that the first variable in the R script is labeled `iter`. It is associated with an iterative algorithm that produces an updated data set of 500 (x,y) observations at each iteration. The fourth field is called `new`, which indicates if point (x,y) is new for a given (x,y) and given iteration. New points appear in red; old ones appear in black.

```
vv<-read.table("c:/vincentg/rfile.txt",header=TRUE);
iter<-vv$iter;
for (n in 0:199) {
  x<-vv$x[iter == n];
  y<-vv$y[iter == n];
  z<-vv$new[iter == n];
  plot(x, y, xlim=c(0,1),ylim=c(0,1),pch=20,col=1+z,
xlab="",ylab="",axes=FALSE);
dev.copy(png, filename=paste("c:/vincentg/Zorm_",n,".png",sep=""));
  dev.off ();
}
```

Produce the Video

There are four different ways to produce your video. When you run the R script, the following happens:

- 200 images (scatter plots) are produced and displayed sequentially on the R Graphic window in a period of about 30 seconds.

- 200 images (one for each iteration or scatter plot) are saved as `Zorm0.png`, `Zorm1.png`, and so on, up to Zorm199 in the target directory.

Then your three options to produce the video are as follows:

1. Caveman style: Film the R Graphic frame sequence with your cell phone.

2. Semi-caveman style: Use a screen-cast tool (for example, ActivePresenter) to capture the streaming plots displayed on the R Graphic window.

3. Use Adobe or other software to automatically assemble the 200 `Zorm*`.png images produced by R.

You can read about other possible solutions (such as open source ffmpeg or the ImageMagick library) at `http://stackoverflow.com/questions/1298100/creating-a-movie-from-a-series-of-plots-in-r`. You could also watch the animation "An R Package for Creating Animations and Demonstrating Statistical Methods" published in the April 2013 issue of the *Journal of Statistical Software*.

A nice thing about these videos is that you can upload them to YouTube. You can check out mine at these URLs:

- `http://www.youtube.com/watch?v=DL4cYD2X9PM`

- `http://www.youtube.com/watch?v=fb0yevGSAxY`

- `http://www.youtube.com/watch?v=QBQIHbQdptk`

- `http://www.youtube.com/watch?v=4oIsB0EdnmQ`

ActivePresenter

You can use ActivePresenter (`http://atomisystems.com`) screen-cast software (free edition), as follows:

- Let the 200 plots automatically show up in fast motion in the R Graphics window.

- Use ActivePresenter to select the area you want to capture (a portion of the R Graphic window, just like for a screen shot, except that it captures streaming content rather than a static image).

- Click Stop when finished and export it to your `.wmv` format and upload to a web server for others to access.

I recently created two high quality videos using ActivePresenter based on a data set with two additional columns using the following, different R script (you can download the data as a 7 MB text file at http://www.datashaping.com/rfile2.txt):

```
vv<-read.table("c:/vincentg/rfile.txt",header=TRUE);
iter<-vv$iter;
for (n in 0:199) {
  x<-vv$x[iter == n];
  y<-vv$y[iter == n];
  z<-vv$new[iter == n];
  u<-vv$d2init[iter == n];
  v<-vv$d2last[iter == n];
  plot(x,y,xlim=c(0,1),ylim=c(0,1), pch=20+z, cex=3*u,
col=rgb(z/2,0,u/2),xlab="", ylab="",axes=TRUE);
  Sys.sleep(0.05); # sleep 0.05 second between each iteration
}
```

You could also try changing the `plot` command to:

```
plot(x,y,xlim=c(0,1),ylim=c(0,1),pch=20,cex=5,col=rgb(z,0,0),
xlab="",ylab="",axes=TRUE);
```

This second R script differs from the first as follows:

- The `dev.copy` and `dev.off` calls are removed to stop producing the PNG images on the hard drive. (You don't need them here because you use screen casts). Producing the PNG files slows down the whole process and creates flickering videos—this step removes most of the flickering.

- The function `Sys.sleep` is used to make a short pause between each frame, which makes the video smoother.

- `rgb` is used inside the plot command to assign a color to each dot: (x, y) gets assigned a color that is a function of z and u, at each iteration.

- The size of the dot (cex) in the plot command now depends on the variable u: That's why you see bubbles of various sizes that grow bigger or shrink.

Note that `d2init` (fourth column in the `rfile2.txt` input data used to produce the video) is the distance between the location of (x,y) at the current iteration and its location at the first iteration. In addition, `d2last` (fifth column) is the distance between the current and previous iterations for each point. The point will be colored in a more intense blue if it made a big move between the current and previous iterations.

The function `rgb` accepts three parameters with values between 0 and 1, representing the intensity in the red, green, and blue frequencies, respectively. For instance, `rgb (0,0,1)` is blue, `rgb (1,1,0)` is yellow, `rgb (0.5,0.5,0.5)` is gray, `rgb (1,0,1)` is purple, and so on. Make sure $0 \leq rgb \leq 1$ otherwise it will crash.

More Sophisticated Videos

You can also create videos that involve points and arrows (not just points) continuously moving from frame to frame. Arrows are attached to points and indicate which cluster a point is moving toward or away from at any given time. Transitions from frame to frame are accelerated over time, and color gradients are also used.

I recently produced a couple of these videos. You can find additional information on them at the following URLs:

- Download the data set at `http://www.datashaping.com/rfile3.txt`.

- View the videos at `http://www.analyticbridge.com/profiles/blogs/shooting-stars`.

Here is the R source code used in this version.

```
vv<-read.table("c:/vincentg/rfile3.txt",header=TRUE);
iter<-vv$iter;
for (n in 1:199) {
  x<-vv$x[iter == n];
  y<-vv$y[iter == n];
  z<-vv$new[iter == n];
  u<-vv$d2init[iter == n];
  v<-vv$d2last[iter == n];
  p<-vv$x[iter == n-1];
  q<-vv$y[iter == n-1];
  u[u>1]<-1;
  v[v>0.10]<-0.10;
  s=1/sqrt(1+n);
  if (n==1) {
    plot(p,q,xlim=c(-0.08,1.08),ylim=c(-0.08,1.09),pch=20,cex=0,
col=rgb(1,1,0),xlab="",ylab="",axes=TRUE   );
  }
  points(p,q,col=rgb(1-s,1-s,1-s),pch=20,cex=1);
  segments(p,q,x,y,col=rgb(0,0,1));
  points(x,y,col=rgb(z,0,0),pch=20,cex=1);
  Sys.sleep(5*s);
  segments(p,q,x,y,col=rgb(1,1,1));
}
segments(p,q,x,y,col=rgb(0,0,1)); # arrows segments
points(x,y,col=rgb(z,0,0),pch=20,cex=1);
```

Statistical Modeling Without Models

Statistical "modeling without models" is a way to do inference, even predictions or computing confidence intervals, without using statistical distributions or models. Sometimes, understanding the physical model driving a system (for instance, the stock market) may be less important than having a trading system that works. Sometimes (as in the stock market), you can try to emulate the system (using Monte Carlo simulations to simulate stock market prices) and fit the data to the simulations without knowing exactly what you are emulating (from a physical or theoretical point of view), as long as it works and can be adapted when conditions or environment (for instance, market conditions) change.

You may be wondering how to get the data needed to produce the previously discussed videos. This section presents details on the algorithms used to produce the data for the videos. I will use my shooting stars video as the example, which means you need a bit of history on the project.

The project began as the result of several of my personal interests and research, including the following:

- Interest in astronomy, visualization, and how physics models apply to business problems

- Interest in systems that produce clusters (as well as birth and death processes) and in visualizing cluster formation with videos rather than charts

- Research on how urban growth could be modeled by the gravitational law

- Interest in creating videos with sound and images synchronized and generated using data

The statistical models behind the videos are birth and death processes—gravitational forces that create clusters that form and die—with points moving from one cluster to another throughout the process, and points coming from far away. Eventually, it became *modeling without models*, a popular trend in data science.

What Is a Statistical Model Without Modeling?

There is a generic mathematical model behind the algorithm used to create the video data, but the algorithm was created first without having a mathematical model in mind. This illustrates a new trend in data science: less and less concern about modeling, and more and more about results.

My algorithm has a bunch of parameters and features that can be fine-tuned to produce anything you want—be it a simulation of a Neyman-Scott cluster process or a simulation of some no-name stochastic process. It's a bit similar to how modern mountain climbing has evolved: from focusing on big names such as Everest in the past, to exploring deeper wilderness and climbing no-name peaks today (with their own challenges), and possibly to mountain climbing on Mars in the future.

You can fine-tune the parameters to:

- Achieve the best fit between simulated data and real business (or other data), using traditional goodness-of-fit testing and sensitivity analysis. Note that the simulated data represents a realization (an instance for object-oriented people) of a spatio-temporal stochastic process.

▪ After the parameters are calibrated, perform predictions (if you speak the statistician's language) or extrapolations (if you speak the mathematician's language).

How Does the Algorithm Work?

The algorithm starts with a random distribution of m mobile points in the [0,1] x [0,1] square window. The points get attracted to each other (attraction is stronger to closest neighbors) and thus, over time, they group into clusters.

The algorithm has the following components:

▪ Creation of n random fixed points (n = 100) on [−0.5, 1.5] × [−0.5, 1.5]. This window is four times bigger than the one containing the mobile points, to eliminate edge effects impacting the mobile points. These fixed points (they never move) also act as some sort of dark matter: they are invisible, they are not represented in the video, but they are the glue that prevents the whole system from collapsing onto itself and converging to a single point.

▪ Creation of m random mobile points (m = 500) on [0,1] × [0,1].

▪ Main loop (200 iterations). At each iteration, compute the distance d between each mobile point (x,y) and each of its m–1 mobile neighbors and n fixed neighbors. A weight w is computed as a function of d, with a special weight for the point (x,y) itself. Then the updated (x,y) is the weighted sum aggregated over all points, and I do that for each point (x,y) at each iteration. The weight is such that the sum of weights over all points is always 1. In other words, replace each point with a convex linear combination of all points.

Some special features of this algorithm include the following:

▪ If the weight for (x,y) (the point being updated) is very high at a given iteration, then (x,y) will barely move.

▪ When negative weights are tested (especially for the point being updated) the results are better. A delicate amount of negative weights also prevents the system from collapsing and introduces a bit of desirable chaos.

▪ Occasionally, one point is replaced by a brand new random point, rather than updated using the weighted sum of neighbors. This is called a "birth." It happens for less than 1 percent of all point updates, and it happens more frequently at the beginning. Of course, you can play with these parameters.

In the Perl source code shown here, the birth process for point $k is simply encoded as:

```perl
if (rand()<0.1/(1+$iteration)) { # birth and death
  $tmp_x[$k]=rand();
  $tmp_y[$k]=rand();
  $rebirth[$k]=1;
}
```

In this source code, in the inner loop over $k, the point ($x, $y) to be updated is referenced as point $k, that is, ($y, $y) = ($moving_x[$k], $moving_y[$k]). Also, in a loop over $l, one level deeper, ($p, $q) referenced as point $l, represents a neighboring point when computing the weighted average formula used to update ($x, $y). The distance *d* is computed using the function distance, which accepts four arguments ($x, $y, $p, and $q) and returns $weight, the weight *w*.

In summary, realistic simulations used to study real-life mechanisms help you understand and replicate the mechanism in the laboratory, even if the mechanism itself is not understood. In this case, these simulations (visualized in videos) help you understand how multiple celestial bodies with various sizes, velocities, and origins work (or anything subject to forces similar to gravitational forces—possibly competitive forces in the market), including how they coalesce, are born, and die. In turn, by fitting data to simulations, you can make predictions, even if the mechanism is not well understood.

Source Code to Produce the Data Sets

Both Perl and R have been used to produce the datasets for the video. You can download the source code for both at http://bit.ly/11Jdi4t.

The Perl code runs much faster than the R code, not because Perl itself is faster, but because of the architecture used in the program: Perl recomputes all of the frames at once and loads them into memory, while R produces each frame only as needed. The advantage of the R version is that it completes all aspects of the process, including producing the data and displaying the video frames.

Three Classes of Metrics: Centrality, Volatility, Bumpiness

This section marks the beginning of a deeper dive into more technical data science information. Let's start with a simple concept. Statistical textbooks focus on centrality (median, average, or mean) and volatility (variance). They don't mention the third fundamental class of metrics: bumpiness. This section begins by considering the relationship between centrality, volatility, and bumpiness. It then discusses the concept of bumpiness and how it can be used. Finally, you will see how a new concept is developed, a robust modern definition is materialized, and a more meaningful definition is created based on, and compatible with, previous science.

Relationships Among Centrality, Volatility, and Bumpiness

Two different data sets can have the same centrality and volatility, but a different bumpiness. Bumpiness is linked to how the data points are ordered, whereas centrality and volatility completely ignore order. So bumpiness is useful for data sets where order matters—in particular, time series. Also, bumpiness integrates the notion of dependence among the data points, whereas centrality and variance do not. Note that a time series can have high volatility (high variance) and low bumpiness. The converse is also true.

Detecting changes in bumpiness is important. The classical example is stock market strategy: an algorithm works well for a while, and then a change in bumpiness makes it fail. Detecting when bumpiness changes can help you adapt your algorithm earlier, and hopefully decrease losses. Low bumpiness can also be associated with stronger, more accurate predictions. When possible, use data with low bumpiness or use bumpiness reduction techniques.

Defining Bumpiness

Given a time series, an intuitive, data science, scale-dependent, and robust metric would be the average acute angle measured on all the vertices. This metric is bounded by the following:

- The maximum is Pi and is attained by smooth time series (straight lines).
- The minimum is 0 and is attained by time series with extreme, infinite oscillations, from one time interval to the other.

This metric is non-sensitive to outliers. It is by all means a modern metric. However, I don't want to reinvent the wheel, and thus I will define bumpiness using a classical "statistic" (as opposed to "data science") metric that has the same mathematical and theoretical appeal and drawbacks as the old-fashioned average (to measure centrality) or variance (to measure volatility).

Bumpiness can be defined as the auto-correlation of lag 1. Figure 4-1 shows three time series with the same mean, variance, and values, but different bumpiness.

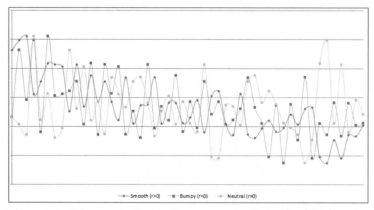

Figure 4-1: Three time series with the same mean, variance, and values, but different bumpiness

Note that the lag 1 auto-correlation is the highest of all auto-correlations, in absolute value. Therefore, it is the single best indicator of the auto-correlation structure of a time series. It is always between –1 and +1. It is close to 1 for smooth time series, close to 0 for pure noise, negative for periodic time series, and close to –1 for time series with huge oscillations. You can produce an *r* close to –1 by ordering pseudo-random deviates as follows: x(1), x(n), x(2), x(n–1), x(3), x(n–2)... where x(k) [k = 1, ..., n] represents the order statistics for a set of n points, with x(1)= minimum, x(n) = maximum.

A better but more complicated definition would involve all the auto-correlation coefficients embedded in a sum with decaying weights. It would be better in the sense that when the value is 0, it means that the data points are truly independent for most practical purposes.

Bumpiness Computation in Excel

You will now consider an Excel spreadsheet showing computations of the bumpiness coefficient *r* for various time series. It is also of interest if you want to learn new Excel concepts such as random number generation with *RAND*, indirect references with *INDIRECT*, *RANK*, and *LARGE*, and other powerful but not well-known Excel functions. Finally, it is an example of a fully interactive Excel spreadsheet driven by two core parameters.

You can download the spreadsheet from `http://bit.ly/KhU41L`. It contains a base (smooth, r > 0) time series in column G and four other time series derived from the base time series:

- Bumpy in column H (r < 0)
- Neutral in column I (r not statistically different from 0)
- Extreme (r = 1) in column K
- Extreme (r = –1) in column M

Two core parameters can be fine-tuned: cells N1 and O1. Note that r can be positive even if the time series is trending down: r does not represent the trend. Instead, a metric that would measure trend would be the correlation with time (also computed in the spreadsheet).

The creation of a neutral time series (r = 0), based on a given set of data points (that is, preserving average, variance, and indeed all values) is performed by reshuffling the original values (column G) in a random order. It is based on using the pseudo-random permutation in column B, itself created using random deviates with RAND, and using the RANK Excel formula. The theoretical framework is based on the Analyticbridge second theorem.

Analyticbridge Second Theorem

A random permutation of non-independent numbers constitutes a sequence of independent numbers. This is not a real theorem per se; however, it is a rather intuitive and easy way to explain the underlying concept. In short, the more data points, the more the reshuffled series (using a random permutation) looks like random numbers (with a prespecified, typically non-uniform statistical distribution), no matter what the original numbers are. It is also easy to verify the theorem by computing a bunch of statistics on simulated reshuffled data: all these statistics (for example, auto-correlations) will be consistent with the fact that the reshuffled values are (asymptotically) independent of each other.

> **NOTE** You can check out the first Analyticbridge theorem at `http://www`
> `.analyticbridge.com/profiles/blogs/how-to-build-simple-accurate-`
> `data-driven-model-free-confidence-in`.

Excel has some issues. In particular, its random number generator has been criticized, and values get recomputed each time you update the spreadsheet, making the results nonreplicable (unless you "freeze" the values in column B).

Uses of Bumpiness Coefficients

Economic time series should always be studied by separating periods with high and low bumpiness, understanding the mechanisms that create bumpiness, and detecting bumpiness in the first place. In some cases, the bumpiness might be too small to be noticed with the naked eye, but statistical tools should detect it.

Another application is in high-frequency trading. Stocks with highly negative bumpiness in price (over short time windows) are perfect candidates for statistical trading because they offer controlled, exploitable volatility—unlike a bumpiness close to zero, which corresponds to uncontrolled volatility (pure noise). And of course, stocks with highly positive bumpiness don't exist anymore. They did 30 years ago: they were the bread and butter of investors who kept a stock or index forever to see it automatically grow year after year.

> **QUESTION**
>
> How do you generalize this definition to higher dimensions—for instance, to spatial processes? You could have a notion of directional bumpiness (north-south or east-west).
>
> Potential application: flight path optimization in real time to avoid serious bumpy air (that is, highly negative wind speed and direction bumpiness).

Statistical Clustering for Big Data

Clustering techniques have already been explored in Chapter 2. Here I describe an additional technique to help cluster large data sets. It can be added to any clustering algorithm. It consists of first creating core clusters using a sample, rather than the entire data set.

Say you have to cluster 10 million points—for instance, keywords. You have a dissimilarity function available as a text file with 100 million entries, each entry consisting of three data points:

- Keyword A
- Keyword B
- Distance between A and B, denoted as d(A,B)

So, in short, you can perform k-NN; (k-nearest neighbors) clustering or some other type of clustering, which typically is $O(n^2)$ or worse, from a computational complexity point of view.

The idea is to start by sampling 1 percent (or less) of the 100 million entries and perform clustering on these pairs of keywords to create a "seed" or "baseline" cluster structure.

The next step is to browse sequentially your 10 million keywords, and for each keyword, find the closest cluster from the baseline cluster structure. If there are 1,000 base clusters, you'll have to perform 10 billion (10,000,000 x 1,000) computations (hash table accesses), a rather large number, but it can easily be done with a distributed architecture (Hadoop).

You could indeed repeat the whole procedure five times (with five different samples), and blend the five different final cluster structures that you obtain. The final output might be a table with 30 million entries, where each entry consist of a pair of keywords A and B and the number of times (if >0) when A and B belong to a same cluster (based on the five iterations corresponding to the five different samples). The final cluster detection algorithm consists of extracting the connected components from these 30 million entries. These entries, from a graph theory point of view, are called ridges, joining two nodes A and B. (Here a node is a keyword.)

What are the conditions for such an algorithm to work? You can assume that each keyword A has on average between 2 and 50 neighboring keywords B such that d(A,B) > 0. The number of such neighbors is usually much closer to 2 than to 50. So you might end up after classifying all keywords with 10 or 20 percent of all keywords isolated (forming single-point clusters).

Of course you'll solve the problem if you work with 50 rather than 5 samples, or samples that represent 25 percent of the data rather than 1 percent, but this is a time-prohibitive approach that poorly and inefficiently leverages statistical sampling. The way to optimize these parameters is by testing: If your algorithm runs very fast and requires little memory, but leaves too many important keywords isolated, then you must increase the sample size or number of samples, or a combination of both. Conversely, if the algorithm is very slow, stop the program and decrease the sample size or number of samples. When you run an algorithm, it is always a good idea to have your program print on the screen (or in a log file) the size of the hash tables as they grow (so you will know when your algorithm has exhausted all your memory and can fix the problem), as well as the steps completed. In short, displaying progress status. For instance:

```
10,000 keywords processed and 545 clusters created
20,000 keywords processed and 690 clusters created,
30,000 keywords processed and 738 clusters created
```

As the program is running, after 21 seconds the first line is displayed on the screen; after 45 seconds the second line is displayed below the first line; after 61 seconds the third line is displayed, and so on. The symbol > is used because it typically shows up on the window console where the program is running. Sometimes, instead of > it's $ or something like $c://home/vincentg/myprograms>.

You can also compute the time used to complete each step (to identify bottlenecks) by calling the time function at the end of each step, and measuring time differences (see http://bit.ly/1e4eRgP for details).

An interesting application of this keyword clustering is as follows: Traditional yellow pages have a few hundred categories and subcategories. The restaurant category has subcategories that are typically all related to type of cuisine: Italian, American, sushi, seafood, and so on. By analyzing and clustering online user queries, you can identify a richer set of subcategories for the restaurant category: type of cuisine, of course (as usual), type of restaurant (wine bar, upscale, pub, family dining, restaurant with view, romantic, ethnic, late dining), type of location (downtown, riverfront, suburban, beach, mountain), or stuff not related to the food itself (restaurant jobs, recipes, menus, restaurant furniture).

NOTE You should prioritize areas that have a high node density, and then assume those areas have a higher chance of being sampled.

Correlation and R-Squared for Big Data

With big data, you sometimes have to compute correlations involving thousands of buckets of paired observations or time series. For instance, a data bucket corresponds to a node in a decision tree, a customer segment, or a subset of observations having the same multivariate feature. Specific contexts of interest include multivariate feature selection (a combinatorial problem) or identification of the best predictive set of metrics.

In large data sets, some buckets contain outliers or meaningless data, and buckets might have different sizes. You need something better than the tools offered by traditional statistics. In particular, you need a correlation metric that satisfies the following conditions:

1. Independent of sample size to allow comparisons across buckets of different sizes: A correlation of (say) 0.6 must always correspond to, for example, the 74th percentile among all potential paired series (X, Y) of size n, regardless of n.

2. The same bounds as old-fashioned correlation for back-compatibility: It must be between –1 and +1, with –1 and +1 attained by extreme, singular data sets, and 0 meaning no correlation.

3. More general than traditional correlation: It measures the degree of monotonicity between two variables X and Y (does X grow when Y grows?) rather than linearity (Y = a + b*X + noise, with a, b chosen to minimize noise). Yet it should not be as general as the distance correlation (equal to zero if and only if X and Y are independent) or the structuredness coefficient defined later in this chapter.

4. Not sensitive to outliers; robust.

5. More intuitive; more compatible with the way the human brain perceives correlations.

Note that R-Squared, a goodness-of-fit measure used to compare model efficiency across multiple models, is typically the square of the correlation coefficient between observations and predicted values, measured on a training set via sound cross-validation techniques. It suffers the same drawbacks and benefits from the same cures as traditional correlation. So I will focus here on the correlation.

To illustrate the first condition (dependence on n), consider the following made-up data set with two paired variables or time series X, Y:

```
X  Y
0  0
1  1
2  0
3  1
4  0
5  1
6  0
7  1
```

Here n = 8 and **r** (the traditional correlation) is equal to r = 0.22. If n = 7 (delete the last observation), then r = 0. If n = 6, r = 0.29. Clearly I observe high correlations when n is even, although, they slowly decrease to converge to 0, for large values of n. If you shift Y one cell down (assuming both X and Y are infinite time series), then correlations for n are now negative! However, this (X, Y) process is supposed to simulate a perfect 0 correlation. The traditional correlation coefficient fails to capture this pattern, for small n.

This is a problem with big data, where you might have tons of observations (monthly home prices and square feet for 300 million homes) but you compute correlations on small buckets (for instance, for all specific types of houses sold in 2013 in a particular ZIP code) to refine home value estimates for houses not on the market by taking into account local fluctuations. In particular, comparisons between buckets of different sizes become meaningless.

Our starting point to improve the standard correlation will be Spearman's rank correlation. It is the traditional correlation but measured on ranked variables. All correlations from the new family that I will introduce in the next section are also based on rank statistics. By working on ranked variables, you satisfy conditions #3 and #4 (although #4 will be further improved with my new correlation). Now denote Spearman's coefficient as **s**.

It is easy to prove:

$$s = 1 - S(X, Y)/q(n)$$

where:

- $S(X, Y) = \text{SUM}\{\ |x(j) - y(j)|^2\ \}$
- $x(j)$, $y(j)$ represent the ranks of observation j, in the X and Y series
- $q(n) = n*(n^{2-1})/6,$

Of course, s satisfies condition #2, by construction. An interesting and important fact, and a source of concern, is that $q(n) = O(n^3)$. In short, $q(n)$ grows too fast.

A New Family of Rank Correlations

Without loss of generality, from now on you can assume that X is ordered and thus $x(j) = j$. The new correlation will be denoted as **t** or t(c) to emphasize that it is a family of correlations governed by the parameter c. Bayesian statisticians might view c as a prior distribution.

The new correlation **t** is computed as follows:

Step A
- Compute $u = \text{SUM}\{\ |x(j) - y(j)|^c\}$
- Compute $v = \text{SUM}\{\ |x(j) - z(j)|^c\}$, where $z(j) = n-1-y(j)$
- $T = T(c) = \min(u, v)$
- Sign = +1 if u<v, –1 if u>v, 0 if u = v

Step B
- $t = t(c) = \text{Sign} * \{\ 1-T(c)/q(n)\ \}$
- $q(n)$ is the maximum value for T(c) computed across all (X, Y) with n observations

Explanation and Discussion

Here are some properties of this new correlation:

- This new correlation is still symmetric. (**t** will not change if you swap X and Y.) Also, if you reverse Y order, then only the sign of the correlation changes. (But this was already true for **s**; prove it as an exercise.)

- It always satisfies condition #2 when $c > 0$. Also, when $c > 0$, **t** = +1 if and only if **s** = +1, and **t** = −1 if and only if **s** = −1.

- It is similar to s (Spearman's) when $c = 2$. However $c = 2$ makes t too sensitive to outliers. Also, $c = 2$ is an artificial value that makes old-style computations and modeling easy. But it is not built with practical purposes in mind, unlike $c = 1$. In short, it is built based on theoretical and historic considerations and suffers drawbacks and criticism similar to old-fashioned R-Squared.

- I conjecture that $q(n) = O(n^{\{c+1\}})$. When c is large, it creates a long, artificial tail for the distribution of $T(c)$. A small c is preferred; otherwise, rare, extremely high values of $T(c)$ artificially boost $q(n)$ and create a **t** that is not well balanced.

- You will focus here on the case $c = 1$.

- You compute the rank distances between X and Y (in u) as well as between X and Z, (in v), where Z is Y in reversed order, and then pick up the smallest between u and v. This step also determines the sign of the correlation.

- In general, **s** and **t** are very similar when the value is close to −1 or +1, but there are significant differences (spread) when the value is close to 0—that is, when you test whether the correlation is 0 or not. Figure 4-2 presents an example showing all $n! = 362{,}880$ potential correlation combinations. Figure 4-3 shows an example where **s** and **t** are very different.

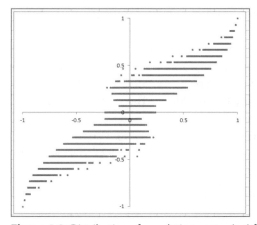

Figure 4-2: Distribution of correlation vector (s, t) for n = 9

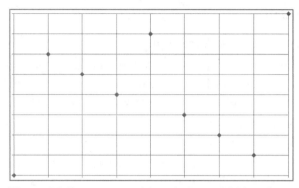

Figure 4-3: Extreme case with s = 0.17, t = –0.26 (n = 9)

NOTE Question: In Figure 4-3, which correlation makes the most sense, **s** or **t**? Answer: Neither is statistically different from 0. However, **t** makes more sense since the two points in the top-right and bottom-left corners look like outliers and make **s** positive (but not **t**, which is less sensitive to outliers).

Asymptotic Distribution and Normalization

Again, I assume that t is defined using c = 1. Simulations where X = (0, 1... n–1) and Y is a random permutation of n elements (obtained by first creating n random numbers then extracting their rank) show that

- t converges faster than s to 0: in one experiment, the observed t averaged more than 30 simulations, for n = 10, it was 0.02; average s was 0.04.
- Average t is also smaller than average s.
- You haven't computed p-values yet, but they will be different, everything else (n, c, test level, null hypothesis that correlation is 0) being equal.

Finally, when t and s are quite different, usually the t value looks more natural, as in Figure 4-3; t < 0 but s > 0 because t is better at eliminating the effect of the two outliers (top-right corner, bottom-left corner). This is critical when you compute correlations across thousands of data buckets of various sizes: You are bound to find outliers in some buckets. And if you look for extreme correlations, your conclusions might be severely biased. (Read the section The Curse of Big Data in Chapter 2 for more information on this.)

Figure 4-4 shows the distribution for T, when n = 10. When n = 10, 97.2 percent of t values are between –0.5 and +0.5. When n = 7, 92.0 percent of t values are between –0.5 and +0.5. So the distribution of t depends on n. Theoretically, when c gets close to 0, what happens?

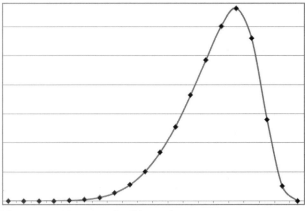

Figure 4-4: Histogram for T (n = 10)

> **NOTE** An interesting fact is that t and s agree most of the time. The classic correlation r between s and t, computed on all n! = 362,880 potential (X, Y) vectors with n = 9 observations, is equal to 0.96.

To estimate the asymptotic distribution of t (when n becomes large), you need to compute q(n). Is there an exact formula for q(n)? I ran a competition to see if someone could come up with a formula, a proof that none exists, or at least an asymptotic formula. Read the next section to find out the details. Let's just say for now that there were two winners—both experts in mathematical optimization—and $1,500 in awards were offered.

Normalization

Because the correlation is in the range [–1, +1] and is thus bounded, I would like a correlation of, for example, 0.5 to always represent the same percentile of t, regardless of n. There are various ways to accomplish this, but it always involves transforming t. Some research still needs to be done. For r or s, you can typically use the Fisher transformation. But it will not work on t, plus it transforms a bounded metric in a nonbounded one, making interpretation difficult.

Permutations

Most of this research and these simulations involve the generation of a large number of permutations for small and large n. This section discusses how to generate these permutations.

One way is to produce all permutations: You can find source code and instructions at `http://bit.ly/171bEzt`. It becomes slow when n is larger than 20; however, it is easy to use MapReduce to split the task on multiple virtual machines, in parallel. Another strategy is to sample enough random permutations to get a good approximation of t's distribution, as well as q(n). There is a one-to-one mapping between permutations of n elements and integer numbers between 1 and n. Each of these numbers can be uniquely represented by an n-permutation and the other way around. Also check the "numbering permutations" section of the Wikipedia article on permutations for details: `http://en.wikipedia.org/wiki/Permutation#Numbering_permutations`). It is slow: $O(n^2)$ to transform a number into a permutation or the other way around. So instead, I used a rudimentary approach (you can download the source code at `http://bit.ly/H4Y1oV`), which is just as fast:

The algorithm to generate a random permutation is as follows:

$$(p(0), p(1), ... , p(n{-}1))$$

For k = 0 to n–1, do

Step 1: Generate p(k) as a random number on {0, ... , n–1}.

Step 2: Repeat Step 1 until p(k) is different from p(0), p(1), ... , p(k–1).

Final Comments

The following comments provide more insight into the differences between the two correlations *s* and *t*.

- If you are interested in using correlations to assess how good your predicted values are likely to be, you can divide your data set into two sets for cross-validation: test and control. Fine-tune your model on the test data (also called the training set), using t to measure its predictive power. But the real predictive power is measured by computing **t** on the control data. The article "Use PRESS, not R-squared to judge predictive power of regression" at `http://bit.ly/14fRoGp` presents a leaving-one-out strategy that accomplishes a similar goal.

- Note that t, unlike s, has a bimodal distribution with a dip around 0. This makes sense because a correlation of 0 means no pattern found (a rare event), whereas different from 0 (but far from –1 or +1) means pattern found—any kind of pattern, however slight—a more frequent event. Indeed, I view this bimodal distribution as an advantage that t has over s.

- t can be used for outlier detection: when |t-s| is large, or |t-r| is large; I have outliers in the data set.

- My t is one of the few metrics defined by an algorithm, rather than a formula. This is a new trend in data science, using algorithms to define stuff.

- The fact that s uses square distances rather than distances (like t) makes it less robust, as outliers heavily weight on s. Although both s and t are based on rank statistics to smooth out the impact of outliers, s is still sensitive to outliers when n is large. And with big data, I see more cases of large n.

■ You could spend years of research on this whole topic of t and random permutations, and write a book or PhD thesis on the subject. Here I did the minimum amount of research to get to a good understanding and solution to the problem. This way of doing data science research is in contrast with slow-paced, comprehensive academic research.

Computational Complexity

The purpose of this section is twofold. First, to solve the problem discussed in the previous section—namely, to find an explicit formula for q(n)—using algorithms (simulations) that involve processing large amount of data. This can help you get familiarized with a number of computer science concepts related to computational complexity. Second, to display an exact mathematical solution proving that sometimes mathematical modeling can beat even the most powerful system of clustered computers to find a solution. Though usually, both work hand in hand.

This function q(n) is at the core of a new type of statistical metrics developed for big data: a nonparametric, robust metric to measure a new type of correlation or goodness of fit. This metric generalizes traditional metrics that have been used for centuries, and it is most useful when working with large ordinal data series, such as rank data. Although based on rank statistics, it is much less sensible to outliers than current metrics based on rank statistics (Spearman's rank correlation), which were designed for rather small n, where Spearman's rank correlation is indeed robust.

Computing q(n)

Start with a caveman approach, and then go through a few rounds of improvements.

Brute Force Algorithm

Brute force consists of visiting all *n!* permutations of n elements to find the maximum q(n). Computational complexity is therefore $O(n!)$—this is terribly slow.

Here's the code that iteratively produces all the n! (factorial n) permutations of n elements stored in an array. It allows you to easily compute stats associated with these permutations and compute aggregates over all or specific permutations. For n>10, it can be slow, and some MapReduce architecture would help. If n>15, you might be interested in sampling rather than visiting all permutations to compute summary stats—more on this later. Because q(n) is a maximum computed on all permutations of size n, this can help you compute n.

This code is also useful to compute all n-grams of a keyword, or, more interesting, in the context of nonparametric statistics. On Stackoverflow.com (`http://bit.ly/1cKCAEA`) you can find the source code in various modern languages, including Python. A Google search for **calculate all permutations** provides interesting links. Here is the Perl code:

```
use List::Permutor;
$n=5;
@array=();
for ($k=0; $k<$n; $k++) { $array[$k]=$k; }
  $permutIter=0;
  my $permutor = new List::Permutor(@array);
  while ( my @permutation = $permutor->next() ) {
   for ($k=0; $k<$n; $k++) { print "$permutation[$k] "; }
  print "\n";
  $permutIter++;
}
```

It couldn't be any easier. You need the Permutor library in Perl. (In other languages no library is needed; the full code is provided.) The easiest way to install the library is as follows, and this methodology applies to any Perl library.

Don't believe people who claim you can use ppm or CPAN to automatically in one click download and install the library. This is by far the most difficult way. Instead, use a caveman install (supposedly the hardest way, but in fact the easiest solution) by doing the following:

1. Do a Google search for **Permutor.pm**.

2. Click SOURCE (at the top of the page) on the Permutor CPAN page (the first link on the Google search results page). This .pm document is a text file (pm is used here as a filename extension, like .doc, .txt, xls).

3. Copy and paste the source code into Notepad, and save it as **Permutor.pm** in the `Perl64/lib/List/` folder (or whatever that folder name is on your machine).

That's it! Note that if you don't have the List library installed on your system (the parent Library for Permutor), you'll first have to download and install List using the same process, but everybody has List on their machine nowadays because it is part of the default Perl package.

First improvement: sampling permutations to estimate q(n). Rather than visiting all permutations, a lot of time can be saved by visiting a carefully selected tiny sample. The algorithm to generate random permutations (p(0), p(1), ..., p(n–1)) was previously mentioned:

```
For k=0 to n-1, do:
Step 1. Generate p(k) as a random number on {0, ... , n-1}
Step 2. Repeat Step 1 until p(k) is different
from p(0), p(1), ... , p(k-1)
End
```

You should also consider the computational complexity of this algorithm, as you compare it with two alternative algorithms:

- **Alternative algorithm I**: Create n random numbers on [0,1], then p(k) is simply the rank of the k-th deviate (k = 0, ..., n–1). From a computational complexity point of view, this is equivalent to sorting, and thus it is O(n log n).

- **Alternative algorithm II**: Use the one-to-one mapping between n-permutations and numbers in 1...n! However, transforming a number into a permutation, using the factorial number representation, is $O(n^2)$.

You would expect the rudimentary algorithm to be terribly slow. Actually, it might never end, running indefinitely, even just to produce p(1), let alone p(n–1), which is considerably harder to produce. Yet it turns out that the rudimentary algorithm is also O(n log n). (Proving this fact would actually be a great job interview question.) Here's the outline.

For positive k strictly smaller than n, you can create p(k) in these ways:

- On the first shot with probability L(k,1) = 1 – k/n
- On the second shot with probability L(k,2) = (k/n) * (1 – k/n)
- On the third shot with probability L(k,3) = (k/n)^2 * (1 – k/n)
- On the fourth shot with probability L(k,4) = (k/n)^3 * (1 – k/n)
- And so on

Note that the number of shots required might be infinite (with probability 0). Thus, on average, you need M(k) = SUM{ j * L(k,j) } = n/(n–k) shots to create p(k), where the sum is positive integers j = 0, 1, 2.... The total number of operations is thus (on average) SUM{M(k)} = n * {1 +1/2 + 1/3 + ... + 1/n}, where the sum is on k = 0,1,...,n–1. This turns out to be O(n log n). Note that in terms of data structure, you need an auxiliary array A of size n, initialized to 0. When p(k) is created (in the last, successful shot at iteration k), you update A as follows: A[p(k)] = 1. This array is used to check if p(k) is different from p(0), p(1), ..., p(k–1), or in other words, if A[p(k)] = 0.

Is O(n log n) the best that you can achieve? No, the algorithm in the next section is O(n), which is better.

Second Improvement: Improving the Permutation Sampler

The Fisher–Yates shuffle algorithm is the best for your purpose. It works as follows:

```
p(k) ← k, k=0,...,n-1
For k=n-1 down to 1, do:
j ← random integer with 0 ≤ j ≤ k
exchange p(j) and p(k)
End
```

This is the best that can be achieved, in terms of computational complexity, for the random permutation generator (that is, it is the fastest algorithm).

A Theoretical Solution

Sometimes, processing vast amounts of data (billions or trillions of random permutations in this case) is not the best approach. A little bit of mathematics can solve your problem simply and elegantly.

In 2013, Jean-Francois Puget, PhD, Distinguished Engineer, Industry Solutions Analytics and Optimization at IBM, found the exact formula and came up with a proof. He was awarded a $1,000 prize by Data Science Central for his solution as the winner of their first theoretical data science competition. If you are interested in applied data science competitions (involving real data sets), you should check `http://www.Kaggle.com`.

Consider Dr. Puget's result:

- Let m be the quotient and let r be the remainder of the Euclidean division of n by 4: $n = 4m + r, 0 \leq r < 4$.

- Let $p(n) = 6m^2 + 3mr + r(r{-}1)/2$.

- Then:

  - $q(n) = p(n)$ if $p(n)$ is even

  - $q(n) = p(n) - 1$ if $p(n)$ is odd

You can find the rather lengthy and complicated proof for this at `www.datashaping.com/Puget-Proof.pdf`.

Structured Coefficient

This section discusses a metric to measure whether a data set has some structure in it. This metric measures the presence or absence of a structure or pattern in data sets. The purpose is to measure the strength of the association between two variables and generalize the modern correlation coefficient discussed in the section Correlation and R-Squared for Big Data in a few ways:

- It applies to non-numeric data—for instance, a list of pairs of keywords, with a number attached to each pair, measuring how close to each other the two keywords are.

- It detects relationships that are not necessarily functional (for instance, points distributed in an unusual domain such as a sphere that has holes in it, and where holes contain smaller spheres that are part of the domain itself).

- It works with traditional, numeric bivariate observations.

The structured coefficient is denoted as **w.** I am working under the following framework:

- I have a data set with n points. For simplicity, consider for now that these n points are n vectors (x, y) where x, y are real numbers.

- For each pair of points {(x,y), (x',y')} I compute a distance d between the two points. In a more general setting, it could be a proximity metric to measure distance between two keywords.

- I order all the distances d and compute the distance distribution, based on these n points.

- Leaving-one-out removes one point at a time and computes the n new distance distributions, each based on n–1 points.

- I compare the distribution computed on n points, with the n ones computed on n–1 points.

- I repeat this iteration, but this time with n–2, then n–3, then n–4 points, and so on.

- You would assume that if there is no pattern, these distance distributions (for successive values of n) would have some kind of behavior uniquely characterizing the absence of structure, behavior that can be identified via simulations. Any deviation from this behavior would indicate the presence of a structure. The pattern-free behavior would be independent of the underlying point distribution or domain, which is an important point. All this would have to be established or tested, of course.

- It would be interesting to test whether this metric can identify patterns such as fractal distribution/fractal dimension.

This type of structured coefficient makes no assumption about the shape of the underlying domains, where the n points are located. These domains could be smooth, bumpy, made up of lines, made up of dual points, have holes, and so on. This type of structured coefficient can be applied to non-numeric data (for example, if the data consists of keywords), time series, spatial data, or data in higher dimensions. It is more generic than many metrics currently used to measure structure, and is entirely data-driven.

Identifying the Number of Clusters

Clustering algorithms have been discussed at large in the previous chapters, as well as this chapter. Here you find a rule of thumb that can be automated and does not require visual inspection by a human being to determine the optimum number of clusters associated with any clustering algorithm.

Note that the concept of cluster is a fuzzy one. How do you define a cluster? Nevertheless, in many applications there is a clear optimum number of clusters. The methodology described here will solve all easy and less easy cases, and will provide a "don't know" answer to cases that are ambiguous.

Methodology

The methodology is described by the following three steps:

1. Create a two-dimensional table with the following rows: number of clusters in row #1 and percentage of variance explained by clusters in row #2.

2. Compute third differences.

3. Compute the maximum for third differences (if much higher than other values) to determine the number of clusters.

This is based on the fact that the piece-wise linear plot of *number of clusters* versus *percentage of variance explained by clusters* is a convex function with an *elbow point* (see Figure 4-5). The elbow point determines the optimum number of clusters. If the piece-wise linear function is approximated by a smooth curve, the optimum would be the point vanishing the second derivative of the approximating smooth curve. This point corresponds to the inflection point on the curve in question. This methodology is simply an application of this "elbow-point detection" technique in a discrete framework (the number of clusters being a discrete number).

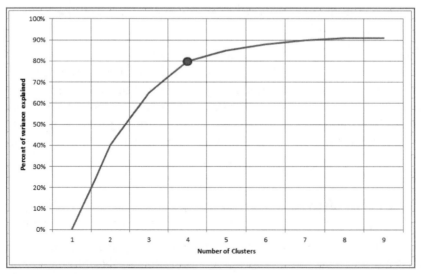

Figure 4-5: Elbow point (circled) used to detect the optimum number of clusters

Example

Row #1 represents the number of clusters (X-axis), and Row #2 is the percentage of variance explained by clusters (Y-axis) in Figure 4-5. Then the third, fourth, and fifth rows are differences (sometimes called *deltas*) from the row just above each of them. For instance, the second number in Row #3 is 15=80-65.

- 1 2 3 4 5 6 7 8 9 ==> number of clusters (X-axis)
- 40 65 80 85 88 90 91 91 ==> percentage of variance explained by clusters (Y-axis)
- 25 15 5 3 2 1 0 ==> first difference on Y-axis
- -10 -10 -2 -1 -1 -1 ==> second difference on Y-axis
- 0 8 1 0 0 ==> third difference on Y-axis

The optimum number of clusters in this example is 4, corresponding to maximum = 8 in the 3rd differences.

> **NOTE** If you already have a strong minimum in the second difference (not the case here), you don't need to go to the third difference: stop at level 2.

Internet Topology Mapping

This section discusses a component often missing, yet valuable for most systems: algorithms and architectures that are dealing with online or mobile data, known as digital data, such as transaction scoring, fraud detection, online marketing, marketing mix and advertising optimization, online search, plagiarism, and spam detection.

I will call it an Internet topology mapping. It might not be stored as a traditional database. (It could be a graph database, a file system, or a set of lookup tables.) It must be prebuilt (for example, as lookup tables with regular updates) to be efficiently used.

Essentially, Internet topology mapping is a system that matches an IP address (Internet or mobile) with a domain name (ISP). When you process a transaction in real time in production mode (for example, an online credit card transaction, to decide whether to accept or decline it), your system has only a few milliseconds to score the transaction to make the decision. In short, you have only a few milliseconds to call and run an algorithm (subprocess), on the fly, separately for each credit card transaction, to decide whether to accept it or reject it. If the algorithm involves matching the IP address with an ISP domain name (this operation is called *nslookup*), it won't work: direct nslookups take between a few hundred and a few thousand milliseconds, and they will slow the system to a grind.

Because of that, Internet topology mapping is missing in most systems. Yet there is a simple workaround to build it:

1. Look at all the IP addresses in your database. Chances are, even if you are Google, 99.9 percent of your traffic is generated by fewer than 100 million IP addresses. Indeed, the total number of IP addresses (the whole universe) consists of fewer than $256^{\wedge 4} = 4{,}294{,}967{,}296$ IP addresses. That's approximately four billion, not that big of a number in the real scheme of big data. Also, many IP addresses are clustered: many IP addresses starting (say) with 120.176.231 are likely part of the same domain. In short, you need to store a lookup table possibly as small as 20 million records (IP ranges/domain mapping) to solve the nslookup issue for 99.9 percent of your transactions. For the remaining 0.1 percent, you can either assign "unknown domain" (not recommended because quite a few IP addresses actually have an unknown domain), or "missing" (better) or perform the caveman, slow nslookup on the fly.

2. Create the lookup table that maps IP ranges to domain names for 99.9 percent of your traffic.

When processing a transaction, access the lookup table created in the last step (stored in memory, or least with some caching available in memory) to detect the domain name. Now you can use a rule system that does incorporate domain names.

Example of rules and metrics based on domain names are:

- Domain extension (.com, .cc, and so on)
- Length of domain name
- Domain name flagged as good (white-listed) or bad (black-listed)
- Patterns found in domain name (for example, digits, a date, flagged keywords, and special characters such as a dash)
- Specific keywords found in a domain name
- Owner of the domain name (Does the owner own other domains, in particular bad domains?)
- Date of creation of a domain name
- Time needed to do the nslookup on IP address in question (0.5 second or 4 seconds?)
- Multiple nslookups needed to find domain attached to this IP address when building IP address or domain name table?
- No domain found
- Is this a subdomain?

This is the *first component* of the Internet topology mapping. The *second component* is a clustering structure—in short, a structure (text file is OK) where a cluster is assigned to each IP address or IP range. Examples of clusters include:

- IP address corresponding to an anonymous proxy.
- .edu proxy.
- Corporate proxy (large with many IPs versus small with a few, heavily used IPs; use a list of top 50,000 companies or websites to help detect corporate domain names).
- Government proxy.
- Static, personal IP.
- Volatile, recycled IP (for example, AOL, Comcast, and mobile IP addresses).
- Isolated IP address versus IP address belonging to a cluster or multiple clusters (either small or large) of IP addresses.
- Well-known ISP: Comcast and so on.
- Mobile IP address.
- IP address is AWS (Amazon Web Services and cloud services) or similar.
- IP address is a mail/web/FTP or API server.

Armed with these components (IP address/domain mapping + IP address cluster structure, aka Internet topology), you can now develop better algorithms: real-time or back-end, end-of-day algorithms. You need the IP address/domain mapping to build the cluster structure. If you have a data scientist on board, it should be easy for her to create this Internet topology mapping and identify the great benefits of using it.

The only issue with creating this product (assuming it will contain 20 million IP address ranges and get updated regularly) is the large amount of time spent in doing millions of slow (0.5 second each) caveman nslookups. Now, there are well-known ranges reserved for AOL and other big ISPs, so probably you will end up doing just 10 million nslookups. Given that 1 percent of them will fail (timing out after two seconds) and that you will have to run nslookup twice on some IP addresses, say that in short, you are going to run 10 million nslookups, each taking on average one second. That's about 2,777 hours, or 115 days.

You can use a MapReduce environment to easily reduce the time by a factor of 20, by leveraging the distributed architecture. Even on one single machine, if you run 25 versions of your nslookup script in parallel, you should make it run four times faster—that is, it would complete in less than a month. That's why I claim that a little guy alone in his garage could create the Internet Topology Mapping in a few weeks or less. The input data set (for example, 100 million IP addresses) would require less than 20 GB of storage, even less when compressed. Pretty small.

Finally, here's a Perl script that automatically performs nslookups on an input file `ips.txt` of IP addresses and stores the results in `outip.txt`. It works on my Windows laptop. You need an Internet connection to make it run, and you should add an error management system to nicely recover if you lose power or you lose your Internet connection.

```
open(IN,"<ips.txt");
open (OUT,">outip.txt");
while ($lu=<IN>) {
  $ip=$lu;
  $n++;
  $ip=~s/\n//g;
  if ($ip eq "") { $ip="na"; }
  `nslookup $ip | grep Name > titi.txt`;
  open(TMP,"<titi.txt");
  $domainName="n/a";
  while ($i=<TMP>) {
    $i=~s/\n//g;
    $i=~s/Name\://g;
    $domainName=$i;
  }
  close(TMP);
  print OUT "$ip\t$domainName\n";
  print "$n> $ip | $domainName\n";
}
close(OUT);
close(IN);
```

In summary, Internet topology mapping is a tool that needs to be created using the steps described here to help in a number of business problems, including spam detection, fraud detection, attribution modeling, digital marketing (including e-mail marketing), publishing (to customize content based on IP address category), and advertising (to optimize relevancy). Traditional algorithms use blacklists or whitelists of IP addresses or IP ranges (a component of the Internet topology mapping), but none, to my knowledge, use IP clusters produced using a clustering algorithm. I have seen business dashboards that show the top 100 IP addresses for a specific metric (traffic volume, amount of fraud, and so on), but this is a really bad business practice since IP addresses are very granular (so the top 100 does not communicate many actionable insights) and a few IP addresses are shared by a very large number of users (mobile IP address proxies in particular). Dashboards based on IP categories derived from Internet topology mapping are more useful to decision makers.

I have also seen IP addresses used as a metric in decision trees, which is also terrible. IP categories or IP clusters should be used in decision trees, rather than a highly granular metric such as IP address. Examples of potential fraud detection rules derived from Internet topology mapping include "corporate IP addresses (unless hacked) should be white-listed" and "IP addresses from universities, associated with computers shared by many students (proxies), are riskier (except some of them where the sys-admin is doing a great job making these networks safe)." The difficulty is not coming up with these two intuitive rules, but rather classifying an IP address as a corporate or university proxy—a problem solved with Internet topology mapping.

Securing Communications: Data Encoding

This section is important, as it illustrates how to develop a real-life application with JavaScript code, how to create a tool that any end user can use from their browser without having to install R, and how to download and/or purchase software or write code. The JavaScript code provided here can be run online or offline from your browser. I believe that in the future, there will be more data science tools that are browser-based and lighter than a full API (I like the fact that it can be run offline from your browser). This code also provides another example of random number generation.

A big issue with data is how to securely transmit it. Here you will see some simple JavaScript code to encode numbers, such as credit card numbers, passwords made up of digits, phone numbers, Social Security numbers, dates such as 20131014, and so on.

The following is an example of an app that anyone can download as a text file, save as an HTML document, and run on their laptop, locally, from a browser (without any Internet connection). I call it an *offline app*, as opposed to a *mobile* or *web* or *social* (Facebook) app. As with most apps, you don't need any programming skills to use it. This one is original in the sense that you don't even need an Internet connection to make it work.

Here's how it works:

1. Open the web app (`datashaping.com/encode.html`) in a separate browser tab.

2. Enter number to encode or decode in the box shown on the web page.

3. Select Encrypt/Decrypt.

4. E-mail the encoded number (it should start with e) to your contact.

5. Your contact uses the same form, enters the encoded number, selects Encrypt/Decrypt, and then the original number is immediately retrieved.

This code is simple (it is by no means strong encryption) and less sophisticated than uuencode. But uuencode is for the tech-savvy, whereas our app is easy to use by any non-technical person. The encoded value is also a text string, and thus easy to copy and paste in any e-mail client. The encoded value has some randomness, in the sense that encoding the same values twice will result in two different encoded values. Finally, it is more secure than it seems at first glance, if you don't tell anyone (except over the phone) where the decoder can be found.

You can make it even more secure by creating a version that accepts parameters. Here's the JavaScript/HTML code (this is the source code of the web page where our application is hosted). You could save it as an HTML document on your local machine, with the filename (for example, encode.html) in a folder (for example, C://Webpages) and then open and run it from a browser on your local machine. The URL for this local web page would be \\/C:/Webpages/encode.html if you use Chrome.

```html
<html>
<script language="Javascript">
<!--
function encrypt2() {
  var form=document.forms[0]
  if (form.encrypt.checked) {
    form.cardnumber.value=crypt(form.cardnumber.value)
  } else {
    form.cardnumber.value=decrypt(form.cardnumber.value)
  }
}
function crypt(string) {
  var len=string.length
  var intCarlu
  var carlu
  var newString="e"
  if ((string.charCodeAt(i)!=101)&&(len>0)) {
    for (var i=0; i<len; i++) {
      intCarlu=string.charCodeAt(i)
      rnd=Math.floor(Math.random()*7)
      newIntCarlu=30+10*rnd+intCarlu+i-48
      if (newIntCarlu<48) { newIntCarlu+=50 }
      if (newIntCarlu>=58 && newIntCarlu<=64) { newIntCarlu+=10 }
      if (newIntCarlu>=90 && newIntCarlu<=96) { newIntCarlu+=10 }
      carlu=String.fromCharCode(newIntCarlu)
      newString=newString.concat(carlu)
    }
    return newString
  } else {
    return string
  }
}
```

```
function decrypt(string) {
  var len=string.length
  var intCarlu
  var carlu
  var newString=""
  if (string.charCodeAt(i)==101) {
    for (var i=1; i<len; i++) {
      intCarlu=string.charCodeAt(i)
      carlu=String.fromCharCode(48+(intCarlu-i+1)%10)
      newString=newString.concat(carlu)
    }
    return newString
  } else {
    return string
  }
}
// -->
</script>

<form>
Enter Number <input type=text name=cardnumber size=19><p>
Encrypt / Decrypt <input type=checkbox name=encrypt
onClick="encrypt2()">
</form>
</html>
```

Summary

This chapter discussed many original, new techniques and recipes used by data scientists to process modern data, including big data. I dived deep enough into the details so that you can reproduce them when needed, but without being too technical, and avoiding jargon and mathematical formulas so that business people can still quickly extract the essence.

Chapter 5 discusses additional techniques that are also part of core data science. While Chapters 4 and 5 contain the most technical material of the book, the transition has been made as smooth as possible by introducing some of the technical material in Chapter 2 (see the section Clustering and Taxonomy Creation for Massive Data Sets).

Data Science
Craftsmanship, Part II

In the previous chapter, you discovered a number of data science techniques and recipes, including visualizing data with data videos, new types of metrics, computer science topics, and questions to ask when choosing a vendor, as well as a comparison between data scientists, statisticians, and data engineers.

In this chapter, you consider material that is less focused on metrics and more focused on applications. It includes discussions on how to create a data dictionary, hidden decision trees, hash joins in the context of NoSQL databases, and the first Analyticbridge Theorem, which provides a simple, model-free, nonparametric way to compute confidence intervals without statistical theory or knowledge.

This chapter is less statistical theory–oriented compared with the previous chapter. The topics discussed in this chapter are typically classified as data analyses rather than statistical or computer analyses. Most of the material has not been published before. Case studies, applications, and success stories are discussed in the next chapter.

The topics discussed in this chapter, such as hidden decision trees, data dictionaries, and hash joins, are important subjects for data scientists because they are at the intersection of statistics and computer science, and are designed to handle big data. Traditional statisticians typically don't learn or use these techniques, but data scientists do.

Data Dictionary

One of the most valuable tools when performing exploratory analyses is building a data dictionary, which offers the following advantages:

▪ Identify areas of sparseness and areas of concentration in high-dimensional data sets.

▪ Identify outliers and data glitches.

▪ Get a good sense of what the data contains and where to spend time (or not) in further data mining.

What Is a Data Dictionary?

A *data dictionary* is a table with three or four columns. The first column represents a label, that is, the name of a variable or a combination of multiple (up to three) variables. The second column is the value attached to the label: the first and second columns actually constitute a name-value pair. The third column is a frequency count: it measures how many times the value (attached to the label in question) appears in the data set. You can add a fourth column to specify the dimension of the label (1 if it represents one variable, 2 if it represents a pair of variables, and so on).

Typically, you include all labels of dimension 1 and 2 with count > threshold (for example, threshold = 5), but no or only few values (the ones with high count) for labels of dimension 3. Labels of dimension 3 should be explored after having built the dictionary for dim 1 and 2, by drilling down on name-value pair of dim 2 that have a high count.

An example of a data dictionary entry is `category~keyword travel~Tokyo 756 2`. In this example, the entry corresponds to a label of dimension 2 (as indicated in column 4), and the simultaneous combination of the two values (travel, Tokyo) is found 756 times in the data set.

The first thing you want to do with a dictionary is to sort it using the following 3-dim index: column 4, then column 1, and then column 3. Then look at the data and find patterns.

Building a Data Dictionary

Browse your data set sequentially. For each observation, store all name-value pair of dim 1 and dim 2 as hash table keys, and increment count by 1 for each of these labels/values. In Perl, it can be performed with code such as `$hash{"$label\ t$value"}++`.

If the hash table grows large, stop, save the hash table on file, and then delete it in memory and resume where you paused, with a new hash table. At the end, merge hash tables after ignoring hash entries where count is too small.

CROSS-REFERENCE The next step after building a data dictionary is exploratory data analysis (EDA). See the section Life Cycle of Data Science Projects later in this chapter.

Hidden Decision Trees

Hidden decision trees (*HDT*) is a technique created and patented by me (see http:// bit.ly/1h9mXZr) to score large volumes of transaction data. It blends robust logistic regression with hundreds of small decision trees (each one representing, for instance, a specific type of fraudulent transaction) and offers significant advantages over both logistic regression and decision trees: robustness, ease of interpretation, no tree pruning, and no node splitting criteria. It makes this methodology powerful and easy to implement, even for someone with no statistical background.

HDT is a statistical and data mining methodology (just like logistic regression, SVM, neural networks, or decision trees) to handle problems with large amounts of data, nonlinearity, and strongly correlated dependent variables. I developed it after discovering how sparse (or noisy) big data usually is, with valuable information (signal) concentrated in just tiny pieces of the data sets — just like stars and matter represent a very tiny fraction of the universe. HDT removes the complexity, instability, arbitrary parameters, and lack of interpretation found in traditional large decision trees. It also eliminates the failure of traditional logistic regressions to identify highly nonlinear structures by blending regression with some sort of decision tree. HDT was first applied in the context of optimum features selection to score credit card transactions to detect fraud. The technique is easy to implement in any programming language. It is more robust than decision trees or logistic regression and helps detect natural final nodes. Implementations typically rely heavily on large, granular hash tables.

No decision tree is actually built (thus the name hidden decision trees), but the final output of a hidden decision tree procedure consists of a few hundred nodes from multiple non-overlapping small decision trees. Each of these parent (invisible) decision trees corresponds, for example, to a particular type of fraud in fraud detection models. Interpretation is straightforward, in contrast with traditional decision trees.

The methodology was first invented in 2003 in the context of credit card fraud detection. It is not implemented in any statistical package at this time. Hidden decision trees are frequently combined with logistic regression in a hybrid scoring algorithm, where 80 percent of the transactions are scored via hidden decision trees, while the remaining 20 percent are scored using a compatible logistic regression type of scoring.

Hidden decision trees take advantage of the structure of large multivariate features typically observed when scoring a large number of transactions, for example, for fraud detection. The technique is not connected with hidden Markov fields.

Potential applications of HDT include the following:

- Fraud and spam detection
- Web analytics
  - Keyword scoring/bidding (ad networks and paid search)
  - Transaction scoring (click, impression, conversion, and action)
  - Click fraud detection
  - Website scoring, ad scoring, landing page or advertiser scoring
  - Collective filtering (social network analytics)
  - Relevancy algorithms
- Text mining
  - Scoring and ranking algorithms
  - Infringement and spam detection
  - Sentiment analysis

The way HDT is applied to these problems is as follows: in a typical machine learning approach, rule sets or *association rules* are used to solve these problems. For instance, if an e-mail message contains the keyword "breast" or other keyword from a keyword blacklist, but not "breast cancer," which is white-listed, then it increases the spam score. If many rules get triggered, the spam score is very high. HDT automatically sets weights to these various rules and automatically detects, among millions (or billions) of rules, which ones should be kept and combined.

Since first developing HDT, I have further refined the model over the past 10 years, as follows:

- 2003: First version applied to credit card fraud detection
- 2006: Application to click scoring and click fraud detection
- 2008: More advanced versions to handle granular and large data sets, such as:
  - **Hidden forests**: Multiple HDTs, each one applied to a cluster of correlated rules
  - **Hierarchical HDTs**: The top structure, not just rule clusters, is modeled using HDTs.
  - **Non-binary rules**: Naive Bayes blended with HDTs.

Implementation

The model presented here is used in the context of click scoring. The purpose is to create predictive scores, where *score* = f(*response*), that is, score is a function of the response. The response is sometimes referred to as the *dependent variable* in statistical and predictive models. Examples of responses include:

- Odds of converting (Internet traffic data — hard or soft conversions)
- CR (conversion rate)
- Probability that transaction is fraudulent

Independent variables are called *features* or rules. They are highly correlated.

Traditional models to be compared with HDTs include logistic regression, decision trees, and naive Bayes.

HDTs use a one-to-one mapping between scores and multivariate features. A *multivariate feature* is a rule combination attached to a particular transaction (that is, a vector specifying which rules are triggered and which ones are not) and is sometimes referred to as a *flag vector* or *node*.

HDT fundamentals based on a typical data set are:

- If you use 40 binary rules, you have 2 at power 40 potential multivariate features.
- If a training set has 10 MM transactions, you will obviously observe 10 MM multivariate features at most, a number much smaller than 2 at power 40.
- 500 out of 10 MM features account for 80 percent of all transactions.
- The top 500 multivariate features have a strong predictive power.
- An alternative algorithm is required to classify the remaining 20 percent of transactions.
- Using neighboring top multivariate features to score the remaining 20 percent of transactions creates bias, as rare multivariate features (sometimes not found in the training set) correspond to observations that are worse than average, with a low score (because they trigger many fraud detection rules).

Implementation Details

Each top node (or multivariate feature) is a final node from a hidden decision tree. There is no need for tree pruning or splitting algorithms and criteria: HDT is straightforward and fast, and can rely on efficient hash tables (where key = feature and value = score). The top 500 nodes, used to classify (that is, score) 80 percent of transactions, come from multiple hidden decision trees—hidden because you never used a decision tree algorithm to produce them.

The remaining 20 percent of transactions are scored using an alternative methodology (typically, logistic regression). Thus HDT is a hybrid algorithm, blending multiple, small, easy-to-interpret, invisible decision trees (final nodes only) with logistic regression.

Note that in the logistic regression, you can use constrained regression coefficients. These coefficients depend on two or three top parameters and have the same sign as the correlation between the rule they represent and the response or score. This makes the regression non-sensitive to high cross correlations among the "independent" variables (rules), which are indeed not independent in this case. This approach is similar to *ridge regression*, *logic regression*, or *Lasso regression*. The regression is used to fine-tune the top parameters associated with regression coefficients. Approximate solutions (you are doing approximate logistic regression here) are—if well designed—almost as accurate as exact solutions but can be far more robust.

You deal with these types of scores:

■ The top 500 nodes provide a score S_1 available for 80 percent of the transactions.

■ The logistic regression provides a score S_2 available for 100 percent of the transactions.

To blend the scores, you would do the following:

■ *Rescale* S_2 using the 80 percent transactions that have two scores, S_1 and S_2. Rescaling means applying a linear transformation so that both scores have the same mean and the same variance. Let S_3 be the rescaled S_2.

■ Transactions that can't be scored with S_1 are scored with S_3.

HDT nodes provide an alternative *segmentation* of the data. One large, medium-score segment corresponds to neutral transactions (triggering no rule). Segments with low scores correspond to specific fraud cases. Within each segment, all transactions have the same score. HDT provide a different type of segmentation than *principal component analysis* (PCA) and other analyses.

Example: Scoring Internet Traffic

Figure 5-1 shows the score distribution with a system based on 20 rules, each one having a low triggering frequency. It has the following features:

■ Reverse bell curve

■ Scores below 425 correspond to unbillable transactions.

■ Spikes at the bottom and top of the score scale

■ 50 percent of all transactions have good scores.

■ Scorecard parameters

- ▪ A drop of 50 points represents a 50 percent drop in the conversion rate.
- ▪ The average score is 650.
- ▪ Model improvement: from reverse bell curve to bell curve
  - ▪ Transaction quality versus fraud detection
  - ▪ Add antirules, perform score smoothing (also removes score caking)

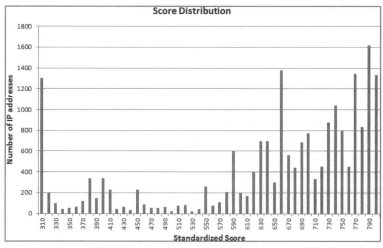

Figure 5-1: Example of score distribution based on HDT

Figure 5-2 shows a comparison of scores with conversion rates (CR). HDTs were applied to Internet data, scoring clicks with a score used to predict chances of conversion (a conversion being a purchase, a click out, or a sign-up on some landing page). Overall, you have a rather good fit.

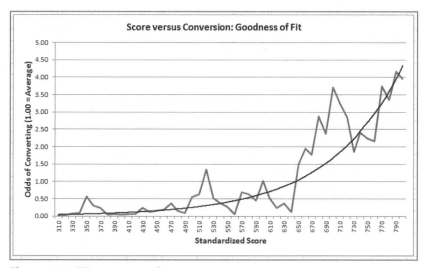

Figure 5-2: HDT scores to predict conversions

Peaks in the figure could mean:

- Bogus conversions (happens a lot if conversion is simply a click out)
- Residual noise
- Model needs improvement (incorporate antirules)

Valleys could mean:

- Undetected conversions (cookie issue, time-to-conversion unusually high)
- Residual noise
- Model needs improvement

Conclusion

HDT is a fast algorithm, easy to implement, and can handle large data sets efficiently, and the output is easy to interpret. It is nonparametric and robust. The risk of *over-fitting* is small if no more than the top 500 nodes are selected and ad hoc cross-validation techniques are used to remove unstable nodes. It offers a built-in, simple mechanism to compute confidence intervals for scores (see the next section).

HDT is an algorithm that can detect multiple types of structures: linear structures via the regression and nonlinear structures via the top nodes. Future directions for HDT could include hidden forests to handle granular data and hierarchical HDTs.

Model-Free Confidence Intervals

Here you can find easy-to-compute, distribution-free, fractional confidence intervals. If observations from a specific experiment (for instance, scores computed on 10 million credit card transactions) are assigned a random bin ID (labeled 1, ⋯ , N) then you can easily build a confidence interval for any proportion or score computed on these k random bins, using the Analyticbridge Theorem described next.

Methodology

Say you want to estimate a parameter p (proportion, mean, it does not matter). You would do the following:

1. Divide your observations into N random buckets.
2. Compute the estimated value for each bucket.
3. Rank these estimates, from p_1 (smallest value) to p_N (largest value).

4. Let p_k be your confidence interval lower bound for p, with k less than N/2.

5. Let p_(N-k+1) be your confidence interval upper bound for p.

The solution is composed of the following:

- [p_k,p_(N-k+1)] is a nonparametric confidence interval for p.
- The confidence level is 2 k/(N+1).

Note that by trying multiple values for k (and for N, although this is more computer-intensive), it is possible to interpolate confidence intervals of any level.

Finally, you want to keep N as low as possible (and k=1 ideally) to achieve the desired confidence interval level. For instance, for a 90 percent confidence interval, N=19 and k=1 work and are optimum.

The Analyticbridge First Theorem

The proof of this theorem relies on complicated combinatorial arguments and the use of the Beta function. Note that the final result does not depend on the distribution associated with your data. In short, your data does not have to follow a Gaussian or any prespecified statistical distribution to make the confidence intervals valid. You can find more details regarding the proof of the theorem in the book *Statistics of Extremes* by E.J. Gumbel (Dover edition, 2004).

Parameters in the Analyticbridge Theorem can be chosen to achieve the desired level of precision, for instance a 95 percent, 99 percent, or 99.5 percent confidence interval. The theorem can also tell you what your sample size should be to achieve a prespecified accuracy level. This theorem is a fundamental result to compute simple, per-segment, data-driven, model-free confidence intervals in many contexts, in particular when generating predictive scores produced via logistic or ridge regression, decision trees, or hidden decision trees (for example, for fraud detection or credit scoring).

The First AnalyticBridge Theorem is shown in Figure 5-3:

Analyticbridge Theorem: *If observations are assigned a random bin ID (labeled 1 ⋯ k), then the estimator $\hat{p}$ of any proportion computed on these k random bins satisfies*

$$P(\hat{p} \leq p_{(1)}) = \frac{1}{k+1} = P(\hat{p} \geq p_{(k)})$$

Also, for m = 1, ⋯, k, we have:

$$P(\hat{p} \leq p_{(m)}) = \frac{m}{k+1} = P(\hat{p} \geq p_{(k-m+1)})$$

Note that $p_{(1)} = \min p_j$ and $p_{(k)} = \max P_j, j = 1 \cdots k$. The $p_{(j)}$'s represent the order statistics, and p_j is the observed proportion in bin j.

Figure 5-3: First AnalyticBridge Theorem

If observations are assigned a random bin ID (labeled 1…k), then the estimator p of any proportion computed on these k random bins satisfies Proba[p < p(1)] = 1/(k+1) = Proba[p > p(k)]. Also, for m = 1,…, k, you have: Proba[p < p(m)] = 1/(k+1) = Proba[p > p(k-m+1)]. Note that p(1) = min p(j) and p(k) =max p(j), j=1…k. The p(j)'s represent the order statistics, and p(j) is the observed proportion in bin j.

You can find the proof of this theorem at `http://bit.ly/1a2hWi7`.

Application

A scoring system designed to detect customers likely to fail on a loan is based on a rule set. On average for an individual customer the probability to fail is 5 percent. In a data set with 1 million observations (customers) and several metrics such as credit score, the amount of debt, salary, and so on, if you randomly select 99 bins, each containing 1,000 customers, the 98 percent confidence interval (per bin of 1,000 customers) for the failure rate is, for example, [4.41 percent or 5.53 percent], based on the Analyticbridge Theorem, with k = 99 and m = 1. (Read the theorem to understand what k and m mean; it's actually easy to understand the signification of these parameters.)

Now, looking at a non-random bin with 1,000 observations consisting of customers with credit score < 650 and less than 26 years old, you see that the failure rate is 6.73 percent. You can thus conclude that the rule credit score < 650 and less than 26 years old is actually a good rule to detect failure rate, because 6.73 percent is well above the upper bound of the [4.41 percent or 5.53 percent] confidence interval.

Indeed, you could test hundreds of rules and easily identify rules with high predictive power by systematically and automatically looking at how far the observed failure rate (for a given rule) is from a standard confidence interval. This allows you to rule out the effect of noise and the process and rank of numerous rules (based on their predictive power; that is, how much their failure rate is above the confidence interval upper bound) at once.

Source Code

One Data Science Central member wrote the following piece of R code to illustrate the theorem. He also created a YouTube video about it, which you can watch at `https://www.youtube.com/watch?v=72uhdRrf6gM`.

```
set.seed(3.1416)
x <- rnorm(1000000,10,2)

analytic_theorem <- function (N,x,med,desv)
{
    length(x)
    meansamples <- rep(NA,N)
```

```
for(i in 1:N){
  meansamples[i]  <- mean(sample(x, length(x)/N, replace = TRUE))
}
meansamples <- sort(meansamples)
confidence <- rep(NA,N/2)
p_lower <- rep(NA,N/2)
p_upper <- rep(NA,N/2)

for(k in 1:N/2){
    confidence[k] <- 2*k/(N+1)
    p_lower[k] <- meansamples[k]
    p_upper[k] <- meansamples[N-k+1]
}

mean_t <- (meansamples[k] + meansamples[N-k+1])/2
x_a <- seq(1:(N/2))
par(mar=c(5,4,4,5)+.1)
plot(x_a, p_upper,type="l", ylim=range(c(med-1*desv, med+1*desv)),
col="blue",xlab="K",ylab="Values")
    lines(x_a, p_lower,type="l",col="red",xaxt="n",yaxt="n",xlab="",
ylab="")
    par(new=TRUE)
    plot(confidence*(N/2),rep(mean_t,N/2),
ylim = range(c(med-1*desv,med+1*desv)),
type="l", col="black",xaxt="n",
yaxt="n",ylab='',xlab='',lty=2)
   axis(3,seq(from=0,to=1,by=.25)*(N/2),las=0,
at=seq(from=0,to=1,by=.25)*(N/2),
labels=c(1,0.75,0.50,0.25,0))
    mtext("Confidence",side=3,line=3)
    legend("bottomright",col=c("red","blue"),lty=1,
legend=c("Lower bound","Upper Bound"))
    legend("topright",legend=c(paste("N=",as.character(N))))
}

for(i in seq(1000,10000,100)) analytic_theorem(i,x,10,2)
```

Random Numbers

Here you consider a simple, modern technique to simulate random numbers based on the decimals of some numbers, such as Pi. Random numbers are used extensively in many statistical applications and Monte Carlo simulations. Also, many rely on faulty techniques to generate random numbers, typically calling a black box function such as Rand() with no idea how good or bad their generator is. Millions of analysts rely on Excel to produce random numbers. But the Excel random generator is notoriously flawed and may cause problems when used in applications where high-quality randomness is a critical requirement. You can find more on how to define and measure randomness, for instance, in the section on the structuredness coefficient in the previous chapter.

This section discusses a random number generator with an infinite period, that is, with no cycling. The period is infinite because it is based on irrational numbers.

One of the best random sets of digits (extensively tested for randomness by hundreds of scientists using thousands of tests in both small and high dimensions) is the decimals of Pi. Despite its random character being superior to most algorithms currently implemented (current algorithms typically use recursive congruence relations or compositions of random permutations and exhibit periodicity), decimals of Pi have two big challenges, making them useless as a random number generator:

- If everybody knows that decimals of Pi are used in many high-security encryption algorithms (to generate undecipherable randomness), then guess what? It loses this great "undecipherable-ness" property.

- Computing millions of decimals of Pi is difficult; it takes a lot of time, much more time than traditional random number generation.

Here is my answer to these two challenges and a proposal for a new random number generator that overcomes these two difficulties:

- Regarding speed, you now have extremely fast algorithms to compute decimals of Pi (see, for instance, the following formulas).

- Regarding using Pi, you should switch to less popular numbers that can be computed via a similar formula to preserve speed and make reverse engineering impossible in encryption algorithms. An example of a fantastic random digit generator would be to use the digits of a number defined by formula [1], with a change like this: Replace the numerators 4, –2, –1, –1 with 3, 1, –2, –2. You get the idea — trillions of random generators could be developed, using variations of the first formula.

Consider the following two fast formulas to compute Pi. The first formula for Pi is:

$$Pi = Sum\{(A+B+C+D)/16^k\},$$ where the sum is over k=0, 1, 2 …; A=4/(8k+1), B=-2/(8k+4), C=-1/(8k+5), and D=-1/(8k+6).

This formula is remarkable because it allows extracting any individual hexadecimal or binary digit of Pi without calculating all the preceding ones.

The second formula for Pi was found by the Chudnovsky brothers in 1987. It delivers 14 digits per term as follows:

$$426880 * SQRT(10005) / Pi = SUM\{ (6k)!(13591409 + 545140134*k)/[(3k)! (k!)^3(-640320)^{(3k)}] \},$$ where the sum is over k=0, 1, 2 ….

It looks like you could derive a recursive formula to compute the k-th digit (in base 16) based on the (k-1)-th digit.

To test for the randomness character of the simulated numbers, consider the digits of Pi as a time series and compute the auto-correlation function (or correlogram) and see if it is statistically different from 0. To perform this test, you would do as follows:

1. Compute auto-correlations $c(k)$ of lag $k = 1, 2, ...,100$, on the first billion digits.

2. Compute $m = \max|c(k)|$.

3. Test if the observed m is small enough by comparing its value (computed on Pi) with a theoretical value computed on a truly random time series of digits. (The theoretical value can be computed using Monte Carlo simulations.)

It would be interesting to study the sum $F(a,b,c,d)$ used in the first formula by replacing the numbers 4, –2, –1, –1 (numerator) with arbitrary a, b, c, d. Of course, $F(4,-2,-1,-1) = \text{Pi}$.

Do interesting numbers $F(a,b,c,d)$ share the two properties listed here, regarding the parameters a, b, c, d? Could the number e=2.71 (or some other beautiful numbers) be a special case of F? For Pi, you have:

$$a + b + c + d = 0$$

$$|a| + |b| + |c| + |d| = 8$$

> **NOTE** Another idea is to use continued fractions to approximate Pi. Denote by p(n) the n-th approximant: $p(n) = A(n) / B(n)$, where A(n) and B(n) are integers defined by simple recurrence relations. Modify these recurrence relations slightly, et voila: You created a new interesting number, with (hopefully) random digits.
>
> Or consider a simple continued fraction such as:
>
> $x = 1/(1 + 1/(1 + 2/(1 + 3/(1 + 4/(1 + 5/(1 + 6/1 + ..))))))$
>
> Despite the strong pattern in the construction of x, its digits show good randomness properties.

Four Ways to Solve a Problem

There can be several ways to solve any problem, and data scientists should always consider multiple options before deciding on a strategy. The following sections present four different ways to solve this problem: You want to increase your presence recognition in certain Google groups by posting more content, but there are so many groups you need to narrow the field to those that are the most popular and active in your target subject.

So you begin by daily identification of the most popular Google groups within a large list of target groups. The only information that is quickly available for each group is the time when the last posting occurred. Intuitively it would appear that the newer the last posting, the more active the group. But there are some caveats to this assumption, such as groups where all postings come from a single user (maybe even a robot), or groups that focus on posting job ads exclusively. Such groups should be eliminated from your list.

Once you identify the groups you want to participate in, you want to ensure your posts actually get read by other group members. For this, your message and subject lines are critical factors (as important as the selection of target groups) to get your postings read and converted to some value. This example problem assumes that your content optimization (the creative part) has been done separately using other data science techniques (for instance to identify, with statistical significance, after removing other factors, which keywords work well in a subject line, depending on audience, using *A/B testing*). So a follow-on assumption is that you have experience in writing great content, and you are now interested in increasing reach while preserving relevancy.

Finally, we assume that you have earned a good blogger score, so your posts are generally accepted and not flagged as spam (this is itself another optimization problem). Indeed, a common issue of modern data science applications is that a problem often requires multiple levels of optimization performed by different teams. This is why it is so critical for the data scientist to acquire domain expertise and business acumen, as well as identifying and talking to the various teams involved.

So the key question is: How do you estimate the volume of activity based on time-to-last-posting for a particular group? You can use the following four approaches to solve this problem.

Intuitive Approach for Business Analysts with Great Intuitive Abilities

The number of posts per time unit is roughly 2x the time since the last posting. If you have a good sense of numbers, you just know that, even if you don't have an analytic degree. There's actually a simple empirical explanation for this. Probably few people have this level of (consistently correct) intuition—maybe none of your employees. If this is the case, this option (the cheapest of the four) must be ruled out.

Note that you don't need to estimate the actual volume of traffic, but instead, just rank the different groups. So a relative volume number (as opposed to the absolute number) is good enough. Such a relative number is obtained by using time elapsed since last posting.

Monte Carlo Simulations Approach for Software Engineers

Any good engineer with no or almost no statistical training can perform simulations of random postings in a group (without actually posting anything), testing various posting frequencies, and for each test, pick up a random (simulated) time and compute time-to-last-posting. Then based on, for example, 20,000 group posting simulations, you can compute (actually, reconstruct) a table that maps time-to-last-transaction to posting volume. Caveat: the engineer must use a good random generator and assess the accuracy of the table, maybe building confidence intervals using the Analyticbridge Theorem described earlier in this chapter: It is a simple technique to use for non-statisticians.

Statistical Modeling Approach for Statisticians

Based on the theory of stochastic processes (Poisson processes) and the Erlang distribution, the estimated number of postings per time unit is indeed 2x the time since last posting. The theory can also give you the variance for this estimator (infinite) and tell you that it's more robust to use time to the second, third, or fourth previous posting, which have finite and known variances. Now, if the group is inactive, the time to previous posting itself can be infinite, but in practice this is not an issue. Note that the Poisson assumption would be violated in this case. The theory also suggests how to combine time to the second, time to the third, and time to the fourth previous posting to get a better estimator. Read my paper "Estimation of the intensity of a Poisson point process by means of nearest neighbor distances" (http://bit.ly/HFyYse) for details. You can even get a better estimator if, instead of doing just one time measurement per day per group, you do multiple measurements per day per group and average them.

Big Data Approach for Computer Scientists

You crawl all the groups every day and count all the postings for all the groups, rather than simply crawling the summary statistics. Emphasis is on using a distributed architecture for fast crawling and data processing, rather than a good sampling mechanism on small data.

Causation Versus Correlation

You know that correlation does not mean causation and that statistical analysis is good at finding correlations. In some contexts (data mining) it does not matter if you discriminate between correlation and causation as long as spurious correlations caused by an external factor are taken care of.

A lot can be done with black-box pattern detection where patterns are found but not understood. For many applications (for example, high-frequency training) it's fine to not care about causation as long as your algorithm works. But in other contexts (for example, root cause analysis for cancer eradication), deeper investigation is needed for higher success. (Although some drugs work, nobody knows why.) And in all contexts, identifying and weighting true factors that explain the cause usually allows for better forecasts, especially if good model selection, model fitting, and cross-validation are performed. But if advanced modeling requires paying a high salary to a statistician for 12 months, maybe the ROI becomes negative and black-box brute force performs better, ROI-wise. In both cases, whether caring about cause or not, it is still science. Indeed, it is actually data science and it includes an analysis to figure out when/whether deeper statistical science is required. And it always involves the cross-validation and design of experiments. Only the statistical theoretical modeling aspect can be ignored. Other aspects, such as scalability and speed, must be considered, and this is science, too: data and computer science.

In special contexts such as *root cause analysis*, you want to identify causes, not correlations. For instance, doing more sports is correlated with lower obesity rates. So someone decides that all kids should have more physical education at school to fight obesity. However, lack of sports is not the root cause of obesity; bad eating habits are, and that's what should be addressed first to fix the problem. Then, replacing sports with mathematics or foreign languages would make children both less obese (once eating habits are fixed) and more educated at the same time.

In all contexts, using predictors that are directly causal typically helps reduce the variance in the model and yields more robust solutions.

How Do You Detect Causes?

If you deal with more than 200 variables, you will find correlations that look significant (from a statistical point of view) but are actually an artifact caused by the large number of variables. For example, simulate 50 observations each with 10,000 variables. Each value in each variable is a simulated random number. Chances are you will find among these 10,000 variables two that are highly correlated, even though the real correlation between any of these two variables is (by design!) zero. As a practical illustration, you can predict chances of lung cancer within the next five years for a given individual either as a function of daily consumption of cigarettes or as a function of an electricity bill. Both are great predictors: the first one is a cause. The second one is not, but it is linked to age. The older you get, the more expensive commodities are due to inflation and this is an indirect (non-causal) factor for lung cancer. You can read more about this in the section about The Curse of Big Data in Chapter 2.

This section summarizes a few techniques that have been used in various contexts to identify causes.

- David Freedman is the author of an excellent book, *Statistical Models: Theory and Practice*, which discusses the issue of causation. It's a unique statistics book in that it gets into the issue of model assumptions. I highly recommend it. It claims to be introductory but I believe that a semester or two of math statistics as a prerequisite can be helpful.

- In the time series context, you can run a VAR and then do tests for Granger causality to see if one variable is actually "causing" the other, where "causing" is defined by Granger. (See any of Granger's books for the technical definition of Granger causality.) The programming language R has a nice package called vars, which makes building VAR models and doing testing extremely straightforward.

- Correlation does not imply causation; although, where there is causation you often but not always have correlation. Causality analysis can be done by learning Bayesian Networks from the data. See the excellent tutorial "A Tutorial on Learning with Bayesian Networks" by David Heckerman at http://research.microsoft.com/apps/pubs/?id=69588.

- Stefan Conrady, who manages the company "Bayesia Networks" (www.bayesia.com) focuses on identifying causation.

- For time series, see http://en.wikipedia.org/wiki/Granger_causality/.

- The only way to discriminate between correlation and coincidence is through a controlled experiment. Design the experiment such that you can test the effect of each parameter independent of the others.

- *Causality*, by Judea Pearl, is a great book on the subject. He discusses this topic in a lot of detail: direct, indirect, confounding, counterfactuals, and so on. Note that the causal model is interested in describing the mechanism (why something is happening)—essentially a deeper understanding than is possible through correlation analysis. A technique used often can be described as follows:

  1. Start with a causal model diagram that will form your hypotheses. (You can use structural equation modeling (SEM) diagrams. I actually use a technique called system dynamics.)

  2. Now find data to confirm or refute the set of hypotheses made in your model. For data that does not exist, you need to perform focused experiments.

  3. Based on data/correlation/sem analysis, refine your causal understanding.

  4. Simulate the model to see if the results are plausible; then refine.

  5. Start using your model; keep refining it as new evidence appears.

A well-known example of detected causality is lung cancer, with smoking having been formally established as a cause rather than a *confounding factor*. For instance, in the United States, lung cancer is correlated with both poverty and smoking. But poverty does not *cause* lung cancer — it is a confounding factor. The fact is that many people living in poverty are smokers, but the real cause of the lung cancer they experience is smoking. You might argue that poverty causes you to smoke, which in turn increases your risk of lung cancer. But no one has ever proved this to be a causal link, as far as I know, and it would still be an indirect link anyway.

Another interesting example is the early effort to identify the cause of the proliferation of malaria-carrying mosquitoes in India. The first identified cause was "bad air" that attracts infected mosquitoes, and thus the implemented solutions focused on improving air quality. It turned out that the real cause was not bad air, but the presence of stagnant water where the malaria-carrying mosquito larvae lived.

Identifying the true cause of a problem is needed in order to develop a proper and effective fix. Whenever a data scientist is asked to do a root cause analysis, it will often involve detecting the *true* cause, not just confounding factors.

Life Cycle of Data Science Projects

The keyword *life cycle* is traditionally used to describe a generic breakdown of tasks applicable to most medium and large projects. A project's life cycle can also be described as its work flow. Designing a work flow for any project, be it software engineering, product development, statistical analysis, or data science, is critical for success. It helps organize tasks in some natural order, provides a big picture of the project, and quickly identifies priorities, issues, options, and milestones. It is also part of *best practices*.

The following describe the main steps in a project's life cycle:

1. Identifying the Problem

    ▪ Identify the type of problem you are faced with (for example, prototyping, proof of concept, root cause analysis, predictive analytics, prescriptive analytics, machine-to-machine implementation, and so on).

    ▪ Identify key people within your organization (and outside) that can help solve the problem.

    ▪ Identify metrics that will be used to measure the success of the solution over baseline (doing nothing).

    ▪ Get specifications, requirements, project details, timeline, priorities, and budget from the appropriate people.

    ▪ Determine the level of accuracy needed.

- Determine if all of the available data is needed.

- Select and build an internal solution versus using a vendor's solution.

- Vendor comparison (usually for analytics, but sometimes also BI or database solutions in smaller companies), select specific benchmarks for evaluation of the progress of the solution, and for comparing vendors.

- Write proposal or reply to RFP (request for proposal).

2. Identifying Available Data Sources

    - Extract (or obtain) and check the sample data using sound sampling techniques, and discuss the fields to make sure you understand the data.

    - Perform EDA (exploratory analysis, data dictionary) on the data.

    - Assess the quality of the data and the value available in it.

    - Identify any data glitches and find work-arounds for them.

    - Ensure that data quality is good enough, and that fields are populated consistently over time.

    - Determine if some fields are a blend of different items (for example, keyword field is sometimes equal to user query and sometimes to advertiser keyword — there is no way to know except via statistical analyses or by talking to business people).

    - Determine how to improve data quality moving forward.

    - Determine if you need to create mini summary tables or a database to help with some of the tasks (such as statistical analyses) in your project.

    - Determine which tool you need (such as R, Excel, Tableau, Python, Perl, Tableau, SAS, and so on).

3. Identifying Additional Data Sources (if needed)

    - Identify what fields should be captured.

    - Determine how granular the data should be.

    - Select the amount of historical data needed.

    - Evaluate if real time data is needed.

    - Determine how will you store or access the data (NoSQL, MapReduce, and so on).

    - Assess the need for experimental design.

4. Performing Statistical Analyses

    - Use imputation methods as needed.

    - Detect and remove outliers.

    - Select your variables (variables reduction).

- Determine if the data is censored (for example, hidden data as in survival analysis or time-to-crime statistics).
- Perform cross-correlation analysis.
- Select your model (as needed), favoring simple models.
- Conduct sensitivity analysis.
- Perform cross-validation and model fitting.
- Measure the data accuracy, providing confidence intervals.

5. Ensuring Proper Implementation and Development

- Ensure the solution is fast, simple, scalable, robust, reusable (FSSRR).
- Determine how frequently you need to update lookup tables, white lists, data uploads, and so on.
- Determine if debugging is needed.
- Assess the need to create an API to communicate with other apps.

6. Communicating Results

- Determine if you need to integrate the results in a dashboard or create an e-mail alert system.
- Decide on dashboard architecture in conjunction with the business users.
- Assess visualization options.
- Discuss potential improvements (with cost estimates).
- Provide training to users about your product or solutions offered to the client as a result of your project.
- Provide support for users such as commenting on code, writing a technical report, explaining how your solution should be used, fine-tuning parameters, and interpreting results.

7. Maintaining the System

- Test the model or implementation using stress tests.
- Regularly update the system.
- Commence the final outsourcing of the system to engineering and business people in your company (once solution is stable).
- Help move the solution to a new platform or vendor, if applicable.

You can use this "life cycle" template and customize it for your projects. It can be used as the skeleton of any proposals you write for a client. Note that not all of these steps are needed in all projects. Some projects are internal and don't need proposals. In other cases, your client (or employer) already has databases, BI, and analytic tools in place, so there's no need to look for vendor solutions to be integrated in your project, or maybe your client/manager wants to keep your work proprietary and not use vendors.

Predictive Modeling Mistakes

As you follow the previous steps to carry out your analysis, you also want to avoid some pitfalls. These mistakes were first mentioned on the Rapid Insight blog. The following list presents a few more. You can read a more detailed version at `http://bit.ly/19vrkeZ`.

Data preparation mistakes can include:

- Including ID fields as predictors
- Using anachronistic variables
- Allowing duplicate records
- Modeling on too small a population
- Not accounting for outliers and missing values
- Joining on a field encoded slightly differently on both tables
- Using hybrid fields, for instance a keyword that is sometimes a user query, sometimes a category
- Poor visualizations that don't communicate well

Modeling mistakes can include:

- Failing to consider enough variables
- Not hand-crafting some additional variables
- Selecting the wrong Y-variable
- Not enough Y-variable responses
- Building a model on the wrong population
- Judging the quality of a model using one measure

To avoid data preparation mistakes, you should spend time with the business people involved in the work to make sure you understand all of the fields. Creating a data dictionary and running a battery of tests on your data will further reduce the chance of glitches. SQL queries that take too long, or return far more data than expected, could be an indicator of bad joins.

Finally, starting with as many variables as possible and narrowing down to an efficient subset is the way to go. Each time you change the model or delete/add variables, you should measure the new performance or lift (decrease in error or residual error or increase in ROI): the less volatile the predictions, the better the model. But avoid over-fitting! Validation can be performed by splitting your data set into two subsets: test and control. When a training set is available, train your model on the test subset, and measure performance on the control subset.

Logistic-Related Regressions

Here you consider a few modern variants of traditional logistic regression, one of the workhorses of statistical science, used in contexts in which the response is binary or a probability. Logistic regression is popular in clinical trials, scoring models, and fraud detection.

Interactions Between Variables

In the context of credit scoring, you need to develop a predictive model using a regression formula such as $Y = \sum w_i R_i$, where Y is the logarithm of odds ratio (fraud versus nonfraud). In a different but related framework, you deal with a logistic regression where Y is binary, for example, Y = 1 means fraudulent transaction, Y = 0 means nonfraudulent. The variables Ri, also referred to as fraud rules, are binary flags, such as:

- High dollar amount transaction
- High risk country
- High risk merchant category

This is the first order model. The second order model involves cross products $R_i * R_j$ to correct for rule interactions. How to best compute the regression coefficients w_i is also referred to as rule weighting. The issue is that rules substantially overlap, making the regression approach highly unstable. One approach consists of constraining the weights, forcing them to be binary (0/1) or to be of the same sign as the correlation between the associated rule and the dependent variable Y. This approach is related to *ridge regression*.

Note that when the weights are binary, this is a typical combinatorial optimization problem. When the weights are constrained to be linearly independent over the set of integer numbers, then each $\sum w_i R_i$ (sometimes called nonscaled score) corresponds to one unique combination of rules. It also uniquely represents a final node of the underlying decision tree defined by the rules. Another approach is *logic regression*, or hidden decision trees, described earlier in this chapter.

First Order Approximation

Now consider an approximate solution to linear regression. Logistic regression is indeed a linear regression on a transformed response, as you will see in the subsection on logistic regression with Excel. So solving the linear regression problem is of interest. In this section you need a minimum of understanding of matrix theory, which can be skipped by people who are not mathematically inclined.

You can solve the regression Y=AX where Y is the response (vector), X the input, and A is the vector of regression coefficients. Consider the following iterative algorithm (k represents the iteration):

$$A_{k+1} = cYU + A_k (I-cXU),$$

where:

- c is an arbitrary constant.

- U is an arbitrary matrix such that YU has the same dimension as A. For instance, U = transposed(X) works.

- A_0 is the initial estimate for A. For instance, A_0 is the correlation vector between the independent variables and the response.

A FEW QUESTIONS

What are the conditions for convergence? Do I have convergence only if the largest eigenvalue (in an absolute value) of the matrix I-cXU is strictly less than 1? In case of convergence, will it converge to the solution of the regression problem? For instance, if c=0, the algorithm converges, but not to the solution. In that case, it converges to A_0.

The parameters are:

n: number of independent variables

m: number of observations

The matrix dimensions are:

A: (1,n) (one row, n columns)

I: (n,n)

X: (n,m)

U: (m,n)

Y: (1,m)

The question arises: Why use an iterative algorithm instead of the traditional solution? There are several reasons, such as:

- You are dealing with an ill-conditioned problem; most independent variables are highly correlated.

- Many solutions (as long as the regression coefficients are positive) provide a good fit, and the global optimum is not that much better than a solution in which all regression coefficients are equal to 1.

- The plan is to use an iterative algorithm to start at iteration #1 with an approximate solution that has interesting properties, move to iteration #2 to improve a bit, and then stop.

Second Order Approximation

You can skip this section if you are not familiar with elementary concepts of matrix theory. Here you need to understand a first order solution to a regression problem in the form:

$$Y = \Sigma\, w_i\, R_i,$$

where Y is the response, w_i are the regression coefficients, and R_i are the independent variables or rules. The number of variables is assumed to be high, and the independent variables are highly correlated.

You want to improve the model by considering a second order regression of the form, such as:

$$Y = \Sigma\, w_i\, R_i + \Sigma\, w_{ij}\, c_{ij}\, m_{ij}\, R_i\, R_j$$

where:

c_{ij} = correlation between R_i and R_j

$w_{ij} = |w_i w_j|^{0.5} * \text{sign}(w_i w_j)$

m_{ij} are arbitrary constants

In practice, some of the R_i's are highly correlated and grouped into rule clusters. These clusters can be identified by using a clustering algorithm on the c_{ij}'s. For example, think of a model with two clusters A and B such as:

$$Y = \Sigma\, w_i\, R_i + m_A\, \Sigma_A\, w_{ij}\, c_{ij}\, R_i\, R_j + m_B\, \Sigma_B\, w_{ij}\, c_{ij}\, R_i\, R_j$$

where:

Σ_A (resp. Σ_B) are taken over all $i < j$ belonging to A (resp. B)

$m_{ij} = m_A$ (constant) if i, j belong to cluster A

$m_{ij} = m_B$ (constant) if i, j belong to cluster B

An interesting case occurs when the cluster structure is so strong that the following results:

$|c_{ij}| = 1$ if i and j belong to the same cluster (either A or B)

$c_{ij} = 0$ otherwise

This particular case results in:

$m_A = 4\, /\, [1 + (1+8k_A)^{0.5}]$

$m_B = 4\, /\, [1 + (1+8k_B)^{0.5}]$

where:

$k_A = \Sigma_A\, |c_{ij}|$ and $k_B = \Sigma_B\, |c_{ij}|$.

NOTE If the cluster structure is moderately strong, with the correlations c_{ij} close to 1, −1, or 0, how accurate is the preceding formula involving k_A and k_B? Here assume that the w_i's are known or approximated. Typically, w_i is a constant or w_i is a simple function of the correlation between Y and R_i.

Alternative Approach

As an alternative to the model described at the beginning of this section, let's consider a simplified model involving one cluster with m_{ij} = constant = m. For instance, the unique cluster could consist of all variables i, j with $|c_{ij}| > 0.70$. The model can be written as:

$$Y = \sum w_i R_i + m \sum w_{ij} c_{ij} R_i R_j$$

You want to find m that provides the best improvement over the first order model, in terms of residual error. The first order model corresponds to m = 0. Now consider the following notations:

$W = \sum w_{ij} c_{ij} R_i R_{j'}$

$V = W - u$, where u = average(W). (Thus V is the centered W, with mean 0.)

$S = \sum w_i R_i$. (average(S) = average(Y) by construction)

Without loss of generality, consider the slightly modified (centered) model:

$$Y = S + mV.$$

Then m is equal to:

$$m = [\, \text{Transposed}(V) * (Y\text{-}S) \,] / [\, \text{Transposed}(V) * V \,]$$

where Y, S, and V are vectors with n rows, and n is the number of observations.

Further Improvements

The alternative approach could be incorporated in an iterative algorithm for credit scoring where at each step a new cluster is added. So at each step you would have the same computation for m, optimizing the residual error on Y = S + mV. However, this time S would contain all the clusters detected during the previous step, and V would contain the new cluster being added to the model.

Regression with Excel

It is worth mentioning that you can perform logistic regression with Excel even without using the data analysis plug-in. If your response is a ratio r between 0 and 1, use the *logit* transformation s = ln{ r/(1-r)}, perform a linear regression on s, and then switch back from s to r using the inverse transform r = exp(s)/{1+exp(s)}.

The multivariate linear regression is available in Excel as the function *linest*. The input is a rectangular data set where the first column is the response (s in this case) and the remaining columns are the independent variables. The output is a vector with all the regression coefficients. Because the output is not a cell but instead an array (linest is an array formula in Excel), you need to specify where the output will be stored in the spreadsheet (in multiple cells) using the keys Ctrl+Shift+Enter simultaneously to select the cells in question. You can get more information on this at `http://office.microsoft.com/en-us/excel-help/linest-function-HP010342653.aspx`.

Experimental Design

Experimental design, sometimes referred to as DOE (design of experiments), A/B testing, multivariate testing (in web analytics), or Taguchi methods (quality control), is a fundamental step in many statistical analyses to make sure a survey or analysis is properly designed and that the data can be exploited and have no uncontrolled bias. Here is an example in a context similar to clinical trials: testing strategies to eliminate addictions.

Interesting Metrics

To monitor a recovering alcoholic and guarantee success, three metrics are critical and are patient-dependent:

- **Time elapsed between drinking events**: 5 days is the minimum for most recovering alcoholics, and you must have been abstinent for 30 days before resuming—not less, not more.
- **Duration of drinking events**: For example, 2 days, such as Friday and Saturday nights.
- **Intensity of drinking events**: For example, 50 percent to 70 percent below the alcoholic period in terms of alcohol consumption.

Rehabilitation centers can identify patients most likely to recover based on these metrics and even reject or accept patients based on answers to these questions.

Segmenting the Patient Population

It is rather well established today that there are four kinds of alcoholics:

- Alcoholic/high functioning
- Alcoholic/not high functioning
- Problem drinker/high functioning
- Problem drinker/not high functioning

You can now introduce a new segment: wants to get drunk versus does not want to get drunk. Both types drink similar amounts and inflict the same damage to their bodies, but the first type appears to be permanently drunk, whereas the second group never appears to be drunk. It could be somewhat associated with the high functioning/not high functioning dichotomy. Assuming it is different, this creates eight segments or alcoholic profiles:

- Alcoholic/high functioning/wants to get drunk
- Alcoholic/not high functioning/wants to get drunk
- Problem drinker/high functioning/wants to get drunk
- Problem drinker/not high functioning/wants to get drunk
- Alcoholic/high functioning/does not want to get drunk
- Alcoholic/not high functioning/does not want to get drunk
- Problem drinker/high functioning/does not want to get drunk
- Problem drinker/not high functioning/does not want to get drunk

Customized Treatments

There are two types of interesting studies that could be made based on this segmentation, assuming you have a good way to assign one of these eight segments to each alcoholic interested in getting cured, and assuming that privacy issues are taken care of. (Alcoholics might be reluctant to be treated, or even classified, due to the fear that it will bite them back.)

1. What is the best segment-dependent treatment for each of these eight segments?

2. Use Markov Chain modeling to create an 8x8 transition probabilities matrix to assess the chances for any alcoholic in any of these eight segments to move from one segment to another segment within the next 6 months. Use this model to assess risks and prioritize who should be treated first and how.

You can add two important states to my Markov Chain: cured and dead. Cured does not mean permanently cured because relapses are possible. Also, the transition probabilities will depend on age, how long people have been in the current state (talking about the eight states discussed previously), how many relapses occur, and so on. So the transition (stochastic) matrix is not 8x8; it is 10x10. Also, people can move from any state (except dead) to any other state.

One goal of this analysis would be to create a new type of rehabilitation center that identifies and serves a minority of patients that are most likely to recover. Such centers would have a 70 percent success rate after 5 years (versus less than 20 percent for most programs), which is great for marketing purposes and costs far less than the typical $20,000 fee because these patients can stop abruptly without experiencing symptoms. Therefore, they require limited medical attention and most of the time no medical attention at all. My guess is that these centers would cater only to the high functioning "does not want to get drunk" alcoholic, using a specific approach for this particular segment.

Note that this framework can be applied to any kind of chemical addiction, maybe even to other addictions such as sex, gambling, or spending; although it would have to be tested first.

Experimental design is an important topic in statistics. It starts with setting the hypothesis and designing the experiment, followed by testing and optimizing it. Common mistakes include under-sampling, not detecting and eliminating confounding variables, wrongly assuming that the observations follow a specific distribution (necessary only for inference purposes), making inferences for data buckets that are too small (it happens when looking at 3x3 interactions on small data sets), having interactions ignored or not incorporated in the test but present in data outside the test, and bias selecting observations to include in your test. For instance, when testing a new drug, if you provide financial incentives to participants, your sample will be not necessarily be representative of the general population.

Analytics as a Service and APIs

An increasing number of individuals and companies now deliver analytics solutions using modern web-based platforms: Data-Applied, DataSpora, and AnalyticBridge, to name a few. See also www.RonCloud.com (R on Cloud) as an example of R programming (the R console) made available as a web app on your browser, allowing you to run sophisticated R programs on your iPad, maybe even on a cell phone. You can find a discussion on RonCloud at http://bit.ly/1cJsvHm.

The concept is at least 10 years old, but because inexpensive web servers can now handle a large bandwidth and can process megabytes of data in a few seconds (even without the cloud), and because Internet users have much faster (broadband) connections, it is possible to develop analytics applications capable of processing millions of observations online, on demand, and in real time, and deliver results via an API or on-the-fly. In some cases, results consist of processed data sets, sometimes fairly large, where one column has been added to the input file: for instance, the new column (the output) is a score attached to each observation. This is a solution being worked on using ad hoc statistical techniques to process data efficiently with hidden decision trees, using little memory and efficient data structures, and thus allowing users to process online on-the-fly large data sets that R or other statistical packages could not process even on a desktop. In fact, these traditional packages (R and Salford Systems) require that all your data be stored in memory, and they typically crash if your input file has more than 500,000 observations, although Hadoop integrations such as RHadoop (R+Hadoop) exist.

Interestingly, this new type of analytics service can rely on popular statistical packages (such as SAS) or can use ad hoc algorithms written in Perl (including production of charts with the GD library), Python, C, C#, or Java. A version based on SAS would be called a SAS web server (extranet or intranet).

How It Works

The steps involved in this are as follows:

1. An API call is made to an external website where SAS is installed; parameters in the API call describe the type of analysis requested (logistic regression and so on).

2. A Perl/CGI script processes the HTTP request, extracts the parameters, and automatically writes a SAS program corresponding to the user's request.

3. The SAS code is run from the Perl script in command-line mode and produces an output file, such as a chart or XML or data file.

4. The Perl script reads the chart, displays it in the browser (if the user is a human being using a web browser), and provides a URL where the user can fetch the chart (in case the user is a web robot executing an API call).

Example of Implementation

One idea is that you must purchase a number of transactions before using the paid service and add dollars regularly. A transaction is a call to the API. The service is accessed via an HTTP call that looks like this:

```
http://www.datashaping.com/AnalyticsAPI?clientID=xxx&
dataSource=yyy&service=zzz&parameters=abc
```

When the request is executed, the following occurs:

1. The script checks if the client has enough credits (dollars).

2. If yes, it fetches the data on the client web server: the URL for the source data is yyy.

3. The script checks if the source data is OK or invalid, or the client server is unreachable.

4. It executes the service zzz, typically a predictive scoring algorithm.

5. The parameter field tells whether you train your predictor (data = training set) or whether you use it for actual predictive scoring (data outside the training set).

6. It processes data fast (a few seconds for 1 MM observations for the training step).

7. It sends an e-mail to the client when done, with the location (on the data shaping server) of the results. (The location can be specified in the API call, as an additional field, with a mechanism in place to prevent file collisions from happening.)

8. It updates the client budget.

All this can be performed without any human interaction. Retrieving the scored data can be done with a web robot and then integrated into the client's database (again, automatically). Training the scores would be charged more than scoring one observation outside the training set. Scoring one observation is a transaction and could be charged as little as $0.0025.

This architecture is for daily or hourly processing but could be used for real time if the parameter is not set to "training." However, when designing the architecture, my idea was to process large batches of transactions, maybe 1 million at a time.

In summary, AaaS and APIs are important topics that should be understood by data scientists. Many times, data is accessed via an API, and some databases offer API access. Also, automated data science (and delivery of results in machine-to-machine communications) relies heavily on APIs and AaaS. Designing APIs is borderline between engineering and data science.

Source Code for Keyword Correlation API

The following is an application of the "Clustering and Taxonomy Creation for Massive Data Sets" described in Chapter 2. This application, used in all search engines, identifies keywords related to a specified keyword, as described previously. This section has everything you need to create your first API from scratch. Just read and download the following, which can keep you busy for a little while!

- The HTML page where the application is hosted. In particular, it contains the web form with all the parameters used by the API. The URL is `http://bit.ly/1de7qoY`.

- The keyword cofrequencies table described earlier. It is saved as 27 files; for instance, kwsum2s_SRCH_CLICKS_p.txt corresponds to keywords starting with the letter p, and kwsum2s_SRCH_CLICKS_0.txt corresponds to keywords not starting with a letter, such as 2013, 98029 (ZIP code), or 1040 (as in "IRS tax form 1040"). It is available at `http://.bit.ly/1de7qoY` as a compressed zip file (7 MB). The uncompressed version consists of 27 files to make it run about 27 times faster.

- The Perl script kw8x3.pl, which can be downloaded from `http://.bit.ly/1aJZBdj`. It computes keyword correlations, given the keyword cofrequencies table with precomputed frequencies.

The application is written in simple Perl but can easily be translated into Python. It does not require special Perl libraries. Later you will consider another example of API that requires downloading special libraries (along with web crawler source code and instructions).

To get the API to work, first install cygwin (available at `http://cygwin.com/install.html`) on your computer or server, and then install Perl (available at `http://www.activestate.com/activeperl/downloads`). If you want the API to work as a web app (as on `www.frenchlane.com/kw8.html`), it has to be installed on a web server. Perl script (files with the .pl extension) must be made executable (usually in a /cgi-bin/ directory) using the UNIX command chmod 755 — in this case, chmod 755 kw8x3.pl. The application can be tested at `www.frenchlane.com/kw8.html`.

Two Examples of an API Call

The following are two examples of how to use the API to find keywords related to the keyword data. Click URL to replicate results. Note that in the first example, the parameter mode is set to Silent, and correl is not specified. In the second example, mode is set to Verbose and correl to $n12/sqrt($n1*$n2) as suggested previously (where n1=x, n2=y, n12=z).

Example 1

- URL for API call: `http://www.frenchlane.com/cgi-bin/kw8x3.pl?query=data&ndisplay=10&sort=Descending&mode=Silent&filter=Yes&boost=&correl=`

- Shortened URL: `http://bit.ly/1biu1mc`

- Results returned:

```
data recovery
data sheet
data base
data cable
data management
recovery
data entry
data protection
data from
data storage
```

Example 2

- URL for API call: `http://www.frenchlane.com/cgi-bin/kw8x3.pl?query=data&ndisplay=10&sort=Descending&mode=Verbose&filter=Yes&boost=&correl=$n12/sqrt($n1*$n2)`

▪ Shortened URL: http://bit.ly/15td3Oi

▪ Results returned:

```
0.282 : data =data recovery= 2143:171:0.245
0.167 : data =data sheet= 2143:60:1.066
0.139 : data =data base= 2143:42:0.571
0.138 : data =data cable= 2143:41:1.414
0.134 : data =data management= 2143:39:0.512
0.121 : data =recovery= 2143:928:0.637
0.116 : data =data entry= 2143:29:1.068
0.112 : data =data protection= 2143:27:1.074
0.105 : data =data from= 2143:24:1
0.103 : data =data storage= 2143:23:1.217
```

Results

Results can be recovered manually from the web app itself with your browser, for instance when you click the provided links, or with a web crawler for batch or real-time processing. Note that the correlation formula used in this example ($n12/sqrt($n1*$n2) is the same as the one described in the section Clustering and Taxonomy Creation for Massive Data Sets of this chapter. The only difference is that in that section, $n1, $n2, and $n12 are respectively called x, y, and z.

In Example 2, the results returned are $n1 = 2143, $n2 = 928, and correlation = 0.121 for the keyword pair {data, recovery}. Note that n1 = 2143 is the number of occurrences of keyword data as reported in the cofrequencies table that you have just downloaded. n2 = 928 is the number of occurrences of keyword recovery, whereas n12 would be the number of simultaneous occurrences of data and recovery (for example, in the same web page or user query), as reported in the cofrequencies table.

One of the tricky parts of this API is that it accepts a user-provided formula to compute the keyword correlations, based on $n1, $n2, and $n12, unless the correl parameter (in the API call) is left empty. Because of this, the API creates an auxiliary Perl script called formula.pl from within kw8x3.pl, in the same directory where the parent script (kw8x3.pl) is located. The parent script then calls the getRho subroutine stored in formula.pl to compute the correlations. Here's the default code for formula.pl:

```
sub getRho{
  my $rho;
  $rho=$n12/sqrt($n1*$n2);
  return($rho)
}
1;
```

The path where formula.pl is stored is `/home/cluster1/data/d/x/a1168268/cgi-bin/`. You will have to change this path accordingly when installing the app on your server. Also, you can improve this API a bit by using a list of stop words — words such as *from, the, how,* and so on, that you want to ignore.

Finally, keep in mind that this is just a starting point. If you want to make it a high quality application, you'll need to add a few features. In particular, you'll have to use a lookup table of keywords that cannot be broken down into individual tokens, such as "New York," "San Francisco," and so on. You'll also have to use a stop list of keywords and do some keyword cleaning. (You can normalize "traveling" as "travel," but not "booking" as "book.") The feed that you use to create your cofrequencies table is also critical: it must contain millions of keywords. If you use too few, your results will look poor. If you use too many, your results will look noisy. In this app, a combination of feeds are used:

- About a million categories and website descriptions from DMOZ (public data)
- Many millions of user queries from search engines (private data)
- Text extracted with a web crawler from several million web pages (public data).

Miscellaneous Topics

This section discusses a few more specialized topics: score preservation (important when you blend data from different clients, different sources, or different time periods, as new data files are no longer compatible with older versions), web crawler optimization (data scientists should be familiar with web crawlers, as a mechanism to extract vast amounts of rich, usually unstructured data), fast database joins, a trick to improve predictive models, and source code to simulate clusters.

Preserving Scores When Data Sets Change

Changes in data can come from multiple sources: for instance, the definition of a visit is suddenly modified in Internet traffic data, resulting in visitor counts suddenly dropping or exploding. Internet log files regularly change, for instance the full user agent string is no longer recorded, impacting traffic quality scores. Or one client has data fields that are not the same or partially overlap only with those from other clients.

How do you handle this issue? The answer is simple: when a change in scores is detected (whether your scoring algorithm or your data has changed), apply the new scores backward to at least two weeks before the change, compare the old and new scores for these two weeks of overlapping scores, and then recalibrate the new scores using these two weeks worth of data to make them consistent (for example, same median, same variance).

If the issue is not temporal but rather the fact that different clients have different data sets, then use a subset of the two data sets, where data fields are compatible and compute scores for both clients on these reduced data sets (and compare with scores computed on full data sets). These four scores (two clients, reduced data, and full data) will be used for recalibration.

The following should be noted when using this approach:

Use change-point, trend-reversal, or slope-change detection algorithms to detect changes. However, the changes you take here are usually brutal and definitely visible with the naked eye, even to a non-statistician (and in many cases, unfortunately, by one of your clients).

When you improve a scoring algorithm, if it improves scores on A but makes them worse on B, then create a hybrid, blended score consisting of an old score for B and a new score for A.

Optimizing Web Crawlers

Web crawling is notoriously slow because it can take up to 2 seconds for an HTTP request to complete. When you crawl billions of web pages, brute force takes billions of seconds. You can assume that the pages that you decide to crawl are carefully chosen so that the caching, browsing, and indexing schedule is already fully optimized.

The following steps increase efficiency (speed) by a factor of 80,000:

1. Use the cloud: split your crawling across 8,000 servers. Speed improvement: 8,000.

2. On each server, run 20 copies of your crawler, in parallel (call it sub-parallelization at the server level). You can expect (based on my experience, assuming each server is used exclusively for this crawling project) to boost speed not by a factor of 20, but maybe as high as 5. Speed improvement so far: 8,000 x 5 = 40,000.

3. Change the timeout threshold (associated with each HTTP request) from 2 seconds to 0.5 seconds. This could improve speed by a factor of 3 (not all web pages require 2 second to download), but then you have to revisit many more pages that failed due to the short 0.5-second threshold. Because of this, the gain is not a factor of 3, but a factor of 2. Note that you should try different values for this threshold until you find one that is optimum. Speed improvement so far: 8,000 x 5 x 2 = 80,000.

4. In addition to changing the timeout threshold, you can change the max size threshold: if a page is more than 24 K, download the first 24 K, and skip the remaining. Of course, although this boosts speed performance, the drawback is information loss.

5. You should also have a black list of websites or web pages that you don't want to crawl because they are consistently slow to load or cause other speed problems (multiple redirects, and so on).

6. Do not revisit the same page over and over; you risk getting stuck in an infinite loop. Use a mechanism where pages previously visited won't be visited again for another, for example, 30 days.

Here's a piece of Perl code to extract a web page: it accesses a Twitter page on big data and copies it on your local machine as `test.html`. The content of the web page is stored in the `$page` (text) variable.

```perl
#!/usr/bin/perl

require LWP::UserAgent;

my $ua = LWP::UserAgent->new;
$ua->timeout(2);
$ua->env_proxy;
$ua->agent("Mozilla/4.0 (compatible; MSIE 7.0; Windows NT 5.1;)");
$ua->max_size(200000);

$url="http://twitter.com/search?q=%23BigData&src=typd";

my $response = $ua->get($url);
if ($response->is_success) {
  $page=$response->content;
  $score=0;
  $success++;
} else {
  $error=$response->status_line;
  print "$error\n";
  $page="-";
}

open(OUT,">test.html");
print OUT "$page\n";
close(OUT);
```

Hash Joins

Hash joins, an option offered by some database vendors, can be efficient, especially when dealing with sparse data. Joins are typically Cartesian products and in many database systems can be slow.

For example, if you join two tables — A and B — each with 1 million rows, with a `where` condition narrowing rows down to 10,000 in table A and a `where` condition narrowing rows to 500,000 in table B, then a solution for an efficient join is to do the following:

1. Identify these 10,000 rows in table A.

2. Put these 10,000 rows in a hash table.

3. Browse the 1 million records from table B with a quick look-up check on the hash table for each of the 500,000 rows in table B, satisfying the `where` criterion associated with table B.

This is far more efficient than having a full Cartesian product, which would involve 1,000,000,000,000 rows. Obviously, the final solution (unless it is an *outer join*) would consist only of 10,000 rows at most. Also, it is easy to write the two or three lines of code required to perform this type of join in a scripting language such as Python or Perl.

Simple Source Code to Simulate Clusters

Following is a short and simple source code to produce nice simulated cluster structures (stored in a text file called `cluster.txt`) and test cluster detection algorithms. The version is written in Perl, and the code is straightforward and easy to adapt to any language: R, C, or Python. You can see simulated clusters produced with the following script at `http://bit.ly/V5FVI2`.

```
`rm cluster.txt`;
$cluster=0;
&seed(1,1);
$cluster++;
&seed(-5,-5);
$cluster++;
&seed(0,0);

#-------------------------------------
sub seed {

local($x,$y)=@_;

$kmax=rand(300);
$x=rand($x)-0.5;
$y=rand($y)-0.5;

#print "==$x == $y\n";
```

```
for ($k=0; $k<$kmax; $k++) {
  $x=$x+rand($1)-0.5;
  $y=$y+rand($1)-0.5;
  $px[$k]=$x;
  $py[$k]=$y;
}
open(OUT,">>cluster.txt");
for ($k=0; $k<$kmax; $k++) {
  print OUT "$cluster\t$px[$k]\t$py[$k]\n";
}
close(OUT);
}
```

New Synthetic Variance for Hadoop and Big Data

This section summarizes many concepts introduced throughout the book, including other synthetic metrics and applied data science theorems produced by the statistical research laboratory at Data Science Central. The two technical notes (you can skip them) can help the math-savvy reader delve deeper into interesting data science research topics ranging from matrix theory (including doubly stochastic orthogonal matrices), convex functions, L^p norms, invariants, geometry in high dimensions, and more. The concept of variance is introduced and generalized in an original way. It is shown that the traditional variance (corresponding to L^2 and described in all textbooks) is the only one that cannot be made scale-invariant using the framework described. Scale-invariant variances are great metrics to detect cluster structures, holes, and uneven point distributions.

Andrew Peterson put it best when he said, "Hadoop is load first, then organize. Database is organize first, then load" (http://linkd.in/1eH7bmb).

Introduction to Hadoop/MapReduce

MapReduce is a framework for processing large amounts of data efficiently. The original problem is "mapped" to smaller problems (which may themselves become "original" problems). Smaller problems are processed in parallel. The results of smaller problems are combined, or "reduced." It works well for processes that can easily be parallelized, such as transactional data processing (scoring), web crawling, processing log data (social network data), and even for tasks such as sorting (which can be decomposed into sorting data subsets followed by a merging step) or manipulating giant — but highly sparse — matrices, using well designed algorithms that exploit the sparsity in the data. It is less efficient to process data sets with significant interactions and dependencies among many data points, such as clustering massive amounts of text. Even in this context, it is still possible to use MapReduce by completely ignoring very weak keyword associations, which represent more than 99.9 percent of keyword associations, in big data sets (for instance, data sets such as the Google keyword index). In cases when strong interactions exist (both short- and long-range), such as in some spatial data, graph databases are a better alternative.

Hadoop is an implementation of MapReduce to help split and merge data to process it in a distributed way, either on a single computer when data is too large to fit in memory (or hash tables grow too large even if data is accessed small buckets at a time) or in a cluster of machines. You can even install it on a single Windows laptop if you first install a Linux environment. It is a file management system more than a traditional database framework, though some SQL layers have been built on top of it. More about Hadoop can be found at `http://bit.ly/1dQVjwf`.

Synthetic Metrics

The new variance introduced here fixes two big data problems associated with the traditional variance and the way it is computed in Hadoop (using a numerically unstable formula). This new metric is synthetic: it was not derived naturally from mathematics, like the variance taught in any statistics 101 course or the variance currently implemented in Hadoop. By *synthetic*, I mean that it was built to address issues with big data (outliers) and the way many big data computations are now done: MapReduce framework, Hadoop being an implementation. It is a different approach to metric design—from data to theory, rather than from theory to data. By theory, I mean statistical models, such as metrics (called statistics by statisticians) derived, for instance, by solving maximum likelihood equations under the assumption of a Gaussian distribution.

These new metrics can be used just like standard metrics for business purposes. Most of the time, they actually generalize standard metrics and can thus be applied in more contexts, while standard metrics are more limited (for instance, with standard metrics, your data must have a Gaussian distribution for the metric to work well, or not too many outliers).

Other synthetic metrics designed in our research laboratory include:

- Predictive power metric, related to entropy (that is, information quantification), used in big data frameworks, for instance to identify optimum feature combinations for scoring algorithms. (See Chapter 6, "Data Science Application Case Studies," for details.)

- Correlation for big data: defined by an algorithm and closely related to the optimum variance metric discussed here. (See Chapter 4, "Data Science Craftsmanship: Part I," for details.)

- Structuredness coefficient: See Chapter 4 for details.

- Bumpiness coefficient: See Chapter 4 for details.

Hadoop, Numerical, and Statistical Stability

There are two issues with the formula used for computing variance in Hadoop. First, the formula used, namely $Var(x_1,\ldots, x_n) = \{SUM(x_i^2)/n\} - \{SUM(x_i)/n\}^2$, is notoriously unstable. For large n, although both terms cancel out somewhat, each one taken separately can take a huge value because of the squares aggregated over billions of observations. It results in numerical inaccuracies, with people having reported negative variances. You can read the comments to my article *The Curse of Big Data* at `http://bit.ly/104jiqU` for details. In addition, there are variance formulas that do not require two passes of the entire data sets that are numerically stable.

Of course, the formula currently used is very easy to implement in a MapReduce environment such as Hadoop. You first split your data into 200 buckets. You compute both sums separately on these 200 data buckets (each computation is simultaneously done on a separate server to decrease computation time by a factor of 200), and then perform 200 aggregations and a final square to get the value for the right term.

My main concern, though, is not about numerical instability but with the fact that in large data sets, outliers are a big problem and will mess up your variance. This variance formula will make variance comparisons across data bins meaningless and will result in highly volatile, inaccurate predictions if the data is used for predictive modeling. The solution is to use a different type of variance, one that is not sensitive to outliers yet is easy to compute with Hadoop.

The Abstract Concept of Variance

Before introducing a new definition of variance, let's first discuss what a variance metric should satisfy. The following are desirable properties, listed in order of importance: #1, #2, and #3 are the most fundamental, whereas #5, #6, and #7 are rarely needed. Property #4 is satisfied by traditional variance, but it leads to some new, interesting types of variance (discussed later in this section) when it is released.

1. The variance is positive. It is equal to 0 only if $x_1 = \ldots = x_n$.
2. The variance (denoted as V) is symmetrical. Any permutation of $(x_1,\ldots,x_n)$ has the same variance as $V(x_1, \ldots, x_n)$.
3. The further away you are from $x_1 = \ldots = x_n$, the higher the variance.
4. The variance is translation-invariant: $V(x_1+c, \ldots, x_n+c) = V(x_1, \ldots, x_n)$ for any constant c.
5. The variance is scale-invariant: $V(cx_1, \ldots, cx_n) = V(x_1, \ldots, x_n)$ for any constant c. Read first the following technical notes for explanations.

6. The variance is invariant under a number of matrix transformations such as rotations or reflections.

7. The variance is bounded, for instance, $V(x_1, ... , x_n) < 1$.

Properties #1 and #2 are mandatory. Property #5 is not necessary; it is easy to derive a scale-invariant variance W from any variance V: define $W(x_1, ... , x_n)$ as $V(x_1, ... , x_n)$ divided by the average $V(x_i, x_j)$ computed on all subsets $\{x_i, x_j\}$ of $\{x_1, ... , x_n\}$ with i<j. Property #7 is not necessary. You can turn any nonbounded variance V into a bounded one using $W = V / (1+V)$. The disadvantage of a non-bounded variance is that a single outlier can make the variance arbitrarily large.

Property #4 is not necessary. You can derive a translation-invariant variance W from V as follows: $W(x_1, ..., x_n) = \max V(x_1+c, ..., x_n+c)$, where the maximum is computed over all c's. This works only when the c achieving maximum V is finite, regardless of $(x_1, ..., x_n)$.

I'd like to redefine property #3 differently. All the variances described here share a property similar to #3 anyway. But strictly speaking, property #3 means that the higher the distance d between $(x_1, ... ,x_n)$ and the line containing the points $(0, ... , 0)$ and $(1, ..., 1)$ in the n-dimensional space, the higher the variance. d is exactly the traditional standard deviation computed on $(x_1, ..., x_n)$, and thus the only variances satisfying property #3 would be monotonic functions of the traditional variance.

The new variance introduced here meets properties #1 and #2. It is defined as follows: let g be an arbitrary strictly convex function, for instance $g(x) = |x|^a$ (with a>1). Then:

$$V(x_1, ... , x_n) = \{SUM(g(x_i))/n\} - g(SUM(x_i)/n).$$

If you use $g(x) = |x|^a$ with a=2, then the formula coincides with the traditional variance. I recommend a much lower value, for instance a=1.25, to solve both the numerical instability and outlier issues. I wish a=1 could be used, but then g would be convex but not strictly convex, and it just does not work. Interestingly, when transforming V (defined using $g(x)= |x|^a$) to make it translation-invariant, you get a new variance W, which works perfectly well even with a=1, making computations faster: it takes far more time to compute $|x|^{1.25}$ than $|x|^1$.

When $g(x) = |x|^a$ and $1 < a < 2$, the c that maximizes $V(x_1+c, ..., x_n+c)$ is $c = -(x_1 + ... + x_n)/n$. I haven't proved this result yet; I invite you to come with a formal proof. But I tested it on several data sets. Clearly, the result no longer holds when a=1 or a=2; if (and only if) a=2, the variance V and its translation-invariant version W are identical. So our final variance, after this transformation, is:

$$W(x1, ... , x_n) = SUM\{g(x_i - u)/n\}, \text{ with } u = (x_1 + ... + x_n)/n,$$
$$g(x) = |x|^a \text{ and a=1.}$$

NOTE W satisfies property #4 (translation-invariant) under the L^a norm. If you transform the W into a scale-invariant variance using the technique previously described, you will end up with a final metric that is good at detecting clusters and data structures with holes: the resulting metric takes higher values when strong cluster patterns are present and conversely, low values when data points are more evenly spread. This works for $1 < a < 2$, as well as for a=1. It does not work for a=2 (standard variance) as the resulting metric would then depend only on n: it would always be equal to $(n-1)/(2n)$ regardless of $(x_1, \ldots ,x_n)$, if a=2. So, the traditional variance is the only variance (with parameter a between 1 and 2) that cannot be made scale-invariant using the approach described here.

As an exercise, compute the variance for a=1, after transforming W (the translation-invariant version of V) to make it scale-invariant, on four data sets with n=10 points:

- The first data set is {0, 1, 2, 3, 4, 5, 6, 7, 8, 9}
- The second data set is {0, 0, 10/3, 9/2, 9/2. 9/2. 9/2, 9, 9, 9}
- The third data set is {0, 0, 0, 0, 0, 9, 9, 9, 9, 9}
- The forth data set is {0, 0, 0, 0, 0, 1, 1, 1, 1, 1}

This can help you understand what a scale-invariant variance is. The values computed on the third and fourth data sets are identical precisely because of the scale-invariant property. Finally, our formula to obtain a scale-invariant variance is $O(n^2)$ in terms of computation, that is, very time-consuming. Everything else discussed here is $O(n)$. How can you improve this $O(n^2)$?

A New Big Data Theorem

The Data Science Central research lab occasionally produces new theorems that have immediate application for better processing of data, both big and small. For example, the formula $V(x_1, \ldots , x_n) = \{SUM(g(x_i))/n\} - g(SUM(x_i)/n)$ defines a variance, satisfying properties #1 and #2, when g is a strictly convex function.

This result — I call it the Fourth AnalyticBridge Theorem — is a direct consequence of *Jensen's inequality*. For those interested, here are three of our previous theorems:

- **First AnalyticBridge Theorem**: Used to build model-free confidence intervals. (Chapter 5)

- **Second AnalyticBridge Theorem**: Used in the context of random permutations. A random permutation of nonindependent numbers constitutes a sequence of independent numbers. (Chapter 4)

- **Third AnalyticBridge Theorem**: Used to prove that a newly defined correlation (used in the context of big data) takes values between –1 and 1. Proved by Jean-Francois Puget in 2013, in our first data science competition. (Chapter 4)

Assuming $X=(x_1, ..., x_n)$ and $Y=(y_1, ...,y_n)$ are two vectors, then $Cov(X, Y) = \{V(X+Y) - [V(X)+V(Y)]\}/2$ defines the traditional covariance, if $g(x)=|x|^a$ and $a=2$. A possible research subject would be to adapt this formula to $1 < a < 2$ and generalize this covariance definition to more than two vectors.

Transformation-Invariant Metrics

It is easy to prove that when $a=2$ (the traditional variance), V satisfies property #4, that is, it is translation invariant: adding a constant to all data points $x_1, ... , x_n$ does not change V. This is no longer true when $1 < a < 2$. For instance, with $n=3$, you have:

- When $a=2$ and x1=3, x2=5, x3=10, then V=8.67
- When $a=2$ and x1=10,003, x2=10,005, x3=10,010, then V=8.67 (unchanged)
- When $a=1.25$ and x1=3, x2=5, x3=10, then V=0.34
- When $a=1.25$ and x1=10,003, x2=10,005, x3=10,010, then V=0.00

This is one of the reasons why I don't like translation invariance and prefer $a=1.25$ over the standard $a=2$.

It can easily be proved that to satisfy the translation-invariant property, the function g must satisfy $g(x) – 2g(x+1) + g(x+2) = $ constant. The only functions g satisfying this constraint are quadratic forms (for instance when a=2), and are thus linked to the traditional variance. Likewise, to satisfy the scale-invariant property, the function g would have to satisfy the equation $g(2x) – 2g(x) = $ constant. There is no strictly convex function satisfying this constraint, so none of our Vs is scale-invariant. But you can use a transformation previously described to build a variance W that is scale-invariant.

NOTE The traditional variance defined by a=2 is also invariant under orthogonal transformations (reflections or rotations) that preserve the mean — that is, it is invariant under linear operators that are both orthogonal and stochastic. In matrix notations, such an operator is an n x n matrix A applied to the column vector $X = (x_1, ..., x_n)'$ and having the sum of each column equal to 1. Here the character ' denotes the transposed vector (from row to column). In short, V(AX) = V(X) if A is such a matrix and a=2.

A particularly interesting case is when A is both doubly stochastic and orthogonal. Then A is a permutation matrix. Such matrices A can be produced using the following iterative algorithm: start with any doubly stochastic matrix A_0; define $A_{k+1} = (A_k – s I) (I – s A'_k)^{-1}$ for k>0. Here you assume 0 < s < 1 for convergence, and the symbol I denotes the n x n identity matrix.

Implementation: Communications Versus Computational Costs

One of the issues with Hadoop and MapReduce is the time spent in data transfers, as you split a task into multiple parallel processes, each running on a different server. It shifts the problem of computational complexity from algorithm complexity to communication or bandwidth costs. By communication, I mean the amount of time moving data around—from a centralized server (database or file management system) or distributed system to memory or to hard disks. How can you optimize these data transfers? How can you optimize in-memory computations? You cannot rely on a built-in function such as variance if it is not properly implemented, as shown here.

Indeed, the variance computation is an interesting problem that illustrates some Hadoop technical challenges. If no efficient built-in algorithm is available, it is necessary to do homemade computations that leverage the MapReduce architecture, at the same time moving as little data as possible over intranet networks (in particular, not downloading all the data once to compute the mean and then again for the variance). Given the highly unstable variance formula (a=2) used in Hadoop, one solution is to stabilize it by removing a large value to all xi's before computing it. After all, with a=2, the variance is translation-invariant, so why not exploit this property? Even better, use a=1.25, which is much more robust against outliers. Or better, its translation-invariant version W, with a=1. But then, you have to write the code yourself, or use some libraries. A much better solution can be found at `http://webmail.cs.yale.edu/publications/techreports/tr222.pdf`.

Final Comments

Much of this discussion focused on a specific parameter **a**, with potential values between 1 and 2. This parameter could be assigned a prior distribution in a Bayesian framework.

Finally, this is an interesting approach to teaching statistics: start with *variance* (the most visual metric), then move to *covariance*, and finally to the *mean*, using the concept of translation independence to introduce the mean. It also shows that such an approach cannot be done with traditional theory (a=2). It works only if a<2.

Summary

This chapter presented material that is less focused on metrics and more focused on applications. It included discussions on how to create a data dictionary (the first step of data exploration), hidden decision trees (a robust data science technique patented by me), hash joins in the context of NoSQL databases, and the first Analyticbridge Theorem, which provides a simple, model-free, nonparametric way to compute confidence intervals without statistical theory or knowledge. The last section was on a new synthetic variance designed for Hadoop that helps solve numerical (instability) and statistical (outlier sensitivity) issues.

Chapter 6 considers case studies, real-life applications, and success stories for various types of projects, ranging from stock market techniques based on data science to advertising mix optimization, fraud and copyright infringement detection, search engine optimization (for search companies), astronomy (forecasting meteorite hits), automated news feed management, e-mail marketing, and relevancy problems (online advertising).

CHAPTER 6

Data Science Application Case Studies

The previous chapter discussed material that should be part of your data science training. The material was less focused on metrics and more on applications. This chapter discusses case studies, real-life applications, and success stories. It covers various types of projects, ranging from stock market techniques based on data science, to advertising mix optimization, fraud detection, search engine optimization, astronomy, automated news feed management, data encryption, e-mail marketing, and relevancy problems (online advertising).

Stock Market

Following is a simple strategy recently used in 2013 to select and trade stocks from the S&P 500, with consistently high returns, based on data science. This section also discusses other strategies, modern trends, and an API that can be used to offer stock signals to professional traders based on technical analysis.

Pattern to Boost Return by 500 Percent

This pattern was found on recent price activity for the 500 stocks that are part of the S&P 500 index. It multiplied the return by factor 5. For each day between 4/24 and 5/23, companies that experienced the most extreme returns—among these 500 companies—were looked at comparing today's with yesterday's closing prices.

Then the daily performance the following day was looked at (again comparing day-to-day close prices), for companies that ranked either #1 or #500. Companies that ranked #1 also experienced (on average) a boost in stock price the next day. The boost was more substantial for companies experiencing a 7.5 percent (or more) price increase. And the return boost on the next day was statistically significant and quite large, so big, in fact, that the total (non-compound) return based on this predictive signal would have been 20 percent over 30 days, versus 4.5 percent for the overall performance of the S&P 500 index.

The following things made it statistically significant:

- It happened throughout the time period in question (not just on a few days).

- It was not influenced by outlier data (a spectacular return one day on one stock and small losses all other days).

- It involved a bunch of different companies (not just three or four).

The return the following day for these companies was positive 15 times out of 20.

Stock Trading Advice and Caveats

These numbers were computed over a small time period, and it happened during a growth (bull market) period. However, you should note the following:

- Patterns never last longer than a few weeks because they are detected by multiple traders and then evaporate.

- Any trading algorithm can benefit from detecting and treating a period of growth, decline, flat and stable, flat but volatile, separately, using the bumpiness coefficient for detection.

Sometimes, when a pattern stops working because of overuse, reversing the strategy (swapping buy and sell, for example, after one week with five bad daily returns) allows you to continue enjoying a good return for a few more weeks, until once again you need to reverse the strategy, creating consecutive, periodic cycles where either the strategy or the reverse strategy is used. Indeed, this pattern probably will not work anymore by the time you read this book because everyone will try to exploit it. But maybe the reverse strategy can work!

You might further increase the return by considering smaller time windows for buying or selling: intraday, or even high-frequency, rather than one buy/sell cycle per day. However, the return on a smaller time window is usually smaller, and the profit can more easily be consumed by:

- Trading (transaction) fees

- Spread: the difference between bid and ask price (usually small, reasonable for fluid stocks like S&P 500)

- Taxes

- Trading errors
- Errors in data used to make predictions
- Numerical approximations

Note that by focusing on the S&P 500, you can eliminate much of the stock market volatility. You can also work with liquid, fluid stocks. This reduces the risk of being a victim of manipulations and guarantees that your buy/sell transactions can be achieved at the wanted price. You can narrow down on stocks with a price above $10 to stay in an even, more robust, predictable environment. You can also check whether looking at extreme daily returns per business category might increase the lift. The S&P 500 data are broken down into approximately 10 main categories.

It is a good idea to do some simulations where you introduce a bit of noise into your data to check how sensitive your algorithm is to price variations. Also, you should not just rely on backtesting, but also walk forward to check whether a strategy will work in the future. This amounts to performing sound cross-validation before actually using the strategy.

How to Get Stock Price Data

You can get months of daily prices at once for all 500 S&P 500 stocks at `http://www.stockhistoricaldata.com/daily-download`. You need to provide the list of all 500 stocks in question. That list, with the stock symbol and business category for each S&P 500 company, is available in a spreadsheet at `http://bit.ly/1apWiRP` as well as on Wikipedia.

On a different note, can you sell stock price forecasts to stock traders? How would you price these forecasts? What would you do with unhappy clients aggressively asking for refunds when your forecast fails?

The conclusion is that you need deep domain expertise, not just pure statistical knowledge, to design professional trading signals that satisfy savvy customers. Dealing with clients (as opposed to developing purely theoretical models) creates potential liabilities and exposure to lawsuits in this context, especially if you sell your signals to people who don't have trading experience.

Optimizing Statistical Trading Strategies

One of the common mistakes in optimizing statistical trading strategies consists of over-parameterizing the problem and then computing a global optimum. It is well known that this technique provides an extremely high return on historical data but does not work in practice. This section investigates this problem, and you see how it can be side-stepped. You also see how to build an efficient six-parameter strategy.

This issue is actually relevant to many real-life statistical and mathematical situations. The problem can be referred to as over-parameterization or over-fitting. The explication as to why this approach fails can be illustrated by a simple example. Imagine you fit data with a 30-parameter model. If you have 30 data points (that is, the number of parameters is equal to the number of observations), you can have a perfect, fully optimized fit with your data set. However, any future data point (for example, tomorrow's stock prices) might have a bad fit with the model, resulting in huge losses. Why? You have the same number of parameters as data points. Thus, on average each estimated parameter of the model is worth no more than one data point.

From a statistical viewpoint, you are in the same situation as if you were estimating the median U.S. salary, interviewing only one person. Chances are your estimation will be poor, even though the fit with your one-person sample is perfect. Actually, you run a 50 percent chance that the salary of the interviewee will be either very low or very high.

Roughly speaking, this is what happens when over-parameterizing a model. You obviously gain by reducing the number of parameters. However, if handled correctly, the drawback can actually be turned into an advantage. You can actually build a model with many parameters that is more robust and more efficient (in terms of return rate) than a simplistic model with fewer parameters. How is this possible? The answer to the question is in the way you test the strategy. When you use a model with more than three parameters, the strategy that provides the highest return on historical data will not be the best. You need to use more sophisticated optimization criteria.

One solution is to add boundaries to the problem, thus performing constrained optimization. Look for strategies that meet one fundamental constraint: reliability. That is, you want to eliminate all strategies that are too sensitive to small variations. Thus, you focus on that tiny part of the parameter space that shows robustness against all kinds of noise. Noise, in this case, can be trading errors, spread, and small variations in the historical stock prices or in the parameter set.

From a practical viewpoint, the solution consists in trying millions of strategies that work well under many different market conditions. Usually, it requires several months' worth of data to have various market patterns and some statistical significance. Then for each of these strategies, you must introduce noise in millions of different ways and look at the impact. You then discard all strategies that can be badly impacted by noise and retain the tiny fraction that are robust.

The computational problem is complex because it is equivalent to testing millions of strategies. But it is worth the effort. The end result is a reliable strategy that can be adjusted over time by slightly varying the parameters. My own strategies are actually designed this way. They are associated with six parameters at most, for instance:

- Four parameters are used to track how the stock is moving (up, neutral, or down).
- One parameter is used to set the buy price.
- One parameter is used to set the sell price.

It would have been possible to reduce the dimensionality of the problem by imposing symmetry in the parameters (for example, parameters being identical for the buy and sell prices). Instead, this approach combines the advantage of low dimensionality (reliability) with returns appreciably higher than you would normally expect when being conservative.

Finally, when you backtest a trading system, optimize the strategy using historical data that is more than 1 month old. Then check if the real-life return obtained during the last month (outside the historical data time window) is satisfactory. If your system passes this test, optimize the strategy using the most recent data, and use it. Otherwise, do not use your trading system in real life.

Improving Long-Term Returns on Short-Term Strategies

This section describes how to backtest a short-term strategy to assess its long-term return distribution. It focuses on strategies that require frequent updates, which are also called adaptive strategies. You examine an unwanted long-term characteristic shared by many of these systems: long-term oscillations with zero return on average. You are presented with a solution that takes advantage of the periodic nature of the return function to design a truly profitable system.

When a strategy relies on parameters requiring frequent updates, you must design appropriate backtesting tools. I recommend that you limit the number of parameters to six. You also learned how to improve backtesting techniques using robust statistical methods and constrained optimization. For simplicity, assume that the system to be tested provides daily signals and needs monthly updates. The correct way to test such an adaptive system is to backtest it one month at a time, on historical data, as the following algorithm does.

For each month in the test period, complete the following steps:

> **Step 1**: Backtesting. Collect the last 6 months' worth of historical data prior to the month of interest. Backtest the system on these 6 months to estimate the parameters of the model.

> **Step 2**: Walk forward. Apply the trading system with the parameters obtained in step 1 to the month of interest. Compute the daily gains.

The whole test period should be at least 18 months long. Thus you need to gather and process 24 months' worth of historical data (18 months, plus 6 extra months for backtesting). Monthly returns obtained sequentially OUT OF SAMPLE (one month at a time) in step 2 should be recorded for further investigation. You are likely to observe the following patterns:

- Many months are performing very well.
- Many months are performing very badly.
- On average, the return is zero.
- Good months are often followed by good months.
- Bad months are often followed by bad months.

You now have all the ingredients to build a long-term reliable system. It's a metastrategy because it is built on top of the original system and works as follows: If the last month's return is positive, use the same strategy this month. Otherwise, use the reverse strategy by swapping the buy and sell prices.

Stock Trading API: Statistical Model

This section provides details about stock price signals (buy/sell signals) based on predictive modeling, previously offered online via an API, to paid clients. In short, this web app is a stock forecasting platform used to get a buy/sell signal for any stock in real time. First consider the predictive model in this section and then the Internet implementation (API) in the following section.

This app relies on an original system that provides daily index and stock trending signals. The nonparametric statistical techniques described here have several advantages:

- **Simplicity**: There is no advanced mathematics involved, only basic algebra. The algorithms do not require sophisticated programming techniques. They rely on data that is easy to obtain.

- **Efficiency**: Daily predictions were correct 60 percent of the time in the tests.

- **Convenience**: The nonparametric system does not require parameter estimation. It automatically adapts to new market conditions. In addition, the algorithms are light in terms of computation, providing forecasts quickly even on slow machines.

- **Universality**: The system works with any stock or index with a large enough volume, at any given time, in the absence of major events impacting the price. The same algorithm applies to all stocks and indexes.

Algorithm

The algorithm computes the probability, for a particular stock or index, that tomorrow's close will be higher than tomorrow's open by at least a specified percentage. The algorithm can easily be adapted to compare today's close with tomorrow's close instead. The estimated probabilities are based on at most the last 100 days of historical data for the stock (or index) in question.

The first step consists of selecting a few price cross-ratios that have an average value of 1. The variables in the ratios can be selected to optimize the forecasts. In one of the applications, the following three cross-ratios were chosen:

- Ratio A = (today's high/today's low) / (yesterday's high/yesterday's low)
- Ratio B = (today's close/today's open) / (yesterday's close/yesterday's open)
- Ratio C = (today's volume/yesterday's volume)

Then each day in the historical data set is assigned to one of eight possible price configurations. The configurations are defined as follows:

- Ratio A > 1, Ratio B > 1, Ratio C > 1
- Ratio A > 1, Ratio B > 1, Ratio C ≤ 1
- Ratio A > 1, Ratio B ≤ 1, Ratio C > 1
- Ratio A > 1, Ratio B ≤ 1, Ratio C ≤ 1
- Ratio A ≤ 1, Ratio B > 1, Ratio C > 1
- Ratio A ≤ 1, Ratio B > 1, Ratio C ≤ 1
- Ratio A ≤ 1, Ratio B ≤ 1, Ratio C > 1
- Ratio A ≤ 1, Ratio B ≤ 1, Ratio C ≤ 1

Now, to compute the probability that tomorrow's close will be at least 1.25 percent higher than tomorrow's open, first compute today's price configuration. Then check all past days in the historical data set that have that configuration. Now count these days. Let N be the number of such days. Then, let M be the number of such days further satisfying the following:

Next day's close is at least 1.25 percent higher than next day's open.

The probability that you want to compute is simply M/N. This is the probability (based on past data) that tomorrow's close will be at least 1.25 percent higher than tomorrow's open. Of course, the 1.25 figure can be substituted by any arbitrary percentage.

Assessing Performance

There are different ways of assessing the performance of your stock trend predictor. Following are two approaches:

- Compute the proportion of successful daily predictions using a threshold of 0 percent instead of 1.25 percent over a period of at least 200 trading days.

- Use the predicted trends (with the threshold set to 0 percent as previously) in a strategy: buy at open, sell at close; or the other way around, based on the prediction.

Tests showed a success rate between 54 percent and 65 percent in predicting the NASDAQ trend. Even with a 56 percent success rate in predicting the trend, the long-term (non-compounded) yearly return before costs is above 40 percent in many instances. As with many trading strategies, the system sometimes exhibits oscillations in performance.

It is possible to substantially attenuate these oscillations using the metastrategy described. In its simplest form, the technique consists of using the same system tomorrow if it worked today. If the system fails to correctly predict today's trend, then use the reverse system for tomorrow.

More generic processes for optimizing models include:

- Automate portfolio optimization by detecting and eliminating stocks that are causing more than average problems, or perhaps stocks with low prices or low volume.

- Use indices rather than stocks.

- Detect time periods when trading should be avoided.

- Incorporate events into your model, such as quarterly corporate reports, job reports, and other economic indicators.

- Provide information on the strength of any pattern detected for any stock on any day, strength being synonymous with confidence interval. A strong signal means a reliable signal, or if you are a statistician, a small confidence interval (increased accuracy in your prediction).

Stock Trading API: Implementation

The system was offered online to paid clients as a web app (web form) and also accessible automatically via an API in real time. When users accessed the web form, they had to provide a stock symbol, a key, and a few parameters, for instance:

- Display strong signals only: if the signal was not deemed strong enough (assuming the user insisted on getting only statistically significant signals), then buy/sell signals were replaced by N/A. The drawback is that users would trade much less frequently, potentially reducing returns but also limiting losses.

- The number of days of historical data used to produce the buy/sell signal is capped at 180.

The key was used to verify that users were on time with payments. An active key meant that users were allowed to run the web app. The web app returned a web page with buy/sell signals to use tomorrow, as well as:

- Historical daily prices for the stock in question

- Daily buy/sell signals predicted for the last 90 days for the stock in question

- Daily performance of the stock predictor for the last 90 days for the stock in question

When the user clicked Submit, a Perl script (say `GetSignals.pl`) was run on the web server to quickly perform the computations on historical data (up to 180 days of daily stock prices for the stock in question) and display the results. The computations required less than 0.5 second per call. Alternatively, the application could be called by a machine (API call via a web robot) using a URL such as `www.DataShaping.com/GetSignals.pl?stock=GE&key=95396745&strength=weak&history=60`.

The results were saved on a web page, available immediately (created on the fly, in real time), that could be automatically accessed via a web robot (machine-to-machine communication) such as `www.DataShaping.com/Results-GE-95396745-weak-60.txt`.

Technical Details

The web app consisted of the following components:

- **Statistical model** embedded in `GetSignals.pl`: see the previous section
- **HTTP requests** embedded in `GetSignals.pl` (the Perl script): to get 180 days' worth of historical data from Yahoo Finance for the stock in question. (The data in question is freely available. Incidentally, accessing it automatically is also done using an API call—to Yahoo this time—and then parsing the downloaded page.) You can find an example of the code for automated HTPP requests in Chapter 5 in the section Optimizing Web Crawlers.
- **Cache system**: Stocks for which historical data had already been requested today had historical prices saved on a server, to avoid calling Yahoo Finance multiple times a day for the same stock.
- **Collision avoidance**: The output text files produced each day were different for each key (that is, each client) and each set of parameters.
- **User or machine interface**: The external layer to access the application (web form or API) by a user or by a machine.

No database system was used, but you could say it was a NoSQL system: actually, a file management system with stock prices accessed in real time via an HTTP request (if not in the cache) or file lookup (if in the cache).

Stock Market Simulations

Although stock market data are widely available, it is also useful to have a simulator, especially if you want to test intraday strategies or simulate growth, decline, or a neutral market.

The statistical process used here is a Markov Chain with infinite state space, to model the logarithm of the stock price (denoted as y). At each iteration, y is augmented by a quantity x (either positive or negative). The possible transitions use notation from the following source code:

- x = pval[0] with probability ptab[0]
- x = pval[1] with probability ptab[1]
- x = pval[6] with probability ptab[6]

Depending on the values in pval and ptab, the underlying process may show a positive trend, a negative trend, or be stationary. In addition, some noise is added to the process to make it more realistic. The simulated data are stored in `datashap.txt`.

For ease, assume the only possible transitions are –1, 0, or +1:

- If ptab[2] = ptab[4], then there is no upward or downward trend.

- If ptab[4] > ptab[2], then the market shows a positive trend.

- If ptab[4] < ptab[2], then the market is declining.

- If ptab[3] is the largest value, then the market is moving slowly.

The transition probabilities are actually proportional to the ptab values. Also, notice that in the source code, ptab[4] is slightly greater than ptab[2], to simulate real market conditions with an overall positive long-term trend (+0.02 percent daily return rate).

You can find a simulation of a perfectly neutral market at `http://bit.ly/1aatvlA`. The X-axis represents the stock price in U.S. dollars. The Y-axis represents the time, with the basic time unit being one day. Surprisingly, and this is counter-intuitive, there is no growth — running this experiment long enough will lead you both below and above the starting point an infinite number of times. Such a memory-less process is known as a *random walk*. The following code, based on the same notations introduced earlier in this section, is used to simulate this type of random walk:

```
#include <stdlib.h>
#include <stdio.h>
#include <time.h>
#include <math.h>

#define N 7

int idx,l;
long k,niter=50000L;
double u,aux;
double ptab[N];
double pval[N];
double aux,p_distrib,x,y=0;
FILE *out;

int main(void)
{

  ptab[0]=0.0;
  ptab[1]=0.0;
  ptab[2]=0.5;
```

```
ptab[3]=0.5;
ptab[4]=0.51;
ptab[5]=0.0;
ptab[6]=0.0;

for (l=0; l<N; l++) { aux+=ptab[l]; }
for (l=0; l<N; l++) { ptab[l]/=aux; }

pval[0]=-3;
pval[1]=-2;
pval[2]=-1;
pval[3]=0;
pval[4]=1;
pval[5]=2;
pval[6]=3;

randomize();
out=fopen("datashap.txt","wt");
fprintf(out,"simulated stock prices - www.datashaping.com \n");

for (k=0L; k<niter; k++) {
        u=((double)rand())/RAND_MAX;
        idx=0;
        p_distrib=ptab[0];
        while (u>p_distrib) {
                idx++;
                p_distrib+=ptab[idx];
        }
        x=pval[idx];
        u=(double)rand()/RAND_MAX;
        x+=0.5*(u-0.5);
        y=y+x;
        fprintf(out,"%lf\n",exp(y/50.0));

}
fclose(out);
return 0;
}
```

Some Mathematics

For those interested in more mathematical stuff, this section presents some deeper results, without diving too deeply into the technical details. You can find here a few mathematical concepts associated with Wall Street. The section on the "curse" of big data in Chapter 2, "Why Big Data Is Different," also discusses statistics related to stock trading.

The following theory is related to the stock market and trading strategies, which have roots in the martingale theory, random walk processes, gaming theory, and neural networks. You see some of the most amazing and deep mathematical results, of practical interest to the curious trader.

Lorenz Curve

Say that you make 90 percent of your trading gains with 5 percent of successful trades. You can write h(0.05) = 0.90. The function h is known as the Lorenz curve. If the gains are the realizations of a random variable X with cdf F and expectation E[X], then

$$h(x) = (\int[0,x] F{-1}(v) \, dv) / E[X], 0 \le x \le 1.$$

To avoid concentrating on too much gain on just a few trades, avoid strategies that have a sharp Lorenz curve. The same concept applies to losses. Related keywords are *inventory management*, *Six Sigma*, *Gini index*, *Pareto distribution*, and *extreme value theory*.

Black-Scholes Option Pricing Theory

The Black-Scholes formula relates the price of an option to five inputs: time to expiration, strike price, value of the underlier, implied volatility of the underlier, and risk-free interest rate. For technical details, check out www.hoadley.net. You can also look at the book *A Probability Path* by Sidney Resnik (Birkhauser, 1998).

The formula can be derived from the theory of Brownian motions. It relies on the fact that stock market prices can be modeled by a geometric Brownian process. The model assumes that the variance of the process does not change over time and that the drift is a linear function of the time. However, these two assumptions can be invalidated in practice.

Discriminate Analysis

Stock picking strategies can be optimized using discriminant analysis. Based on many years of historical stock prices, it is possible to classify all stocks in three categories—bad, neutral, or good—at any given time. The classification rule must be associated with a specific trading strategy, such as buying at close today and selling at close 7 days later.

Generalized Extreme Value Theory

What is the parametric distribution of the daily ratio high/low? Or the 52-week high/low? And how would you estimate the parameter for a particular stock? Interdependencies in the time series of stock prices make it difficult to compute an exact theoretical distribution. Such ratios are shown in Figure 6-1.

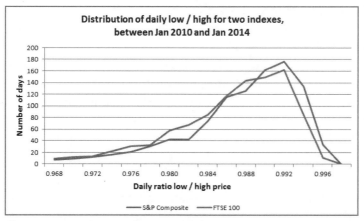

Figure 6-1: Dow Jones and NASDAQ daily ratios

The distribution is characterized by two parameters: mode and interquartile. The FTSE 100 (international index) has a much heavier left tail than the NASDAQ, though both distributions have the same mean, making it more attractive to day traders. As a rule of thumb, indexes with a heavy left tail are good to have higher volatility and returns, but they are riskier.

Random Walks and Wald's Identity

Consider a random walk in Z (positive and negative integers), with transition probabilities P(k to k+1)=p, P(k to k)=q, P(k to k–1)=r, with p+q+r=1. The expected number of steps for moving above any given starting point is infinite if p is smaller than r. It is equal to 1/(p–r) otherwise.

This result, applied to the stock market, means that under stationary conditions (p=r), investing in a stock using the buy-and-hold strategy may never pay off, even after an extremely long period of time.

Arcsine Law

This result explains why 50 percent of the people consistently lose money, whereas 50 percent consistently see gains. Now compare stock trading to coin flipping (tails = loss, heads = gain). Then:

- The probability that the number of heads exceeds the number of tails in a sequence of coin-flips by some amount can be estimated with the Central Limit Theorem, and the probability gets close to 1 as the number of tosses grows large.

- The law of long leads, more properly known as the arcsine law, says that in a coin-tossing game, a surprisingly large fraction of sample paths leaves one player in the lead almost all the time, and in very few cases will the lead change sides and fluctuate in the manner that is naively expected of a well-behaved coin.

▪ Interpreted geometrically in terms of random walks, the path crosses the X-axis rarely, and with increasing duration of the walk, the frequency of crossings decreases and the lengths of the "waves" on one side of the axis increase in length.

New Trends

Modern trading strategies include crawling Twitter postings to extract market sentiment broken down by industry, event modeling, and categorization (impact of announcements, quarterly reports, analyst reports, job reports, and economic news based on keywords using statistical modeling), as well as detection of patterns such as the following:

▪ **Short squeeze**: A stock suddenly heavily shorted tanking very fast, sometimes on low volume, recovering just as fast. You make money on the way up if you missed the way down.

▪ **Cross correlations with time lags**: Such as "If Google is up today, Facebook will be down tomorrow."

▪ **Market timing**: If the Asian market is up early in the morning, the NYSE will be up a few hours later.

▪ **After-shocks (as in earthquakes)**: After a violent event (Lehman & Brothers bankruptcy followed by an immediate stock market collapse), for a couple of days, the stock market will experience extreme volatility both up and down, and it is possible to model these waves ahead of time and get great ROI in a couple of days. Indeed, some strategies consist in keeping your money in cash for several years until such an event occurs, then trading heavily for a few days and reaping great rewards, and then going dormant again for a few years.

▪ **Time series technique**: To detect macro-trends (change point detection, change of slope in stock market prices)

These patterns use data science — more precisely, pattern detection — a set of techniques that data scientists should be familiar with. The key message here is that the real world is in an almost constant state of change. Change can be slow, progressive, or abrupt. Data scientists should be able to detect when significant changes occur and adapt their techniques accordingly.

Encryption

Encryption is related to data science in two different ways: it requires a lot of statistical expertise, and it helps make data transmission more secure. Credit card encoding is discussed in Chapter 4 "Data Science Craftsmanship, Part I." I included JavaScript code for a specific encoding technique that never encodes the same message identically because of random blurring added to the encoded numbers. This section discusses modern steganography: the art and science of hiding messages in multimedia documents, e-mail encryption, and captcha technology. The steganography discussion can help you become familiar with image processing techniques.

Data Science Application: Steganography

Steganography is related to data encryption and security. Imagine that you need to transmit the details of a patent or a confidential financial transaction over the Internet. There are three critical issues:

- Make sure the message is not captured by a third party and decrypted.
- Make sure a third party cannot identify who sent the message.
- Make sure a third party cannot identify the recipient.

Having the message encrypted is a first step, but it might not guarantee high security. Steganography is about using mechanisms to hide a confidential message (for example, a scanned document such as a contract) in an image, a video, an executable file, or some other outlet. Combined with encryption, it is an efficient way to transmit confidential or classified documents without raising suspicion.

Now consider a statistical technology to leverage 24-bit images (bitmaps such as Windows BMP images) to achieve this goal. Steganography, a way to hide information in the lower bits of a digital image, has been in use for more than 30 years. A more advanced, statistical technique is described that should make steganalysis (reverse engineering steganography) more difficult: in other words, safer for the user.

Although you focus here on the widespread BMP image format, you can use the technique with other lossless image formats. It even works with compressed images, as long as information loss is minimal.

A Bit of Reverse Engineering Science

The BMP image format created by Microsoft is one of the best formats to use for steganography. The format is open source and public source code is available to produce BMP images. Yet there are so many variants and parameters that it might be easier to reverse-engineer this format, rather than spend hours reading hundreds of pages of documentation to figure out how it works. Briefly, this 24-bit format is the easiest to work with: it consists of a 54-bit header, followed by the bitmap. Each pixel has four components: RGB (red, green, and blue channels) values and the alpha channel (which you can ignore). Thus, it takes 4 bytes to store each pixel.

Go to http://bit.ly/19B7YVO for detailed C code about 24-bit BMP images. One way to reverse-engineer this format is to produce a blank image, add one pixel (say, purple) that is 50 percent Red, 50 percent Blue, 0 percent Green, change the color of the pixel, and then change the location of the pixel to see how the BMP binary code changes. That's how the author of this code figured out how the 256-color BMP format (also known as the 8-bit BMP format) works. Here, not only is the 24-bit easier to understand, but it is also more flexible and useful for steganography.

To hide a secret code, image, or message, you first need to choose an original (target) image. Some original images are great candidates for this type of usage; some are poor and could lead you to being compromised. Images that you should avoid are color poor, or images that have areas that are uniform. Conversely, color-rich images with no uniform areas are good candidates. So the first piece of a good steganography algorithm is a mechanism to detect images that are good candidates, in which to bury your secret message.

New Technology Based on One-to-Many Alphabet Encoding

After you detect a great image to hide your message in, here is how to proceed. Assume that the message you want to hide is a text message based on an 80-char alphabet (26 lowercase letters, 26 uppercase letters, 10 digits, and a few special characters such as parentheses). Now assume that your secret message is 300 KB long (300,000 1-byte characters) and that you are going to bury it in a 600 x 600 pixel x 24-bit image (that is, a 1,440 KB image; 1,440 KB = 600 x 600 x (3+1) and 3 for the RGB channels, 1 for the alpha channel; in short, each pixel requires 4 bytes of storage). The algorithm consists of the following:

Step 1: Create a (one-to-many) table in which each of the 80 characters in your alphabet is associated with 1,000 RGB colors, widely spread in the RGB universe, and with no collision (no RGB component associated with more than one character). So you need an 80,000-record lookup table, each record being 3 bytes long. (So the size of this lookup table is 240 KB.) This table is somewhat the equivalent of a key in encryption systems.

Step 2: Embed your message in the target image:

- 2.1. Preprocessing: in the target image, replace each pixel that has a color matching one of the 80,000 entries from your lookup table with a close neighboring color. For instance, if pixel color R=231, G=134, B=098 is both in the target image and in the 80,000-record lookup table, replace this color in the target image with (say) R=230, G=134, B=099.

- 2.2. Randomly select 300,000 pixel locations in the target 600 x 600 image. This is where the 300,000 characters of your message are going to be stored.

- 2.3. For each of the 300,000 locations, replace the RGB color with the closest neighbor found in the 80,000-record lookup table.

The target (original) image will look exactly the same after your message has been embedded into it.

How to Decode the Image

Look for the pixels that have an RGB color found in the 80,000 RGB color lookup table, and match them with the characters that they represent. It should be straightforward because this lookup table has two fields: character (80 unique characters in your alphabet) and RGB representations (1,000 different RGB representations per character).

How to Post Your Message

With your message securely encoded, hidden in an image, you would think that you just have to e-mail the image to the recipient, and he will easily extract the encoded message. This is a dangerous strategy because even if the encrypted message cannot be decoded, if your e-mail account or your recipient's e-mail account is hijacked (for example, by the NSA), the hijacker can at least figure out who sent the message and/or to whom.

A better mechanism to deliver the message is to anonymously post your image on Facebook or other public forum. You must be careful about being anonymous, using bogus Facebook profiles to post highly confidential content (hidden in images using the steganography technique), as well as your 240 KB lookup table, without revealing your IP address.

Final Comments

The message hidden in your image should not contain identifiers, because if it is captured and decoded, the hijacker might be able to figure out who sent it, and/or to whom.

Most modern images contain metatags, to help easily categorize and retrieve images when users do a Google search based on keywords. However, these metatags are a security risk: they might contain information about who created the image and his IP address, timestamp, and machine ID. Thus it might help hijackers discover who you are. That's why you should alter or remove these metatags, use images found on the web (not created by you) for your cover images, or write the 54 bytes of BMP header yourself. Metatags should not look fake because this could have your image flagged as suspicious. Reusing existing images acquired externally (not produced on your machines) for your cover images is a good solution.

One way to increase security is to use a double system of lookup tables (the 240 KB tables). Say you have 10,000 images with embedded encoded messages stored somewhere on the cloud. The lookup tables are referred to as keys, and they can be embedded into images. You can increase security by adding 10,000 bogus (decoy) images with no encoded content and two keys: A and B. Therefore, you would have 20,002 images in your repository. You need key A to decode key B, and then key B to decode the other images. Because all the image files (including the keys) look the same, you can decode the images only if you know the filenames corresponding to keys A and B. So if your cloud is compromised, it is unlikely that your encoded messages will be successfully decoded by the hijacker.

NOTE If you reference the book *Steganography in Digital Media* by Jessica Friedrich (published by Cambridge University Press, 2010), there is no mention of an algorithm based on alphabet lookup tables. (Alphabets are mentioned nowhere in the book, but are at the core of the author's algorithm.) Of course, this does not mean that the author's algorithm is new, nor does it mean that it is better than existing algorithms. The book puts more emphasis on steganalysis (decrypting these images) than on steganography (encoding techniques).

Solid E-Mail Encryption

What about creating a startup that offers encrypted e-mail that no government or entity could ever decrypt, offering safe solutions to corporations that don't want their secrets stolen by competitors, criminals, or the government?

For example, consider this e-mail platform:

- It is offered as a web app for text-only messages limited to 100 KB. You copy and paste your text on some web form hosted on some web server (referred to as A). You also create a password for retrieval, maybe using a different app that creates long, random, secure passwords. When you click Submit, the text is encrypted and made accessible on some other web server (referred to as B). A shortened URL displays on your screen: that's where you or the recipient can read the encrypted text.

- You call (or fax) the recipient, possibly from and to a public phone, and provide him with the shortened URL and password necessary to retrieve and decrypt the message.

- The recipient visits the shortened URL, enters your password, and can read the unencrypted message online (on server B). The encrypted text is deleted after the recipient has read it, or 48 hours after the encrypted message was created, whichever comes first.

- The encryption algorithm (which adds semi-random text to your message prior to encryption, and also has an encrypted timestamp and won't work if semi-random text isn't added first) is such that the message can never be decrypted after 48 hours (if the encrypted version is intercepted) because a self-destruction mechanism is embedded into the encrypted message and into the executable file. And if you encrypt the same message twice (even an empty message or one consisting of just one character), the two encrypted versions will be very different, of random length and at least 1 KB in size, to make reverse-engineering next to impossible. Maybe the executable file that does perform the encryption would change every 3 to 4 days for increased security and to make sure a previously encrypted message can no longer be decrypted. (You would have the old version and new version simultaneously available on B for just 48 hours.)

- The executable file (on A) tests if it sits on the right IP address before doing any encryption, to prevent it from being run on, for example, a government server. This feature is encrypted within the executable code. The same feature is incorporated into the executable file used to decrypt the message, on B.

- A crime detection system is embedded in the encryption algorithm to prevent criminals from using the system by detecting and refusing to encrypt messages that seem suspicious (child pornography, terrorism, fraud, hate speech, and so on).

- The platform is monetized via paid advertising by attracting advertising clients, such as antivirus software (for instance, Symantec) or with Google Adwords.

- The URL associated with B can be anywhere, change all the time, or be based on the password provided by the user and located outside the United States.

- The URL associated with A must be more static. This is a weakness because it can be taken down by the government. However, a work-around consists of using several specific keywords for this app, such as ArmuredMail, so that if A is down, a new website based on the same keywords will emerge elsewhere, allowing for uninterrupted service. (The user would have to do a Google search for ArmuredMail to find one website— a mirror of A—that works.)

- Finally, no unencrypted text is stored anywhere.

Indeed, the government could create such an app and disguise it as a private enterprise; it would in this case be a honeypot app.

Note that no system is perfectly safe. If there's an invisible camera behind you filming everything you do on your computer, this system offers no protection for you—though it would still be safe for the recipient, unless he also has a camera tracking all his computer activity. But the link between you and the recipient (the fact that both of you are connected) would be invisible to any third party. And increased security can be achieved if you use the web app from an anonymous computer—maybe from a public computer in some hotel lobby.

To further improve security, the system could offer an e-mail tool such as `www.BlackHoleMail.com` that works as follows:

- Bob (bob@nsa.com) wants to send a message to John (john@ge.com).
- Bob encrypts john@ge.com. It becomes x4ekh8vngalkgt.
- Bob's e-mail is sent to x4ekh8vngalkgt@BlackHoleMail.com.
- BlackHoleMail.com forwards the message to john@ge.com after decrypting the recipient's e-mail address.
- John does not know who sent the message. He knows it comes from x4ekh-8vngalkgt@BlackHoleMail.com, but that's all he knows about the sender.

Encrypted e-mail addresses work for 48 hours only, to prevent enforcement agencies from successfully breaking into the system. If they do, they can reconstruct only e-mail addresses used during the last 48 hours. In short, this system makes it harder for the NSA and similar agencies to identify who is connected to whom.

A double-encryption system would be safer:

- You encrypt your message using C. (The encrypted version is in text format.)
- Use A to encrypt the encrypted text.
- Recipient uses B to decrypt message; the decrypted message is still an encrypted message.
- Then the recipient uses C to fully decrypt the doubly encrypted message.
- You can even use more than two layers of encryption.

Captcha Hack

Here's an interesting project for future data scientists: designing an algorithm that can correctly identify the hidden code 90 percent of the time and make recommendations to improve captcha systems.

Reverse-engineering a captcha system requires six steps:

1. Collect a large number of images so that you have at least 20 representations of each character. You'll probably need to gather more than 1,000 captcha images.
2. Filter noise in each image using a simple filter that works is as follows: (a) each pixel is replaced by the median color among the neighboring pixels and (b) color depth is reduced from 24-bit to 8-bit. Typically, you want to use filters that remove isolated specks and enhance brightness and contrast.

3. Perform image segmentation to identify contours, binarize the image (reduce depth from 8-bit to 1-bit, that is, to black and white), vectorize the image, and simplify the vector structure (a list of nodes and edges saved as a graph structure) by re-attaching segments (edges) that appear to be broken.

4. Perform unsupervised clustering in which each connected component is extracted from the previous segmentation. Each of them should represent a character. Hopefully, you've collected more than 1,000 sample characters, with multiple versions for each of the characters of the alphabet. Now have a person attach a label to each of these connected components, representing characters. The label attached to a character by the person is a letter. Now you have decoded all the captchas in your training set, hopefully with a 90 percent success rate or better.

5. Apply machine learning by harvesting captchas every day, applying the previous steps, and adding new versions of each character (detected via captcha daily harvests) to your training set. The result: your training set gets bigger and better every day. Identify pairs of characters that are difficult to distinguish from each other, and remove confusing sample characters from training sets.

6. Use your captcha decoder to extract the chars in each captcha using steps 2 and 3. Then perform *supervised clustering* to identify which symbols they represent, based on your training set. This operation should take less than 1 minute per captcha.

Your universal captcha decoder will probably work well with some types of captchas (blurred letters), and maybe not as well with other captchas (where letters are crisscrossed by a network of random lines).

Note that some attackers have designed technology to entirely bypass captchas. Their system does not even "read" them; it gets the right answer each time. They access the server at a deeper level, read what the correct answer should be, and then feed the web form with the correct answer for the captcha. Spam technology can bypass the most challenging questions in sign-up forms, such as factoring a product of two large primes (more than 2,000 digits each) in less than 1 second. Of course, they don't extract the prime factors; instead they read the correct answer straight out of the compromised servers, JavaScript code, or web pages.

Anyway, this interesting exercise will teach you a bit about image processing and clustering. At the end, you should be able to identify features that would make captchas more robust, such as:

■ Use broken letters, for example, a letter C split into three or four separate pieces.

■ Use multiple captcha algorithms; change the algorithm each day.

■ Use special chars in captchas (parentheses and commas).

- Create holes in letters.
- Encode two-letter combinations (for example, ab, ac, ba, and so on) rather than isolated letters. The attacker will then have to decode hundreds of possible symbols, rather than just 26 or 36, and will need a much bigger sample.

Fraud Detection

This section focuses on a specific type of fraud: click fraud generated directly or indirectly by ad network affiliates, generating fake clicks to steal money from advertisers. You learn about a methodology that was used to identify a number of Botnets stealing more than 100 million dollars per year. You also learn how to select features out of trillions of feature combinations. (Feature selection is a combinatorial problem.) You also discover metrics used to measure the predictive power of a feature or set of features.

CROSS-REFERENCE For more information, see Chapter 4 for Internet technology and metrics for fraud detection, and Chapter 5 for mapping and hidden decision trees.

Click Fraud

Click fraud is usually defined as the act of purposely clicking ads on pay-per-click programs with no interest in the target website. Two types of fraud are usually mentioned:

- An advertiser clicking competitors' ads to deplete their ad spend budgets, with fraud frequently taking place early in the morning and through multiple distribution partners: AOL, Ask.com, MSN, Google, Yahoo, and so on.
- A malicious distribution partner trying to increase its income, using click bots (clicking Botnets) or paid people to generate traffic that looks like genuine clicks.

Although these are two important sources of non-converting traffic, there are many other sources of poor traffic. Some of them are sometimes referred to as invalid clicks rather than click fraud, but from the advertiser's or publisher's viewpoint, there is no difference. Here, consider all types of non-billable or partially billable traffic, whether it is the result of fraud, whether there is no intent to defraud, and whether there is a financial incentive to generate the traffic in question. These sources of undesirable traffic include:

- **Accidental fraud**: A homemade robot not designed for click fraud purposes running loose, out of control, clicking on every link, possibly because of a design flaw. An example is a robot run by spammers harvesting e-mail addresses. This robot was not designed for click fraud purposes, but still ended up costing advertisers money.

▪ **Political activists**: People with no financial incentive but motivated by hate. This kind of clicking activity has been used against companies recruiting people in class action lawsuits, and results in artificial clicks and bogus conversions. It is a pernicious kind of click fraud because the victim thinks its PPC campaigns generate many leads, whereas in reality most of these leads (e-mail addresses) are bogus.

▪ **Disgruntled individuals**: It could be an employee who was recently fired from working for a PPC advertiser or a search engine. Or it could be a publisher who believes he has been unjustifiably banned.

▪ **Unethical people in the PPC community**: Small search engines trying to make their competitors look bad by generating unqualified clicks, or shareholder fraud

▪ **Organized criminals**: Spammers and other internet pirates used to run bots and viruses who found that their devices could be programmed to generate click fraud. Terrorism funding falls in this category and is investigated by both the FBI and the SEC.

▪ **Hackers**: Many people now have access to homemade web robots. Although it is easy to fabricate traffic with a robot, it is more complicated to emulate legitimate traffic because it requires spoofing thousands of ordinary IP addresses—not something any amateur can do well. Some individuals might find this a challenge and generate high-quality emulated traffic, just for the sake of it, with no financial incentive.

This discussion encompasses other sources of problems not generally labeled as click fraud but sometimes referred to as invalid, non-billable, or low-quality clicks. They include:

▪ **Impression fraud**: Impressions and clicks should always be considered jointly, not separately. This can be an issue for search engines because of their need to join large databases and match users with both impressions and clicks. In some schemes, fraudulent impressions are generated to make a competitor's CTR (click-through rate) look low. Advanced schemes use good proxy servers to hide the activity. When the CTR drops low enough, the competitor ad is not displayed anymore. This scheme is usually associated with self-clicking, a practice where an advertiser clicks its own ads though proxy servers to improve its ranking, and thus improve its position in search result pages. This scheme targets both paid and organic traffic.

▪ **Multiple clicks**: Although multiple clicks are not necessarily fraudulent, they end up either costing advertisers money when they are billed at the full price or costing publishers and search engines money if only the first click is charged for. Another issue is how to accurately determine that two clicks—say 5 minutes apart—are attached to the same user.

- **Fictitious fraud**: Clicks that appear fraudulent but are never charged for. These clicks can be made up by unethical click fraud companies. Or they can be the result of testing campaigns and are called click noise. A typical example is the Google bot. Although Google never charges for clicks originating from its Google bot robot, other search engines that do not have the most updated list of Google bot IP addresses might accidentally charge for these clicks.

Continuous Click Scores Versus Binary Fraud/Non-Fraud

Web traffic isn't black or white, and there is a whole range from low quality to great traffic. Also, non-converting traffic might not necessarily be bad, and in many cases can actually be good. Lack of conversions might be due to poor ads or poorly targeted ads. This raises two points:

- **Traffic scoring**: Although as much as 5 percent of the traffic from any source can be easily and immediately identified as totally unbillable with no chance of ever converting, a much larger portion of the traffic has generic quality issues—issues that are not specific to a particular advertiser. A traffic scoring approach (click or impression scoring) provides a much more actionable mechanism, both for search engines interested in ranking distribution partners and for advertisers refining their ad campaigns.

- A generic, universal scoring approach allows advertisers with limited or no ROI metrics to test new sources of traffic, knowing beforehand where the generically good traffic is, regardless of conversions. This can help advertisers substantially increase their reach and tap into new traffic sources as opposed to obtaining small ROI improvements from A/B testing. Some advertisers converting offline, victims of bogus conversions or interested in branding, will find click scores most valuable.

A scoring approach can help search engines determine the optimum price for multiple clicks (such as true user-generated multiple clicks, not a double click that results from a technical glitch). By incorporating the score in their smart pricing algorithm, they can reduce the loss due to the simplified business rule "one click per ad per user per day."

Search engines, publishers, and advertisers can all win because poor quality publishers can now be accepted in a network, but are priced correctly so that the advertiser still has a positive ROI. And a good publisher experiencing a drop in quality can have its commission lowered according to click scores, rather than being discontinued outright. When its traffic gets better, its commission increases accordingly based on scores.

To make sense for search engines, a scoring system needs to be as generic as possible. Click scores should be designed to match the conversion rate distribution using generic conversions, taking into account bogus conversions and based on *attribution analytics* (discussed later in this section) to match a conversion with a click through correct user identification. An IP can have multiple users attached to it, and a single user can have multiple IP addresses within a 2-minute period. Cookies (particularly in server logs, less so in redirect logs) also have notorious flaws, and you should not rely on cookies exclusively when dealing with advertiser server log data.

I have personally designed scores based on click logs, relying, for instance, on network topology metrics. The scores were designed based on advertiser server logs, also relying on network topology metrics (distribution partners, unique browsers per IP cluster, and so on) and even on impression-to-click-ratio and other search engine metrics, as server logs were reconciled with search engine reports to get the most accurate picture. Using search engine metrics to score advertiser traffic enabled designing good scores for search engine data, and the other way around, as search engine scores are correlated with true conversions.

When dealing with advertiser server logs, the reconciliation process and the use of appropriate tags (for example, Google's gclid) whenever possible allow you to not count clicks that are artifacts of browser technology.

Advertiser scores are designed to be a good indicator of the conversion rate. Search engine scores use a combination of weights based both on expert knowledge and advertiser data. Scores should have been smoothed and standardized using the same methodology used for credit card scoring. The best quality assessment systems rely on both real-time and less granular scores, such as end of day.

The use of a smooth score based on solid metrics substantially reduces false positives. If a single rule is triggered, or even two rules are triggered, it might barely penalize the click. Also, if a rule is triggered by too many clicks or not correlated with true conversions, it is ignored. For instance, a rule formerly known as "double click" (with enough time between the two clicks) has been found to be a good indicator of conversion and was changed from a rule into an anti-rule whenever the correlation is positive. A click with no external referral but otherwise normal will not be penalized after score standardization.

Mathematical Model and Benchmarking

The scoring methodology I have developed is state-of-the-art, and based on almost 30 years of experience in auditing, statistics, and fraud detection, both in real time and on historical data. It combines sophisticated cross-validation, design of experiments, linkage, and unsupervised clustering to find new rules, machine learning, and the most advanced models ever used in scoring, with a parallel implementation and fast, robust algorithms to produce at once a large number of small overlapping decision trees. The clustering algorithm is a hybrid combination of unique decision-tree technology with a new type of PLS logistic stepwise regression to handle tens of thousands of highly redundant metrics. It provides meaningful regression coefficients computed in a short amount of time and efficiently handles interaction between rules.

Some aspects of the methodology show limited similarities with ridge regression, tree bagging, and tree boosting (see `http://www.cs.rit.edu/~rlaz/prec20092/ slides/Bagging _ and _ Boosting.pdf`). Now you can compare the efficiency of different systems to detect click fraud on highly realistic simulated data. The criterion for comparison is the mean square error, a metric that measures the fit between scored clicks and conversions:

- **Scoring system with identical weights**: 60 percent improvement over a binary (fraud/non-fraud) approach

- **First-order PLS regression**: 113 percent improvement over a binary approach

- **Full standard regression (not recommended because it provides highly unstable and non-interpretable results)**: 157 percent improvement over a binary approach

- **Second-order PLS regression**: 197 percent improvement over a binary approach, an easy interpretation, and a robust, nearly parameter-free technique

- **Substantial additional improvement**: Achieved when the decision trees component is added to the mix. Improvement rates on real data are similar.

Bias Due to Bogus Conversions

The reason bogus conversions are elaborated on is because their impact is worse than most people think. If not taken care of, they can make a fraud detection system seriously biased. Search engines that rely on presales or non-sales (soft) conversions, such as sign-up forms, to assess traffic performance can be misled into thinking that some traffic is good when it actually is poor, and the other way around.

Usually, the advertiser is not willing to provide too much information to the search engine, and thus conversions are computed generally as a result of the advertiser placing some JavaScript code or a clear gif image (beacon) on target conversion pages. The search engine can then track conversions on these pages. However, the search engine has no control over which "converting pages" the advertiser wants to track. Also, the search engine cannot see what is happening between the click and the conversion, or after the conversion. If the search engine has access to presale data only, the risk for bogus conversions is high. A significant increase in bogus conversions can occur from some specific traffic segment.

Another issue with bogus conversions arises when an advertiser (for example, an ad broker) purchases traffic upstream and then acts as a search engine and distributes the traffic downstream to other advertisers. This business model is widespread. If the traffic upstream is artificial but results in many bogus conversions—a conversion being a click or lead delivered downstream—the ad broker does not see a drop in ROI. She might actually see an increase in ROI. Only the advertisers downstream start to complain. When the problem starts being addressed, it might be too late and may have already caused the ad broker to lose clients.

This business flaw can be exploited by criminals running a network of distribution partners. Smart criminals will hit this type of "ad broker" advertiser harder. The criminals can generate bogus clicks to make money themselves, and as long as they generate a decent number of bogus conversions, the victim is making money too and might not notice the scheme.

A Few Misconceptions

It has been argued that the victims of click fraud are good publishers, not advertisers, because advertisers automatically adjust their bids. However, this does not apply to advertisers lacking good conversion metrics (for example, if the conversion takes place offline) nor to smaller advertisers who do not update bids and keywords in real time. It can actually lead advertisers to permanently eliminate whole traffic segments, and lack the good ROI when the fraud problem gets fixed on the network. On some second-tier networks, impression fraud can lead an advertiser to be kicked out one day without the ability to ever come back. Both the search engine and the advertiser lose in this case, and the one who wins is the bad guy now displaying cheesy, irrelevant ads on the network. The website user loses, too, because all good ads have been replaced with irrelevant material.

Finally, many systems to detect fraud are still essentially based on outlier detection and detecting shifts from the average. But most fraudsters try hard to look as average as possible, avoiding expensive or cheap clicks, using the right distribution of user agents, and generating a small random number of clicks per infected computer per day, except possibly for clicks going through large proxies. This type of fraud needs a truly multivariate approach, looking at billions of combinations of several carefully selected variables simultaneously and looking for statistical evidence in billions of tiny click segments to unearth the more sophisticated fraud cases impacting a large volume of clicks.

Statistical Challenges

To some extent, the technology to combat click fraud is similar to what banks use to combat credit card fraud. The best systems are based on statistical scoring technology because the transaction—a click in the context—is usually not either bad or good.

Multiple scoring systems based on IP scores and click scores and metric mix (feature) optimization are the basic ingredients. Because of the vast amount of data, and potentially millions of metrics used in a good scoring system, combinatorial optimization is required, using algorithms such as Markov Chain Monte Carlo or simulated annealing.

Although scoring advertiser data can be viewed as a regression problem, the dependent variable being the conversion metric, scoring search engine data is more challenging because conversion data are not readily available. Even when dealing with advertiser data, there are several issues to address. First, the scores need to be standardized. Two identical ad campaigns might perform differently if the landing pages are different. The scoring system needs to address this issue.

Also, although scoring can be viewed as a regression problem, it is a difficult one. The metrics involved are usually highly correlated, making the problem ill-conditioned from a mathematical viewpoint. There might be more metrics (and thus more regression coefficients) than observed clicks, making the regression approach highly unstable. Finally, the regression coefficients—also referred to as weights—must be constrained to take only a few potential values. The dependent variable being binary, you are dealing with a sophisticated ridge logistic regression problem.

The best technology actually relies on hybrid systems that can handle contrarian configurations, such as "time < 4 am" is bad, "country not US" is bad, but "time < 4 am and country = UK" is good. Good cross validation is also critical to eliminate configurations and metrics with no statistical significance or poor robustness. Careful metric (feature) binning and a fast distributed feature optimization algorithm are important.

Finally, design of experiments to create test campaigns—some with a high proportion of fraud and some with no fraud—and usage of generic conversion and proper user identification are critical. And remember that failing to remove bogus conversions will result in a biased system with many false positives. Indeed, buckets of traffic with conversion rates above 10 percent should be treated separately from buckets of traffic with conversion rates below 2 percent.

Click Scoring to Optimize Keyword Bids

Click scoring can do many things, including:

- Determine optimum pricing associated with a click
- Identify new sources of potentially converting traffic
- Measure traffic quality in the absence of conversions or in the presence of bogus conversions

- Predict the chance of conversion for new keywords (with no historical data) added to a pay-per-click campaign
- Assess the quality of distribution ad network partners

These are just a few of the applications of click scoring. Also note that scoring is not limited to clicks, but can also involve impressions and metrics such as clicks per impression.

From the advertiser's viewpoint, one important application of click scoring is to detect new sources of traffic to improve total revenue in a way that cannot be accomplished through A/B/C testing, traditional ROI optimization, or SEO. The idea consists of tapping into delicately selected new traffic sources rather than improving existing ones.

Now consider a framework in which you have two types of scores:

- **Score I**: A generic score computed using a pool of advertisers, possibly dozens of advertisers from the same category
- **Score II**: A customized score specific to a particular advertiser

What can you do when you combine these two scores? Here's the solution:

- Scores I and II are good. This is usually one of the two traffic segments that advertisers are considering. Typically, advertisers focus their efforts on SEO or A/B testing to further refine the quality and gain a little edge.

- Score I is good and score II is bad. This traffic is usually rejected. No effort is made to understand why the good traffic is not converting. Advertisers rejecting this traffic might miss major sources of revenue.

- Score I is bad and score II is good. This is the other traffic segment that advertisers are considering. Unfortunately, this situation makes advertisers happy: they are getting conversions. However, this is a red flag, indicating that the conversions might be bogus. This happens frequently when conversions consist of filling web forms. Any attempt to improve conversions (for example, through SEO) are counter-productive. Instead, the traffic should be seriously investigated.

- Scores I and II are bad. Here, most of the time, the reaction consists of dropping the traffic source entirely and permanently. Again, this is a bad approach. By reducing the traffic using a schedule based on click scores, you can significantly lower exposure to bad traffic and at the same time not miss the opportunity when the traffic quality improves.

The conclusion here is that, in the context of keyword bidding on pay-per-click programs such as Google Adwords, click scores aggregated by keyword are useful to predict conversion rates for keywords with little or no history. These keywords represent as much as 90 percent of all keywords purchased and more than 20 percent of total ad spend. These scores are also useful in real time bidding.

Automated, Fast Feature Selection with Combinatorial Optimization

Feature selection is a methodology used to detect the best subset of features out of dozens or hundreds of features (also called *variables* or *rules*). "Best" means with highest *predictive power*, a concept defined in the following subsection. In short, you want to remove duplicate features, simplify a bit the correlation structure (among features) and remove features that bring no value, such as features taking on random values, thus lacking predictive power, or features (rules) that are almost never triggered (except if they are perfect fraud indicators when triggered).

The problem is combinatorial in nature. You want a manageable, small set of features (say, 20 features) selected from, for example, a set of 500 features, to run the *hidden decision trees* (or some other classification/scoring technique) in a way that is statistically robust. But there are 2.7×10^{35} combinations of 20 features out of 500, and you need to compute all of them to find the one with maximum predictive power. This problem is computationally intractable, and you need to find an alternative solution. The good thing is that you don't need to find the absolute maximum; you just need to find a subset of 20 features that is good enough.

One way to proceed is to compute the predictive power of each feature. Then, add one feature at a time to the subset (starting with 0 feature) until you reach either of the following:

- 20 features (your limit)
- Adding a new feature does not significantly improve the overall predictive power of the subset. (In short, convergence has been attained.)

At each iteration, choose the feature to be added from the two remaining features with the highest predictive power. You will choose (between these two features) the one that increases the overall predictive power most (of the subset under construction). Now you have reduced your computations from 2.7×10^{35} to $40 = 2 \times 20$.

> **NOTE** An additional step to boost predictive power: remove one feature at a time from the subset, and replace it with a feature randomly selected from the remaining features (from outside the subset). If this new feature boosts an overall predictive power of a subset, keep it; otherwise, switch back to the old subset. Repeat this step 10,000 times or until no more gain is achieved (whichever comes first).

Finally, you can add two or three features at a time, rather than one. Sometimes, combined features have far better predictive power than isolated features. For instance, if feature A = country, with values in {USA, UK} and feature B = hour of the day, with values in {"day – Pacific Time", "night – Pacific Time"}, both features separately have little if any predictive power. But when you combine both of them, you have a much more powerful feature: UK/night is good, USA/ night is bad, UK/day is bad, and USA/day is good. Using this blended feature also reduces the risk of false positives/false negatives.

Also, to avoid highly granular features, use lists. So instead of having feature A = country (with 200 potential values) and feature B = IP address (with billions of potential values), use:

- Feature A = country group, with three lists of countries (high risk, low risk, neutral). These groups can change over time.

- Feature B = type of IP address (with six to seven types, one being, for instance, "IP address is in some whitelist" (see the section on IP Topology Mapping for details).

Predictive Power of a Feature: Cross-Validation

This section illustrates the concept of predictive power on a subset of two features, to be a bit more general. Say you have two binary features, A and B, taking two possible values, 0 or 1. Also, in the context of fraud detection, assume that each observation in the training set is either Good (no fraud) or Bad (fraud). The fraud status (G or B) is called the *response* or *dependent variable* in statistics. The features A and B are also called *rules* or *independent variables*.

Cross-Validation

First, split your training set (the data where the response—B or G—is known) into two parts: control and test. Make sure that both parts are data-rich: if the test set is big (millions of observations) but contains only one or two clients (out of 200), it is data-poor and your statistical inference will be negatively impacted (low robustness) when dealing with data outside the training set. It is a good idea to use two different time periods for control and test. You are going to compute the predictive power (including rule selection) on the control data. When you have decided on a final, optimum subset of features, you can then compute the predictive power on the test data. If the drop in predictive power is significant in the test data (compared with the control), something is wrong with your analysis. Detect the problem, fix it, and start over again. You can use multiple control and test sets. This can give you an idea of how the predictive power varies from one control set to another. Too much variance is an issue that should be addressed.

Predictive Power

Using the previous example with two binary features (A, B) taking on two values (0, 1), you can break the observations from the control data set into eight categories:

- A=0, B=0, response = G
- A=0, B=1, response = G
- A=1, B=0, response = G
- A=1, B=1, response = G
- A=0, B=0, response = B
- A=0, B=1, response = B
- A=1, B=0, response = B
- A=1, B=1, response = B

Now denote as $n_1, n_2 \ldots n_8$ the number of observations in each of these eight categories, and introduce the following quantities:

$$P_{00} = n_5 / (n_1 + n_5), P_{01} = n_6 / (n_2 + n_6), P_{10} = n_7 / (n_3 + n_7), P_{11} = n_8 / (n_4 + n_8)$$
$$p = (n_5 + n_6 + n_7 + n_8) / (n_1 + n_2 + \ldots + n_8)$$

Assume that p, measuring the overall proportion of fraud, is less than 50 percent (that is, $p<0.5$, otherwise you can swap between fraud and non-fraud). For any r between 0 and 1, define the W function (shaped like a W), based on a parameter **a** ($0 < a < 1$, and I recommend **a** = 0.5–p) as follows:

$$W(r) = 1 - (r/p), \text{ if } 0 < r < p$$
$$W(r) = a * (r-p) / (0.5-p), \text{ if } p < r < 0.5$$
$$W(r) = a * (r-1+p) / (p-0.5), \text{ if } 0.5 < r < 1-p$$
$$W(r) = (r-1+p) / p, \text{ if } 1-p < r < 1$$

Typically, $r = P_{00}, P_{01}, P_{10},$ or P_{11}. The W function has the following properties:

- It is minimum and equal to 0 when r = p or r = 1–p, that is, when r does not provide any information about fraud/non-fraud.
- It is maximum and equal to 1 when r=1 or r=0, that is, when you have perfect discrimination between fraud and non-fraud in a given bin.
- It is symmetric: W(r) = W(1–r) for $0 < r < 1$. So if you swap Good and Bad (G and B), it still provides the same predictive power.

Now define the predictive power:

$$H = P_{00} W(P_{00}) + P_{01} W(P_{01}) + P_{10} W(P_{10}) + P_{11} W(P_{11})$$

The function H is the predictive power for the feature subset {A, B}, having four bins, 00, 01, 10, and 11, corresponding to (A=0, B=0), (A=0, B=1), (A=1, B=0), and (A=1, B=1). Although H appears to be remotely related to *entropy*, H was designed to satisfy nice properties and to be parameter-driven, because of **a**. Unlike entropy, H is not based on physical concepts or models; it is actually a synthetic (though useful) metric.

Note that the weights P_{00}... P_{11} in H guarantee that bins with low frequency (that is, a low-triggering rate) have low impact on H. Indeed, I recommend setting W(r) to 0 for any bin that has less than 20 observations. For instance, the triggering rate for bin 00 is $(n_1 + n_5) / (n_1 + \ldots + n_8)$, observations count is $n_1 + n_5$, and $r = P_{00} = n_5 / (n_1 + n_5)$ for this bin. If $n_1 + n_5 = 0$, set P_{00} to 0 and $W(P_{00})$ to 0. I actually recommend doing this not just if $n_1 + n_5 = 0$ but also whenever $n_1 + n_5 < 20$, especially if p is low. (If p is very low, say, $p < 0.01$, you need to over-sample bad transactions when building your training set and weight the counts accordingly.) Of course, the same rule applies to P_{01}, P_{10}, and P_{11}. Note that you should avoid feature subsets that have a large proportion of observations spread across a large number of almost empty bins, as well as feature subsets that produce a large number of empty bins. Observations outside the training set are likely to belong to an empty or almost empty bin and lead to high-variance predictions. To avoid this drawback, stick to binary features, select up to 20 features, and use the (hybrid) hidden decision tree methodology for scoring transactions. Finally, P_{ij} is the naive estimator of the probability P(A=i, B=j) for i,j = 0,1.

The predictive power H has interesting properties:

■ It is always between 0 and 1, equal to 0 if the feature subset has no predictive power and equal to 1 if the feature subset has maximum predictive power.

■ A generic version of H (not depending on p) can be created by setting p=0.5. Then the W functions are not shaped like a W anymore; they are shaped like a V.

Data Structure and Computations

You can pre-compute all the bin counts n_i for the top 20 features (that is, features with highest predictive power) and store them in a small hash table with at most 2×2^{20} entries (approximately 2 million; the factor is 2 because you need two measurements per bin: number of Bs, and number of Gs). An entry in this hash table would look like this:

$Hash{01101001010110100100_G} = 56,

meaning that Bin # 01101001010110100100 has 56 good (G) observations.

The hash table is produced by parsing your training set one time, sequentially: for each observation, compute the flag vector (which rules are triggered, that is, the 01101001010110100100 vector in this example), check if it's good or bad, and update (increase count by 1) the associated hash table entry accordingly, with the following instruction:

$Hash{01101001010110100100_G}++

Then, whenever you need to measure the predictive power of a subset of these 20 features, you don't need to parse your big data set again (potentially billions of observations), but instead, just access this small hash table. This table contains all you need to build your flag vectors and compute scores for any combination of features that is a subset of the top 20.

You can even do better than top 20, maybe top 30. Although this would create a hash table with 2 billion entries, most of these entries would correspond to empty bins and thus would not be in the hash table. Your hash table might contain only 200,000,000 entries, maybe too big to fit in memory, and requiring a MapReduce/Hadoop implementation.

Even better: build this hash table for the top 40 features. Then it will fully solve your feature selection problem described earlier. However, now your hash table could have up to 2 trillion entries. But if your data set has only 100 billion observations, then, of course, your hash table cannot have more than 100 billion entries. In this case, I suggest that you create a training set with 20 million observations so that your hash table will have at most 20 million entries (probably less than 10 million with all the empty bins) and thus can fit in memory.

You can compute the predictive power of a large number (say, 100) of feature subsets by parsing the big 40-feature input hash table obtained in the previous step. Then for each flag vector and G/B entry in the input hash table, loop over the 100 target feature subsets to update counts (all the n_i) for these 100 feature subsets. These counts are stored/updated in an output hash table. The key in the output hash table has two components: feature ID and flag vector. You then loop over the output hash table to compute the predictive power for each feature subset. This step can be further optimized.

Association Rules to Detect Collusion and Botnets

An example of *collusion* is when multiple affiliates (or sub-publishers) are associated in the same fraud scheme and share the same resources. Typically, this a Botnet, that is, a set of computer IP addresses infected with a virus that automatically clicks once a day (at most) from each infected machine.

Association rules are fraud detection rules that try to correlate two fraudsters via an external metric. For instance, when an affiliate A is identified as fraudulent, you look at all the IP addresses attached to it. If 50 percent or more of these IP addresses also appear exclusively in association with another affiliate B (and nowhere else), then chances are that B is also part of the fraudulent scheme. Even better: now you look at all the IP addresses attached to B, and you discover that another affiliate, say C, shares 10 percent of them exclusively. Now you've found yet another participant in the fraud scheme. I have successfully identified several additional sources of fraud associated with one fraudster using this technique.

Another rule falling in the same category is the proportion of short visits (less than 20 seconds) that involve two clicks associated with two little, unknown affiliates or referral domains. When this proportion is above some threshold (say, 20 percent of all visits for a specific affiliate), you are likely dealing with fraud. By creating the list of all affiliates found in these two-click visits and then looking at other visits that also involve these affiliates as well as other affiliates, you can detect a larger proportion of bad affiliates.

Finally, Botnets used in click fraud are typically involved in other criminal activities as well and controlled by one operator. So detecting these Botnets with a click fraud detection algorithm can also help detect other crimes: spam, phishing, ID theft, and so on.

Extreme Value Theory for Pattern Detection

Because criminals don't put too much effort into creating artificial traffic that looks, from a statistical point of view, similar to natural traffic, their traffic is full of extreme events that make detection easier. These event probabilities can be estimated (in natural traffic) via Monte Carlo simulations. When discovering an event (in suspicious traffic) with a probability of occurrence below one chance in 1 million, it is a red flag. Of course, if you are tracking billions of events, you will have false positives. Read the section on the curse of big data (Chapter 2) to see how to address this issue. Rare events that were successfully used to detect fraud include:

- Visits with a consistent, perfect 50.00 percent conversion rate, day after day, from the same referral

- A spike in the number of IP addresses that generate exactly eight clicks per day, day after day. (When you plot the distribution of clicks per IP for a specific affiliate or keyword, you see a spike for the value 8.)

- IP addresses with 3+ days of activity per week, with little traffic each day (one or two clicks at most). If you have an affiliate with 40 percent of IP addresses having this pattern, this is an extremely rare event (for most websites) and a red flag.

- A large portion of your traffic (say, 5 percent) has the exact same click score when using your scoring algorithm. This is suspicious.

- Specific keywords found on the web page where the click is taking place: "Viagra," or some JavaScript tags mostly found on fraudulent websites—or even an empty page!

- Domain name patterns, such as an affiliate using dozens of domains, the vast majority with names such as xxx-and-yyy.com (for instance, chocolate-and-car.com).

All these rules have been successfully used to detect fraud. Multiple rules must be triggered before confirming fraud. For instance, in one case, the bad affiliate simultaneously had the domain name pattern, the identical scores pattern, and the empty web page pattern. It was first discovered because all its clicks had the same score. And by further analyzing the data, I discovered and created the two other rules: domain pattern and empty page pattern.

Digital Analytics

The borderline between data science and other domains, in particular business intelligence (what business analysts do), is not clear. In smaller companies, startups, and non-traditional companies (which hire a significant share of data scientists), several of the project types discussed in this section are handled by one person — the data scientist — who also plays a part-time role as business analyst. Being polyvalent allows you to command higher salaries and experience increased job security.

Domain expertise is critical to succeed in data analytics. A lot of domain expertise is shared with you here, with a focus on rules of thumb and principles that stay valid over time (such as solid SEO principles, e-mail campaign optimization, ad matching, and so on), even though the digital/ad tech industry is constantly changing.

Some of the techniques discussed in this section are typically implemented by vendors (Comscore, Rocket Fuel, and others), search engines (such as Bing, Google, Yahoo), ad networks such as AdKnowledge, or savvy publishers, rather than by advertisers themselves. Advertisers rely on vendors, though large advertisers such as eBay or Cars.com also develop and integrate their own proprietary tools on top of vendor tools. It is important for you to learn about the type of data science work (digital analytics) done by vendors and search engines, because collectively they hire more data scientists than all advertisers combined.

CROSS-REFERENCE For a more traditional data science discussion related to digital analytics, read the section Big Data Problem That Epitomizes the Challenges of Data Science in Chapter 2.

Online Advertising: Formula for Reach and Frequency

How do you effectively compute the reach and frequency of ads for advertisers? The formula discussed here computes reach and frequency for online advertisers to help them determine how many impressions they must purchase to achieve their goals. It is provided to illustrate that sometimes, it is easier to spend two hours to reinvent the wheel, solve the problem mathematically, and get an efficient solution than to spend hours trying to find the solution in the literature or blindly run expensive simulations or computations the way computer scientists traditionally do.

How many ad impressions should an advertiser purchase to achieve a specified reach on a website? I have investigated the problem and found a simple mathematical solution:

$$\text{Reach} = \text{Unique Users} - \text{SUM}\{ U_k * (1 - P)^k\}$$

The sum is over all positive integers k = 1, 2, and so on. U_k is the number of users turning exactly *k* pages in the given time period. So you need to compute the distribution of page views per unique user during the targeted time period to compute U_k. *P* is the ratio of purchased impressions by total pages.

The number of unique users who see the ad *n* times during the time period in question is given by:

$$\text{SUM}\{ U_k * C(k, n) * P^n (1 - P)^{k-n}\}$$

The sum is over all positive integers *k* greater or equal to *n*. C(k, n) = k! / [n! (k–n)!] are the binomial coefficients.

In this context, "unique user" represents a user that is counted as one user regardless of the number of visits during the time period in question. A user is a human being, thus robots (web crawlers) should be filters. The IAB (Internet Advertising Bureau) provides definitions, directives, and best practices on how to measure unique users and filter robots. Users are typically tracked via cookies. In the past, many counting methods resulted in a single user being counted multiple times, thus the term "unique user" was created to distinguish users from visits. (Defining concepts such as "unique user" is also part of the data scientist's job.)

E-Mail Marketing: Boosting Performance by 300 Percent

We improved our own open rates on Data Science Central by 300 percent and dramatically improved total clicks and click-through rates using the following strategies, based on data analysis:

- Remove subscribers who did not open the newsletter during the last eight deployments. This produced a spectacular increase in the open rate and also significantly improved our "spam score," because the newsletter's chances of ending up in a spam box or a spam trap is reduced to almost 0.

- Segment of the subscriber base to better target members, for instance to send a UK conference announcement to members located in Europe, but not to members in Asia or America.

- Detect and stop sending messages that produce low open rates.

- Capture member information (profession, experience, industry, location, and so on) on sign-up to create better segments.

- Grow your subscriber list by:

  - Offering great products for free to subscribers only, for instance e-books, requesting that visitors subscribe to your newsletter if they want to download the book.

  - Requesting that new LinkedIn group members become a member of your community. (The IEEE organization is using the same strategy.)

- A/B testing in real time when deploying an e-mail blast: try three different subject lines with 3,000 subscribers, and then use the subject line with highest click-through rate for the remaining subscribers.

- Identify patterns in subject lines that work well:

  - Research reports from well-respected companies

  - Case studies, success stories

  - Announcement about 10 great articles recently published in top news outlets

  - Salary surveys, job ads from great companies, data science programs from top universities

  - Not using the same great keywords over and over because it kills efficiency. (Poor subject titles that change each time work better than great subject titles that are overused.)

As a result, our mailing list management vendor informed us that our open rate is far above average — and they manage 60,000 clients from small to multi-million e-mail lists!

Optimize Keyword Advertising Campaigns in 7 Days

SEO (search engine optimization) and SEM (search engine marketing) companies regularly hire data scientists, so you need to have a good grasp of how to implement solid, general SEM principles. Here's an example application that is based on careful analysis of keyword performance on Google Analytics:

1. Identify 10 top, high-volume, well-targeted keywords for your business. These are your seed keywords.

2. Create large lists of bid keywords: use Google tools to identify "related keywords" that are related to your seed keywords.

3. Grow further by finding keywords that are related to the keywords obtained in the previous step.

4. Use Google AdWords tools to find keywords that are on your web page, and most important, on your competitors' web pages, choosing the website selection under Find Keywords under Add Keywords when you manage your ad group. Only pick keywords that have a moderate to high volume, and skip keywords with high competition. (Competition and volume statistics are provided by Google on the same page.)

5. Create a campaign, and then add one ad group for all these 2,000 or so keywords. Select your target market (for example, North America + Europe and Google Search + Partners Search) in your campaign settings. Set a max bid that is three or four times higher than what you want.

6. Create four or five different ads so that at least one of them will have a great CTR and will boost click volume.

7. After 4 hours, check your traffic report and pause all keywords with a CTR < 0.20 percent and impression count > 400. This will boost your CTR, further improve your campaigns, and eventually improve your ROI. Then, reduce your max bid by 10 percent because you are probably burning your budget too quickly.

8. On day #2: Check the stats again: Remove low CTR keywords, and reduce the max bid by 10 percent.

9. On day #3: Check the stats again: Remove low CTR keywords, and reduce the max bid by 10 percent. Then isolate keywords with high volume and good CTR, and put them in a separate campaign or ad group. If you are still burning your daily budget too fast, improve targeting by excluding some country and excluding display advertising or other sources of lower traffic quality.

10. On day #4 to #7: Proceed as for day #3, but be less aggressive in your efforts to reduce your max bid: if your CPC goes down too much too quickly, your campaign will collapse.

11. By day #8, you should have several ad groups, each with maybe 50 keywords, which are stable and great for your website, plus a huge ad group (the leftovers of day #1 to #7) that will continue to work as well, requiring occasional monitoring.

Automated News Feed Optimization

Here is another application where data science can help. Each year, billions of dollars are poured into online advertising programs (display and pay-per-click advertising) in an effort to attract visitors to websites. Those websites that attract a high volume of visitors do so because they have great content.

Producing great content can be time-consuming and expensive, so nearly every website publisher wants to automate their content production. In addition, displaying the right content to the right user at the right time dramatically increases ad revenue. Analytic techniques can be used to achieve the goal of relevant and highly targeted content.

For example, at Data Science Central we have achieved the first steps of automated content creation. Our news feed system harvests news from keyword-targeted Google news, selected Twitters and blogs, and also content that we create. Our news feed aggregator was created without writing a single line of code, instead using various widgets, Twitter feeds, and Feedburner. Our analytics news shows up on AnalyticBridge, LinkedIn, and many other places, and is updated in real time to drive good traffic to our websites.

Bigger companies are hiring analytic professionals to optimize these processes. For website publishers and anyone generating online advertising revenue, content is king. My first experiments have proved that optimizing content and news has a bigger impact than optimizing advertising campaigns in terms of increasing advertising revenue. The increased revenue comes from two sources:

- More traffic and more returning users, thus more page views and more conversions.

- Most important is more relevant traffic and higher quality traffic with higher conversion rates, in the attempt to produce news and content that will attract and retain users that also share an interest in the advertisers' products and services.

The fact that Data Science Central is a social network does not play a major role in this dynamic (assuming that spam control has been taken care of effectively). What is critical is content quality and dynamic content, thus our focus on real time news and on including (in our feeds) micro-blogs from a number of small, well-respected data scientists. With strategies such as these, you can turn a social network into a profitable website with growing revenue.

Competitive Intelligence with Bit.ly

Competitive intelligence is part of business intelligence, and is a sub-domain of market research. Bit.ly allows you to check the popularity of web pages published by you or your competitors. It also allows you to see how much traffic you contribute to a web page (one that's your own or some external web page that you promote as part of a marketing campaign), versus how much traffic other people or your competitors generate for the same web page.

Bit.ly, a URL shortener (like tinyurl.com), is the standard tool used in LinkedIn e-mail blasts to shorten long URLs with several tags. (The reason is that LinkedIn blasts are text-only.) Yet, bit.ly offers much more than redirect services; it also has interesting reporting capabilities.

This reporting capability is an example of an excellent big data application, provided you are aware of its simple yet incredibly powerful dashboard. It is also a classic example of big data that is useless unless you are aware of the features coming with it and how to leverage it.

Here is a useful example. Consider Figure 6-2, which shows a screenshot of a bit.ly dashboard:

TIME	sort by Date Created	CLICKS VIA YOUR SHORTLINK		TOTAL CLICKS	TOTAL SAVES
		Past 7 days	Total		
12:23p	**Selected articles from top news outlets -...** www.datasciencecentral.com/profiles/blogs/selecte...		53	65	2
Apr 17 9:46p	**Selected articles posted this week - Anal...** www.analyticbridge.com/profiles/blogs/selected-arti...		816	842	2
Apr 17 7:22p	**goPivotal** gopivotal.com/?utm_source=DSC&utm_medium=emai...		626	626	1
Apr 17 5:15p	**goPivotal** gopivotal.com/		155	269	9
Apr 14 9:24p	**Three classes of metrics: centrality, vola...** www.analyticbridge.com/profiles/blogs/three-class...		102	155	5
Apr 10 10:23a	**Google search: three bugs to fix with bet...** www.analyticbridge.com/profiles/blogs/google-sear...		142	178	4
Apr 10 10:22a	**Weekly Digest - April 8 - Big Data News** www.bigdatanews.com/profiles/blogs/weekly-dige...		102	107	2
Apr 10 10:10a	**Career Alert - April 10 - AnalyticBridge** www.analyticbridge.com/group/analyticjobs/forum/t...		686	686	1
Apr 9 2:38p	**Advanced Business Analytics, Data Mini...** www.linkedin.com/groups/Advanced-Business-Ana...		1	2	1
Apr 7 6:40p	**The Face of the New University - Data S...** www.datasciencecentral.com/profiles/blogs/the-fac...		734	811	4

Figure 6-2: Bit.ly dashboard

You can find the amount of traffic (page views) from your bit.ly redirects in the "Clicks via Your Shortlink" column. Keep in mind that the same link might have been shortened by other people. That's why there is an extra column labeled "Total Clicks" that tells you the total traffic coming to the target URL, both from you and from other people who used bit.ly to shorten the same URL.

NOTE Other important competitive intelligence tools besides bit.ly include Quantcast.com, Compete.com, and Alexa.com (which is the least reliable).

Assess Traffic from the Competition

Assessing traffic from the competition is useful for website publishers or media companies. For the goPivotal link created at 5:15 p.m. (Figure 6-2), 155 clicks are from me and another 114 are from competitors. So I delivered better than competitors on this one. Of course, not everyone uses bit.ly in their marketing campaigns, but many do because it offers traffic statistics by referrer, country, and day to the client. Simply add a + sign at the shortened URL `https://bit.ly/11xTDUD+`.

Note that the goPivotal link created at 7:22 p.m. contains special proprietary tags and is thus tracked separately. (The bit.ly URL is different, although it points to the same page.) That's why it has 0 clicks attributable to third parties.

Assess Traffic from People Who Shared Your Link

Still continuing with Figure 6-2, the link for "Three classes of metrics" is internal to Data Science Central, so I know that the extra 53 clicks (53 = 155–102) are from people who shared the article with others using bit.ly. If you click "Three Classes of Metrics" on the bit.ly dashboard, then you know who shared the link and how much traffic they generated (in this case, 53 clicks). This information allows you to track who contributes solid traffic to your website.

RealTime bit.ly

RealTime bit.ly is still a beta project (you can access it at `http://rt.ly/`), but if you use the real-time feature it allows you to fine-tune e-mail campaigns in real time, via A/B testing. For example, if you want to send an e-mail to 100,000 subscribers, you would:

1. Send version A to 2,500 contacts and B to another 2,500 contacts, randomly selected.

2. Wait 10 minutes (even less if possible); see which one performs better (say it's B).

3. Deploy the whole campaign to the remaining 95,000 contacts, using version B of your message.

For instance, the difference between A and B is the subject line, and the success metric is the open rate or click-out rate. For instance, in A, subject line = "Weekly Digest - April 22" and in B, subject line = "Best articles from DSC." Note that usually when doing e-mail campaign optimization, you are not interested in optimizing just one campaign, but actually *all* your campaigns. If you want to optimize one campaign, subject line B would win. For global, long-term optimization, A will win.

Measuring Return on Twitter Hashtags

Building a great list of Twitter followers and judiciously using #hashtags seems to be the Holy Grail to grow traffic and reap rewards from social media. A good reference on the subject is the Mashable article *"How to Get the Most Out of Twitter #Hashtags"* which can be accessed at `http://mashable.com/2009/05/17/twitter-hashtags/`.

The reality is very different. First, when did you read a Tweet for the last time? Probably long ago. Also, hashtags tend to discourage people from clicking your link. In practice, even with 6,000 real followers, a Tweet will generate 0 clicks at worst and 20 clicks at best. This is true if you count only clicks coming straight from your Tweet and ignore indirect traffic and the multiplier effect described next.

Here's an example of a Tweet with two hashtags, in case you've never seen one before:

> "naXys to Focus on the Study of Complex Systems": `http://ning.it/12EFrsc` `#bigdata #datascience`

Is It Really That Bad?

No, it actually works. First, if your Tweet gets re-Tweeted, it is not difficult to generate tons of additional clicks that can be attributed to Twitter (and even more from other sources), even for subjects as specialized as data science. The Twitter multiplier can be as high as 3.

For instance, a great article published in our Data Science Central weekly digest gets 800 clicks that are directly attributed to the eBlast sent to more than 60,000. After 12 months, the article has been viewed 12,000 times. When you analyze the data, you find that 2,400 of the total visits can be attributed to Twitter (people reposting your link and sharing it via Twitter).

There are also some other positive side effects. Some publishers run web crawlers to discover, fetch, and categorize information, and #hashtags are one of the tools they use to detect and classify pieces of news. Data Science Central is one of them—both as a crawler and as a crawlee. The same publishers also publish lists of top data scientists. Their lists are based on who is popular on specific hashtags regardless of whether the Tweets in questions are generated automatically (syndicated content) or by a human being.

And while a Tweet full of special characters is a deterrent for the average Internet user, it is much less so for geeks. (If you read this book, chances are that you are, at least marginally, a geek.) However, you must still comply with the following rules:

- You don't have more than two hashtags per Tweet.
- The hashtags are relevant.
- 50 percent of your Tweets have no hashtags.

Otherwise, people will stop reading what you post and then you are faced with the challenge of finding new followers faster than you are losing old ones.

Hashtags are particularly suited to comment on a webinar as it goes live: INFORMS could use the #INFORMS2013 hashtag for people commenting on their yearly conference. Hashtags are also helpful to promote or discuss some event. For instance, we created #abdsc to reward bloggers Tweeting about us.

Still, it is not so easy to be listed under *Top* rather than *All People* on Twitter when posting a Tweet. And if you are not in the Top list, your hashtag has no value. In addition, you can be a victim of hashtag hijacking: hashtag spammers abusing a popular hashtag to promote their own stuff.

Figure 6-3 is based on recent posts at Data Science Central tracked via bit.ly and shows that a blog post can easily see its traffic statistics triple (right-most column), thanks to other people who like what you wrote and re-Tweet or re-post it on their blogs. Note that the fewer internal clicks, the bigger the multiplier: when we don't do much to promote one of our posts, then other bloggers promote it on our behalf. The most extreme case here is one internal click with multiplier 53.

TIME	sort by Date Created	CLICKS VIA YOUR BITLY LINK		TOTAL CLICKS
		Past 7 days	Total	
May 26 11:42p	New pattern to predict stock prices, mul... www.analyticbridge.com/profiles/blogs/new-pattern...		75	183
May 26 1:23p	Reverse clustering for tactical warfare - ... www.analyticbridge.com/profiles/blogs/reverse-clu...		47	70
May 26 12:29a	La solitude du thésard de fond - Héloïse ... www.scienceshumaines.com/la-solitude-du-thesar...		4	93
May 24 9:56p	Why is it so hard to count this way? - An... www.analyticbridge.com/forum/topics/why-is-it-so-...		216	216
May 23 9:26a	Big Analytics 2013 Atlanta - Confirm Ide... www.cvent.com/events/big-analytics-2013-atlanta/r...		472	472
May 22 10:01p	Data Scientist Demographics - Data Scie... www.datasciencecentral.com/profiles/blogs/data-s...		69	257
May 22 5:54p	Data Science eBook by Analyticbridge - ... www.datasciencecentral.com/profiles/blogs/data-a...		304	387
May 22 2:12p	Visual analytics for everyone	Tableau S... www.tableausoftware.com/trial/tableau-software?...		1	53
May 22 12:48p	Now, choose a right career for your chil... www.business-standard.com/article/companies/no...		8	40
May 18 4:50p	How to choose an analytic tool? - Data S... www.datasciencecentral.com/forum/topics/how-to-...		27	69

Figure 6-3: Clicks multiplier achieved through social networks

Will Hashtags Work for You?

An easy way to check whether hashtags provide a lift is to perform some A/B testing. You can use the following protocol:

1. Over a 14-day time period, Tweet two links each day: one at noon and one at 6 p.m.

2. The first day, in the morning, add the hashtag #datascience to your Tweet. Don't add a hashtag in the evening.

3. On the second day, do the reverse: no hashtag at noon, but add a hashtag #datascience at 6 p.m.

4. Keep alternating noon and 6 p.m. to determine when to add the hashtag.

5. Attach a specific query string to each link, for instance, `?date=0528&hashtag =yes&time=6pm` to the URL you are Tweeting (before shortening the URL). This is for tracking purposes.

6. Use **bit.ly** to shorten your URLs.

For example, your Tweet (hashtag version) could be something like this:

Testing Twitter hashtags performance `https://bit.ly/11wpSXi` #datascience #hashtagABtest

Note that when you click `https://bit.ly/11wpSXi`, the query string shows up in the reconstructed URL in your browser (after the redirect). What's more, you can monitor how many clicks you get by looking at `https://bit.ly/11wpSXi+` (same bit.ly URL, with + added at the end).

After 20 days, you can now perform a statistical analysis to check the following:

▪ Hashtags boost the number of direct clicks.

▪ Hashtags boost the multiplier effect discussed earlier.

You can detect if click variations are explained by time, weekend/weekday, or some other factor such as link and whether hashtags positively contribute, and quantify this contribution.

Real-Time Detection of Viral Tweets

Micro-memes are emergent topics for which a hashtag is created, used widely for a few days, and then disappears. How can they be detected and leveraged? Journalists and publishers are particularly interested in this.

TrendSpottr and Top-Hashtags are websites offering this type of service. However, they rely on sample data—a major drawback to discover new, rare events that suddenly spike. It is especially difficult because these memes use made-up keywords that never existed before, such as #abdsc or #hashtagABtest.

Also, Top-Hashtag worked with Instagram, but not with Twitter, last time I checked. Hashtags also work on Google+. For data science, the most interesting large social networks are LinkedIn (more professional), Google+, Quora (more geeky), and Twitter. So identifying in real time new trends that are emerging on these networks is important.

One solution consists of following the most influential people in your domain and getting alerts each time one of their new hashtags get 10+ Tweets. If some new hashtag from an unknown person starts creating a lot of buzz, these influencers (at least some of them) will quickly notice, and you will, too, because you follow the influencers. Just pick up the right list of keywords and hashtags to identify top influencers: data science, Hadoop, big data, business analytics, visualization, predictive modeling, and so on. Some lists of top influencers are publicly available.

The key message of this discussion is twofold: currently, good algorithms to detect signal from noise and categorize Tweets are yet to be developed, and they involve data science and NLP (natural language processing). Such algorithms are particularly useful to website publishers, content managers, and journalists.

Improving Google Search with Three Fixes

These big data problems probably impact many search engines, which is one piece of evidence that there is still room for new startups to invent superior search engines. Data scientists are well equipped to identify these problems and quantitatively measure whether they are big or small issues, to help prioritize them. These problems can be fixed with improved analytics and data science. Here are the problems and the solutions.

Outdated Search Results

Google does not do a good job of showing new or recently updated web pages. Of course, new does not mean better, and the Google algorithm favors old pages with a good ranking, on purpose—maybe because the ranking for new pages is less reliable or has less history. (That's why I created statistical scores to rank web pages with no history.) To solve this problem, the user can add **2013** to Google searches. And Google could do that, too, by default. For instance, compare search results for the query **data science** with those for **data science 2013**. Which one do you like best? Better, Google should allow you to choose between "recent" versus "permanent" search results when you do a search.

The issue here is to correctly date web pages, which is a difficult problem because webmasters can use fake timestamps to fool Google. But because Google indexes most pages every couple of days, it's easy to create a Google timestamp and keep two dates for each (static) web page: date when first indexed and date when last modified. You also need to keep a 128-bit signature (in addition to related keywords) for each web page to easily detect when it is modified. The problem is more difficult for web pages created on the fly.

Wrongly Attributed Articles

You write an article on your blog. It then gets picked up by another media outlet, say *The New York Times*. Google displays *The New York Times* version at the top and sometimes does not even display the original version at all, even if the search query is the title of the articles, using an exact match. You might argue that *The New York Times* is more trustworthy than your little unknown blog or that your blog has a poor page rank. But this has two implications:

It creates a poor user experience. To the Google user, the Internet appears much smaller than it actually is.

Webmasters can use unfair strategies to defeat Google: using smart Botnet technology with the right keyword mix to manufacture tons of organic Google queries, but manufacture few clicks—only on their own links. This will lower the organic CTR for competitors but boost yours. It is expected that this "attack" would fix your content attribution problem.

Another, meaner version of the CTR attack consists of hitting the culprit website with lots of organic Google clicks (Google redirects) but no Google impression. This could fool Google algorithms into believing that the website in question is engaging in CTR fraud by manipulating click-in ratios, and thus get them dropped from Google. At the same time it will create a terrible impression-to-conversion (click-out) ratio for advertisers showing up on the incriminated landing pages, hitting display ads particularly hard, causing advertisers to drop the publisher. In short, this strategy could automatically take care of copyright infringement using two different levers at once: click in and click out. It must be applied to one violator at a time (to avoid detection) until they are all gone. If properly executed, nobody will ever know who did the attack; maybe nobody will ever find out that an attack took place.

One easy way for Google to fix the problem is, again, to correctly identify the first version of an article, as described in the previous paragraph.

Favoring Irrelevant Web Pages

Google generates a number of search result impressions per week for every website, and this number is extremely stable. It is probably based on the number of pages, keywords, and popularity (page rank) of the website in question, as well as a bunch of other metrics (time to load, proportion of original content, niche versus generic website, and so on). If every week Google shows exactly 10,000 impressions for your website, which page or keyword match should Google favor?

Google should favor pages with low bounce rate. In practice, it does the exact opposite.

Why? Maybe if a user does not find your website interesting, he performs more Google searches and the chance of him clicking a paid Google ad increases. So bad (landing page) user experience financially rewards Google.

How do you fix it? If most users spend little time on a web page (and Google can easily measure time spent), that web page (or better, that web page or keyword combination) should be penalized in the Google index to show up less frequently. Many publishers also use Google Analytics, which provides Google with additional valuable information about bounce rate and user interest at the page level.

However, you might argue that if bounce rate is high, maybe the user found the answer to his question right away by visiting your landing page, and thus the user experience is actually great. I disagree, since at Data Science Central, each page displays links to similar articles and typically results in subsequent page views. Indeed, the worst bounce rate is associated with Google organic searches. More problematic is the fact that the bounce rate from Google organic is getting worse (while it's getting better for all other traffic sources), as if the Google algorithm lacks machine learning capabilities or is doing a poor job with new pages added daily. In the future, longer articles broken down into two or three pages will hopefully improve the bounce rate from Google organic (and from other sources as well).

Improving Relevancy Algorithms

Here you focus on ad relevancy in the context of online advertising such as search engine advertising. When you see ads on search result pages or elsewhere, the ads that display in front of your eyes (should) have been highly selected to maximize the chance that you convert and generate ad revenue for the publisher or search engine.

If you think you see irrelevant ads, either they are priced cheaply or Google's ad relevancy algorithm is not working well. Sometimes it's due to cheap ads, sometimes poor scoring, and you could argue that sometimes it's because the advertiser is doing a poor job of keyword selection and targeting.

Ad scoring algorithms used to be simple, the score being a function of the max bid paid by the advertiser and the CTR. This led to abuses: an advertiser could generate bogus impressions to dilute competitor CTR, or clicks on its own ads to boost its own CTR, or a combination of both, typically using proxies or Botnets to hide the scheme, thus gaining unfair competitive advantage over search engines. Note that search engines use traffic quality scores. Indeed, I have been hired in the past, as a data scientist, to reverse engineer some of these traffic quality algorithms, as well as perform stress tests to see what makes them fail.

Recently, in addition to CTR and max bid, ad networks have added ad relevancy to their ad scoring mix (that is, in the algorithm used to determine which ads you will see, and in which order). In short, ad networks don't want to display ads that will make the user frustrated — it's all about improving user experience and reducing churn to boost long-term profits. How Does Ad Relevancy Scoring Work?

There are three components in the mix:

- The user visiting a web page hosting the ad in question
- The web page where the ad is hosted
- The ad itself, that is, its text or visual content, or other metrics such as size, and so on

The fourth important component—the landing page—is not considered in this short discussion. (Good publishers scrape advertiser landing pages to check the match between a text ad and its landing page, and eliminate bad adware.)

The Solution

You will need to create three taxonomies:

- **Taxonomy A** to categorize returning users based on their interests, member profile, or web searching history
- **Taxonomy B** to categorize web pages that are hosting ads, based on content or publisher-provided keyword tags
- **Taxonomy C** to categorize ads, based on text ad content, or advertiser-provided keywords to describe the ad (such as bid keyword in PPC campaigns, or ad title)

The two important taxonomies are B and C, unless the ad is displayed on a generic web page, in which case A is more important than B. So ignore taxonomy A for now. *The goal is to match a category from Taxonomy B with one from Taxonomy C.* Taxonomies may or may not have the same categories, so in general it will be a fuzzy match where, for instance, the page hosting the ad is attached to the categories Finance/Stock Market in Taxonomy B, while the ad is attached to the categories Investing/Finance in Taxonomy C. So you need to have a system in place to measure distances between categories belonging to two different taxonomies.

How to Build a Taxonomy

There are a lot of vendors and open source solutions available on the market, but if you want to build your own taxonomies from scratch, here's one way to do it:

1. Scrape the web (DMOZ directory with millions of precategorized web pages that you can download freely is a good starting point), extract pieces of text that are found on the same web page, and create a distance to measure proximity between pieces of text.
2. Clean and stem your keyword data.

3. Leverage your search query log data: two queries found in the same session are closer to each other (with respect to the preceding distance) than arbitrary queries.

4. Create a table with all pairs of "pieces of text" that you have extracted and that are associated (for example, found on the same web page or same user session). You will be OK if your table has 100 million such pairs.

Say that (X, Y) is such a pair. Compute n1 = # of occurrences of X in your table, n2 = # of occurrences of Y in your table, and n12 = # of occurrences where X and Y are associated (for example, found on the same web page). A metric that tells you how close X and Y are to each other would be R = n12 / SQRT(n1 x n2). With this dissimilarity metric (used for instance at http://www.frenchlane.com/kw8.html) you can cluster keywords via hierarchical clustering and eventually build a taxonomy—which is nothing more than an unsupervised clustering of the keyword universe with labels manually assigned to (say) the top 20 clusters, with each representing a category.

Ad Rotation Problem

When an advertiser uses (say) five versions of an ad for the same landing page and the same AdWords keyword group (keywords purchased on Google), how frequently should each of the five ads show up? From Google's perspective, the optimum is achieved by the ad providing the highest revenue per impression, whether the advertiser is charged by impression (CPM model) or by the click (pay-per-click). For the advertiser, the ad commanding the lowest cost-per-click (CPC) is sometimes the optimum one, although it might generate too few clicks.

However, Google cannot just simply show 100 percent of the time the ad with the highest revenue per impression. This metric varies over time, and in 2 weeks the optimum ad could change, as users get bored seeing the same ad all the time or new keywords are purchased. So Google will show the five ads, semi-randomly. The optimum ad is displayed much more frequently, and the worst one very rarely.

But how do you define "much more frequently" and "very rarely"? Of course, it depends on the impression-to-click ratio multiplied by the CPC. Interestingly, it seems that Google has chosen a logarithm relationship between how frequently an ad is displayed and its CTR (impression-to-click ratio). The CPC is ignored in Google's model, at least in this example.

What do you think about Google's choice of a logarithmic distribution? Is it:

▪ Arbitrary?

▪ Coincidental? (More tests would show that the relation found is wrong and just happened by chance for this specific ad campaign.)

▪ The result of deep investigations by Google data scientists?

And why is the CPC decoupled? Maybe to avoid fraud and manipulations by advertisers.

If you check the figures at `http://www.analyticbridge.com/group/webanalytics/forum/topics/ad-serving-optimization` you'll see that the optimum ad is served 76.29 percent of the time, and the second best one only 10.36 percent of the time, despite both having a similar CTR and a similar CPC. The CPC is not taken into account, just the CTR; models involving CTR have a worse R^2 (goodness of fit). Models other than logarithmic have a worst R^2 than logarithmic.

Miscellaneous

This section discusses a few data science applications in various other contexts. These applications are routinely encountered in today's markets.

Better Sales Forecasts with Simpler Models

A common challenge is how to make more accurate sales forecasts. The solution is to leverage external data and simplify your predictive model. In 2000, I was working with GE's analytic team to improve sales forecasts for NBC Internet, a web portal owned by NBC. The sales/finance people were using a basic formula to predict next month sales based mostly on sales from the previous month. With GE, I started to develop more sophisticated models that included time series techniques (ARMA—auto regressive models) and seasonality but still were entirely based on internal sales data.

Today, many companies still fail to use the correct methodology to get accurate sales forecasts. This is especially true for companies in growing or declining industries, or when volatility is high due to macroeconomic, structural factors. Indeed, the GE move toward using more complex models was the wrong move: it did provide a small lift but failed to generate the huge lift that could be expected switching to the right methodology.

The Right Methodology

Most companies with more than 200 employees use independent silos to store and exploit data. Data from the finance, advertising/marketing, and operation/inventory management/product departments are more or less independent and rarely merged together to increase ROI. Worse, external data sources are totally ignored.

Even each department has its own silos: within the BI department, data regarding paid search, organic search, and other advertising (print, TV, and so on) are treated separately by data analysts that don't talk to each other. Although lift metrics from paid search (managed by SEM people), organic search (managed by SEO people), and other advertising are clearly highly dependent from a business point of view, interaction is ignored and the different channels are independently—rather than jointly—optimized.

If a sale results from a TV ad seen 3 months ago, together with a Google ad seen twice last month, and also thanks to good SEO and landing page optimization, it will be impossible to accurately attribute the dollar amount to the various managers involved in making the sale happens. Worse, sales forecasts suffer from not using external data and econometric models.

For a startup (or an old company launching a new product), it is also important to accurately assess sales growth using auto-regressive time series models that take into account advertising spend and a decay function of time. In the NBC Internet example, TV ads were found to have an impact for about 6 months, and a simple but good model would be:

$$Sales(t) = g\{ f(sales(t-1, t-2, ... , t-6), a_1*SQRT[AdSpend(t-1)] + ... + a_6*SQRT[AdSpend(t-6)] \}$$

where the time unit is 1 month (28 days is indeed better), and both g and f are functions that need to be identified via cross-validation and model fitting techniques (the f function corresponding to the ARMA model previously mentioned).

Following is a list of factors influencing sales:

■ Pricing optimization (including an elementary price elasticity component in the sales forecasting model), client feedback, new product launch, and churn should be part of any basic sales forecasts.

■ Sales forecasts should integrate external data, in particular:

  ■ Market share trends: Is your company losing or gaining market share?

  ■ Industry forecasts (growth or decline in your industry)

  ■ Total sales volume for your industry based on competitor data. (The data in question can easily be purchased from companies selling competitive intelligence.)

  ■ Prices from your top competitors for same products, in particular, price ratios (yours versus the competition's).

  ■ Economic forecasts: Some companies sell this type of data, but their statistical models have flaws, and they tend to use outdated data or move very slowly to update their models with fresh data.

A Simple Model

Identify the top four metrics that drive sales among the metrics that I have suggested (do not ignore external data sources—including a sentiment analysis index by product, that is, what your customers write about your products on Twitter), and create a simple regression model. You could get it done with Excel (use the data analysis plug-in or the linest function) and get better forecasts than you would using a more sophisticated model based only on internal data coming from just one of your many data silos.

How to Hire a Good Sales Forecaster

You need to hire some sort of a management consultant with analytic acumen who will interact with all departments in your organization, gather, merge, and analyze all data sources from most of your silos, integrate other external data sources, and communicate with both executives and everybody in your organization who owns or is responsible for a data silo. He will recommend a solution. Conversations should include data quality issues, which metrics you should track moving forward, and how to create a useful dashboard for executives.

Better Detection of Healthcare Fraud

The Washington Education Association (WEA, in Washington State) is partnering with Aon Hewitts (Illinois), a verification company, to eliminate a specific type of health insurance fraud: teachers reporting non-qualifying people as dependents, such as an unemployed friend with no health insurance. The fraud is used by "nice" people (teachers) to provide health insurance to people who would otherwise have none, by reporting them as spouses or kids.

Interestingly, I saw the letter sent to all WEA teachers. It requires them to fill out lots of paperwork and provide multiple identity proofs (tax forms, birth certificates, marriage certificates, and so on) similar to ID documents (I9 form) required to be allowed to work for a company.

It is easy to cheat on the paper documentation that you have to mail to the verification company (for example, by producing fake birth certificates or claiming you don't have one, and so on). In addition, asking people to fill out so much paperwork is a waste of time and natural resources (trees used to produce paper) and results in lots of errors, privacy issues, and ID theft risk, and costs lots of money for WEA.

So why don't they use modern methods to detect fraud: data mining techniques to detect suspicious SSNs, identifying SSNs reported as dependent by multiple households based on IRS tax data, SSNs not showing up in any tax forms submitted to the IRS, address mismatch detection, and so on? (Note that a 5-day-old baby probably has no record in the IRS database, yet he is eligible as a dependent for tax or health insurance purposes.)

Why not use data mining technology, instead of paper, to get all of the advantages that data mining offers over paper? What advantages does paper offer? I don't see any.

Attribution Modeling

I was once asked to perform a study for NBC. It was running advertising using a weekly mix of TV shows at various times to promote its Internet website. I was asked to identify which TV shows worked best to drive new users to the website. Each week, it was using pretty much the same mix of 10 to 12 shows out of 20 different shows. GRT data (number of eyeballs who watched a particular TV show at a particular time) were collected, as well as weekly numbers of new users, over a 6-month time period. No A/B testing was possible, so the problem was quite complicated.

Here's how I solved the problem. I computed a distance for all pairs of weeks {A, B}, based on which TV shows were used in the weeks in question, as well as the total GRT of each week (high GRT results in many new users unless the TV ad is really bad). I then looked at pairs of weeks that were very similar (in terms of GRTs and show mixes) and close in time (no more than 2 months apart). I focused on pairs where week A had one more show, say show S, compared with week B. Week B did not have S but instead had an extra show not shared with A, say show T. Actually, it was a bit more complicated than that. I allowed not just one, but two different shows. But for the sake of simplicity, stick with this example: show S in week A and not in week B, and show T in week B but not in week A. If week A had more new users than B, I would adjust the performance index of shows S and T as follows: $P(S) = P(S) + 1$, $P(T) = P(T) - 1$. The converse was done; A had fewer new users than B.

To identify the best performing shows, all that was left to do was to rank shows by their performance indexes. *Law & Order* was the winner and was used more often in the mix of TV shows used to promote the website.

Forecasting Meteorite Hits

This example can be used for training purposes as part of the curriculum to become a data scientist. This section describes the different steps involved in a typical, real analysis: from understanding the problem (how to forecast meteorite hits) to providing an answer.

Conclusions are based on manual estimates, which make sense in this context. This section also describes how much a consultant would charge for this analysis, disproving the fact that data scientists are expensive.

The conclusions of the statistical analysis are different from what you've read in the press recently: the Russian meteor is an event said to occur once every 40 years, according to journalists.

Following is a statistical analysis in eight steps:

1. Define the scope of analysis. This is a small project to be completed in 10 hours of work or less, billed at $100/hour. Provide the risk of meteorite hit per year per meteorite size.

2. Identify data and caveats. You can find and download the data set at `http://osm2.cartodb.com/tables/2320/public#/map`.

   Data about identified meteors—those that have not hit Earth yet but occasionally fly by—are not included in this analysis. Identifying and forecasting the number of such meteors would be the scope of another similar project.

3. Data cleaning: the data seem comprehensive, but they are messy. The database seems to take years to get updated (many fewer meteorites in 2000–2010 than one decade earlier). Some years have very little data. The number of meteorites started to explode around 1974, probably the year when collecting data started. Five fields are of special interest: meteorite type, size, year, and whether the date corresponds to "when it fell" or "when it was found." Another field not considered here is location. Discard data prior to 1900.

4. Exploratory analysis: Some strong patterns emerge, despite the following:

   ▪ Messy data

   ▪ Recent years with missing observations or data glitches

   ▪ Massive meteorites that are both extremely rare and extremely big—creating significant volatility in the number of tons per year

   ▪ The fact that most meteorites are found (rather than being seen falling) with unknown time lags between "discovery" and "fall." And "found" sometimes means a fragment rather than the whole rock.

   These patterns are:

   ▪ Smaller meteorites are now detected because of the growing surface of inhabited land and better instruments.

   ▪ The frequency of hits decreases exponentially with size (measured in grams in the data set).

   ▪ Grouping by size using a logarithmic scale and grouping by decade makes sense.

5. The actual analysis: you can find the Excel spreadsheet with data and formulas at `http://bit.ly/1gaiIMm`. It helps to include the "found" category in the analysis (despite its lower accuracy); otherwise, the data set is too small. The data are summarized (grouped by decade and size) on the Analysis

tab in the spreadsheet, using a basic Excel function such as Concatenate, Countif, Averageif, log, int.

There are nine group sizes with at least one observation: from size 0 for the smallest meteorites to size 8 representing a 9 to 66 ton meteorite—like the one that exploded over Russia. According to the data set, no size 8 was found in the last 40 years, and maybe this is why people claim that the 2013 Russian bang occurs every 40 years. But there were five occurrences between 1900 and 1950. Not sure how reliable these old numbers are. Here, the size is computed as $INT(0.5 * \log m)$ where m is the mass of the meteorite in grams.

Also look at size ratios, defined as the number of meteorites of size k divided by the number of meteorites of size k + 1 (for a given decade), to build a predictive model. Analyze how variations occur in these ratios, as well as ratio variations across decades for a fixed size k.

A quick regression where Y = ratio (1950–2010 aggregated data) and X = size shows a perfect linear fit ($R^2 > 0.98$), as shown in the top figure at `http://www.analyticbridge.com/profiles/blogs/great-statistical-analysis-forecasting-meteorite-hits`. In the figure, I have excluded size 0 (it has its own problems), as well as sizes 8 and 7, which are rare (only one occurrence for size 8 during the time period in question). The total number of meteorites across all sizes is 31,690.

I tried separate regressions (size versus ratio) for each decade to see if a pattern emerges. A pattern does emerge, although it is easier to detect with the brain than with a computer: the slope of the regression decreases over time (very, very roughly and on average), suggesting that more small meteorites have been found recently, whereas the number of large meteorites does not increase much over time (for size 5+).

6. Model selection: two decades show relatively good pattern stability and recency: 2000–2010 and 1990–2000. Likewise, sizes 5 and 4 show pattern stability (growth over time for size 4, rather flat for size 5). I used these two time periods and sizes to build initial forecasts and estimating slopes, eventually providing two predictions for the chance of a hit (lower and upper bound) for any size. The span (or confidence interval) grows exponentially with size, as you would expect.

The ratios in white font/red background in the spreadsheet represent manual estimates (sometimes overwriting actual data) based on interpolating the most stable patterns. No cross-validation was performed. Much of the validation consisted of identifying islands of stability in the ratio summary table in cells Y1:AG8.

7. Prepare forecasts, as shown in Figure 6-4.

Meteorite Size	Meteorite Weight	Unit	Occur every... (in years)	
			Upper bound (1)	Lower bound (2)
0	0	grams		
1	6	grams		
2	54	grams		
3	402	grams		
4	3	kilograms		
5	22	kilograms	0.2	0.2
6	163	kilograms	1.3	1.3
7	1,203	kilograms	10.3	8.7
8	9	tons	99.5	65.4
9	66	tons	1,114	556
10	485	tons	14,153	5,281
11	3,585	tons	200,971	55,448
12	26,489	tons	3,155,244	637,651
13	195,730	tons	54,270,201	7,970,639
14	1,446,257	tons	1,014,852,765	107,603,626
15	10,686,475	tons	20,500,025,853	1,560,252,571
16	78,962,960	tons	444,850,561,020	24,183,914,855
17	583,461,743	tons	#############	399,034,595,112
(1) based on 2000-2009 data				
(2) based on 1990-1999 data				
9 tons means: from 9 to 66 tons.				

Figure 6-4: Predicting meteorite hits based on size

A formula to compute yearly occurrences as a function of actual weight can easily be derived:

$$\text{Yearly\_Occurrences}(weight) = 1/(A + B* \log(weight))$$

Here's an exercise for you: estimate A and B based on Figure 6-4.

Based on the table, it makes the "every 40 year" claim for the 2013 Russian bang plausible. The Russian meteorite might have exploded louder than expected because of the angle, composition, or velocity. Or maybe the weight of the meteorite is based on the strength of its explosion, rather than the other way around.

There were no meteorites of sizes 9, 10, 11, or 12 in the data set and few of size 8, so the associated risks (for these sizes) are based on pure interpolation. Yet they constitute the most interesting and valuable part of this study.

8. Followup: A more detailed analysis would involve predictions broken down by meteor type (iron and water), angle, and velocity. Also, the impact of population growth could be assessed in this risk analysis. In this small analysis, it is indeed implicitly factored in. Also, you could do some more conventional cross-validation, maybe making a prediction for 2013, and see how close you are for meteorites of sizes 0 to 4. Discussing this with the client can provide additional work for the consultant and more value for the client.

This is a small analysis and there is not a real metric to measure model performance or ROI on this project. Many projects do, just not this one. It is also unusual for a statistician or data scientist to make intelligent guesses and handmade predictions. It is commonplace in engineering, though.

Data Collection at Trailhead Parking Lots

This section illustrates that data science can be used in many different contexts. It also focuses on experimental design and sampling, a domain of statistical science that should be included in data science. Finally, it shows that "no data" does not mean you can't do anything. Data scientists should be able to tell how to first create (in a way that helps data science) and then track data, when the data are initially absent.

Trailhead parking lots are notorious for crime activity. These remote, unpatrolled locations, hidden in dense forests, attract all sorts of bad people. One original crime is thieves stealing the park fees paid by hikers. These fees consist of $5 bills inserted by trail users (hikers) in an envelope and dropped in a locked mailbox at the trailhead. These wooden boxes are easy to break and repair, for the purpose of stealing some of the $5 bills. A smart thief would probably visit 10 trailhead parking lots with lots of hikers once a week, at night, and steal 50 percent of the envelopes. (Stealing 100 percent would attract the police's attention.) It could easily generate a $50,000 income a year, with little work and low risk—especially because there are so many agencies involved in charging and collecting these fees. A smart thief would steal only $5,000 a year from each agency but would target 10 different agencies associated with 10 different popular hikes.

I'm not saying this crime is happening, but it is a possibility. Another type of crime would be perpetrated by official employees collecting these fees and keeping a small percentage for themselves.

How would you detect this crime? Installing webcams might be too expensive in these remote locations with no Internet and no cell phone service. How can you prevent this crime from happening? And how can you make sure every hiker pays the fee—usually $5 per day? Now answer some of these questions.

We asked readers on Data Science Central to answer the question: how can you detect crime and fix it with data science? The answers, which offer real data science solutions, include using experimental design, creating data, tracking numbers on dollar bills or money collected by employees, employee rotation, and others. (If you would like to see more of the answers in more detail, see `http://www.analyticbridge.com/profiles/blogs/how-would-you-detect-and-stop-this-type-of-crime` in the comments section.)

Other Applications of Data Science

Data science is applied in many other domains and industries. For instance:

- **Oil industry**: Use statistical models to detect oil fields by drilling as few wells as possible. If you could drill 10 wells, 5 producing oil, 5 not producing oil, and assuming the shape of the oil field is a convex domain, then the problem consisted of estimating the border of the domain (oil field), based on 5 outside and 5 inside points, and then drill wells with a high probability of finding oil.

- **Credit scoring**: One of the issues preventing new models from being created and deployed is regulations. Larger banks have statisticians that work on credit models for loans and the models must be approved by regulators, the FDIC (see `http://1.usa.gov/1aLJ9aa`). New methodology pioneered by John Elder, for better scoring, relies on *ensemble methods*. Note that similar statistical modeling regulations that can kill data science innovation apply to clinical trials.

Data science applications cover most fields: sensor data, mobile data, smart grids (optimizing electrical networks and electricity pricing), econometrics, clinical trials, operations research (optimizing business processes), astronomy, plagiarism and copyright infringement detection, and even computational chemistry (designing new molecules to fight cancer).

Summary

This chapter discussed case studies, real-life applications, and success stories involving data science. It covered various types of initiatives, ranging from stock market techniques to advertising mix optimization, fraud detection, search engine optimization (for search companies), astronomy (forecasting meteorite hits), automated news feed management, data encryption, e-mail marketing, and various relevancy problems (online advertising).

The next chapter focuses on helping you get employed as a data scientist. It includes sample resumes, more than 90 job interview questions, companies that routinely hire data scientists, and typical job titles for data scientists.

Launching Your New Data Science Career

Chapter 6 discussed case studies, real-life applications, and success stories covering various types of data science initiatives. This chapter focuses on helping you get employed as a data scientist, starting with 90 job interview questions (including questions on how to solve small, real-life data science problems), exercises to test your visual analytic skills, career moves from statistician to data scientist, examples of well-known data scientists and the skills they have, and finally, typical job titles (few are actually called data scientists, though this is changing) and salary surveys.

Job Interview Questions

These are mostly open-ended questions that prospective employers may ask to assess the technical horizontal knowledge of a senior candidate for a high-level position, such as a director, as well as of junior candidates. The answers to some of the key questions can be found at `http://bit.ly/1cGlFA5`.

Questions About Your Experience

- What is the biggest data set you have processed, and how did you process it? What were the results?
- Tell me two success stories about your analytic or computer science projects. How was lift (or success) measured?

- Have you been involved in database design and data modeling?

- Have you been involved in dashboard creation and metric selection? What do you think about BIRT?

- What features of Teradata do you like?

- How do you handle missing data? What imputation techniques do you recommend?

- Have you been working with white lists? Positive rules (in the context of fraud or spam detection)? Have you optimized code or algorithms for speed in SQL, Perl, C++, Python, and so on? How and by how much?

- Is it better to spend 5 days developing a 90 percent accurate solution or 10 days for 100 percent accuracy? Does this depend on the context?

- How can you prove that one improvement you've brought to an algorithm is an improvement over not doing anything? Are you familiar with A/B testing, and have you been able to make such tests truly successful (give examples)?

- Do you know or have you used data reduction techniques other than PCA? What do you think of step-wise regression? What kind of step-wise techniques are you familiar with? When is full data better than reduced data or samples?

- Are you familiar with extreme value theory, Monte Carlo simulations, or mathematical statistics (or anything else) to correctly estimate the chance of a rare event?

- Do you have any experience with using APs, programming APIs, Google or Amazon.com APIs, or AaaS (Analytics as a Service)?

- When is it better to write your own code rather than using a data science software package?

- Which tools do you use for visualization? What do you think of Tableau, R, and SAS? Do you know how to efficiently represent five dimensions in a chart or in a video?

- What types of clients have you been working with: internal, external, sales/finance/marketing/IT people? Do you have consulting experience? Have you dealt with vendors, including vendor selection and testing?

- Are you familiar with software life cycle? With IT project life cycle—from gathering requests to maintenance? (Read the section Life Cycle of Data Science Projects in Chapter 5 for details.)

- Are you a lone coder? A production person (developer)? Or a designer (architect)?

- Are you familiar with pricing optimization, price elasticity, inventory management, competitive intelligence? Give examples.

- Have you used time series models, cross-correlations with time lags, correlograms, spectral analysis, and signal processing and filtering techniques? In which context?

- Which data scientists do you admire most? Which startups?

- How did you become interested in data science?

- What did you do today? Or what did you do this week/last week?

- What/when is the latest data mining book/article you read? What/when is the latest data mining conference/webinar/class/workshop/training you attended? What/when is the most recent programming skill that you acquired?

- What are your favorite data science websites? Who do you admire most in the data science community and why? Which company do you admire most?

- What/when/where is the last data science blog post you wrote?

- Who are the best people you have recruited and where are they today?

Technical Questions

- What are lift, KPI, robustness, model fitting, design of experiments, and the 80/20 rule?

- What are collaborative filtering, n-grams, MapReduce, and cosine distance?

- What is probabilistic merging (aka fuzzy merging)? Is it easier to handle with SQL or other languages? Which languages would you choose for semi-structured text data reconciliation?

- Toad or Brio or any other similar clients are quite inefficient to query Oracle databases. Why? What would you do to increase speed by a factor of 10 and be able to handle far bigger outputs?

- What are hash table collisions? How are they avoided? How frequently do they happen?

- How can you make sure a MapReduce application has good load balance? What is load balance?

- Is it better to have 100 small hash tables or one big hash table in memory, in terms of access speed (assuming both fit within RAM)? What do you think about in-database analytics?

- Why is Naive Bayes so bad? How would you improve a spam detection algorithm that uses Naive Bayes?

- What is star schema? What are lookup tables?

- Can you perform logistic regression with Excel, and if so, how, and would the result be good?

- Define quality assurance, Six Sigma, and Design of Experiments. Give examples of good and bad designs of experiments.

- What are the drawbacks of general linear model? Are you familiar with alternatives (Lasso, ridge regression, and boosted trees)?

- Do you think 50 small decision trees are better than one large one? Why?

- Give examples of data that do not have a Gaussian distribution or lognormal. Give examples of data that have a chaotic distribution.

- Why is mean square error a bad measure of model performance? What would you suggest instead?

- What is a cron job?

- What is an efficiency curve? What are its drawbacks, and how can they be overcome?

- What is a recommendation engine? How does it work?

- What is an exact test? How and when can simulations help when you do not use an exact test?

- What is the computational complexity of a good, fast clustering algorithm? What is a good clustering algorithm? How do you determine the number of clusters? How would you perform clustering on 1 million unique keywords, assuming you have 10 million data points—each one consisting of two keywords and a metric measuring how similar these two keywords are? How would you create this 10-million-data-points table?

- Should removing stop words be Step 1, rather than Step 3, in the search engine algorithm described in the section Big Data Problem Epitomizing the Challenges of Data Science in Chapter 2?

General Questions

- Should click data be handled in real time? Why? In which contexts?

- What is better: good data or good models? And how do you define "good"? Is there a universal good model? Are there any models that are definitely not so good?

- How do you handle missing data? What imputation techniques do you recommend?

- Compare SAS, R, Python, and Perl.

- What is the curse of big data? (See section The Curse of Big Data in Chapter 2.)

- What are examples in which MapReduce does not work? What are examples in which it works well? What are the security issues involved with the cloud? What do you think of EMC's solution offering a hybrid approach—to both an internal and external cloud—to mitigate the risks and offer other advantages (which ones)? (You can find more information about key players in this market in the section The Big Data Ecosystem in Chapter 2, and especially in the online references provided in this section.)

- What is sensitivity analysis? Is it better to have low sensitivity (that is, great robustness) and low predictive power, or vice versa? How can you perform good cross-validation? What do you think about the idea of injecting noise into your data set to test the sensitivity of your models?

- Compare logistic regression with decision trees and neural networks. How have these technologies been vastly improved over the last 15 years?

- Is actuarial science a branch of statistics (survival analysis)? If not, how so? (You can find more information about actuarial sciences at `http://en.wikipedia .org/wiki/Actuarial _ science` and `http://www.dwsimpson.com/`.)

- What is root cause analysis? How can you identify a cause versus a correlation? Give examples. (You can find information on this in Chapter 5, "Data Science Craftsmanship, Part II.")

- How would you define and measure the predictive power of a metric?

- Is it better to have too many false positives, or too many false negatives?

- Have you ever thought about creating a startup? Around which idea/concept?

- Do you think that a typed login/password will disappear? How could they be replaced?

- What do you think makes a good data scientist?

- Do you think data science is an art or a science?

- Give a few examples of best practices in data science.

- What could make a chart misleading, or difficult to read or interpret? What features should a useful chart have?

- Do you know a few rules of thumb used in statistical or computer science? Or in business analytics?

- What are your top five predictions for the next 20 years?

- How do you immediately know when statistics published in an article (for example, newspaper) are either wrong or presented to support the author's point of view, rather than correct, comprehensive factual information on a specific subject? For instance, what do you think about the official monthly unemployment statistics regularly discussed in the press? What could make them more accurate?

- In your opinion, what is data science? Machine learning? Data mining?

Questions About Data Science Projects

- How can you detect individual paid accounts shared by multiple users? This is a big problem for publishers, digital newspapers, software developers offering API access, the music and movie industry (file sharing issues), and organizations offering monthly flat-fee access to single users to view or download content.

- How can you optimize a web crawler to run much faster, extract better information, and better summarize data to produce cleaner databases?

- How would you come up with a solution to identify plagiarism?

- You are about to send 1 million e-mails (marketing campaign). How do you optimize delivery? How do you optimize response? Can you optimize both separately?

- How would you turn unstructured data into structured data? Is it really necessary? Is it OK to store data as flat text files rather than in a SQL-powered RDBMS?

- How would you build nonparametric confidence intervals for scores?

- How can you detect the best rule set for a fraud detection scoring technology? How can you deal with rule redundancy, rule discovery, and the combinatorial nature of the problem (for finding optimum rule set—the one with best predictive power)? Can an approximate solution to the rule set problem be OK? How would you find an OK approximate solution? How would you decide it is good enough and stop looking for a better one?

- How can you create keyword taxonomies?

- What is a Botnet? How can it be detected?

- How does Zillow's algorithm work to estimate the value of any home in the United States?

- How can you detect bogus reviews or bogus Facebook accounts used for bad purposes?

- How would you create a new anonymous digital currency (focusing on the aspects of security)? How do you protect this currency against Internet pirates? How do you make it easy for stores to accept it? (For instance, each transaction has a unique ID used only once and expiring after a few days, and the space for unique IDs is very large to prevent hackers from creating valid IDs just by chance.)

- You design a robust nonparametric statistic (metric) to replace correlation or R-Squared that is independent of sample size, always between –1 and +1 and based on rank statistics. How do you normalize for sample size? Write an algorithm that computes all permutations of n elements. How do you sample permutations (that is, generate tons of random permutations) when n is large, to estimate the asymptotic distribution for your newly created metric? You may use this asymptotic distribution for normalizing your metric. Do you think that an exact theoretical distribution might exist, and therefore, you should find it and use it rather than wasting your time trying to estimate the asymptotic distribution using simulations?

▪ Here's a more difficult, technical question related to the previous one. There is an obvious one-to-one correspondence between permutations of n elements and integers between 1 and factorial n. Design an algorithm that encodes an integer less than factorial n as a permutation of n elements. What would be the reverse algorithm used to decode a permutation and transform it back into a number? **Hint**: An intermediate step is to use the factorial number system representation of an integer. You can check this reference online to answer the question. Even better, browse the web to find the full answer to the question. (This will test the candidate's ability to quickly search online and find a solution to a problem without spending hours reinventing the wheel.)

▪ How many "useful" votes will a Yelp review receive?

▪ Can you estimate and forecast sales for any book, based on Amazon.com public data? **Hint**: See http://www.fonerbooks.com/surfing.htm.

▪ This question is about experimental design (and a bit of computer science) using LEGOs®. Say you purchase two sets of LEGOs® (one set to build a car and a second set to build another car). Now assume that the overlap between the two sets is substantial. There are three different ways that you can build the two cars. The first step consists of sorting the pieces (LEGOs®) by color and maybe also by size. The three ways to proceed are:

1. Sequentially: Build one car at a time. This is the traditional approach.

2. Semi-parallel system: Sort all the pieces from both sets simultaneously so that the pieces will be blended. Some in the red pile will belong to car A; some will belong to car B. Then build the two cars sequentially, following the instructions in the accompanying leaflets.

3. In parallel: Sort all the pieces from both sets simultaneously, and build the two cars simultaneously, progressing simultaneously with the two sets of instructions.

Which is the most efficient way to proceed?

NOTE To test these assumptions and help you become familiar with the concept of distributed architecture, you can have your kid build two LEGO® cars, A and B, in parallel and then two other cars, C and D, sequentially. If the overlap between A and B (the proportion of LEGO® pieces that are identical in both A and B) is small, then the sequential approach will work best. Another concept that can be introduced is that building an 80-piece car takes more than twice as much time as building a 40-piece car. Why? (The same also applies to puzzles.)

- How can you design an algorithm to estimate the number of LinkedIn connections your colleagues have? The number is readily available on LinkedIn for your first-degree connections with up to 500 LinkedIn connections. However, if the number is above 500, it just says "500+." The number of shared connections between you and any of your LinkedIn connections is always available.

For this question, you are provided with the solution below as a learning tool. First, let's introduce some notations:

- A is you.

- B is one of your connections.

- y is your number of connections (easily available).

- x is the unknown number of connections that B has (unknown if x > 500).

- z is the number of shared connections between A and B (easily available).

- N is the size (number of LinkedIn members) of the LinkedIn cloud or large network you belong to (must be estimated).

  Basic formula: P(C is a shared connection) = P(C is connected to you) × P(C is connected to B) = (y/N) × (x/N) = (x × y) / (N × N). Thus x = (z × N) / y, or N = (x × y) / z.

  Step 1: Compute N

  To build the table shown in Figure 7-1, I sampled a few of my connections that have fewer than 500 connections to find out what x and z were. My number of connections is y=9,670.

  A first approximation (visual analytics without using any tool other than my brain!) yields N = (x × y) / z = (approx.) 500 × 9,670 / 5 = (approx.) 1 million. So my N is 1 million. Yours might be different. Note that the number of people on LinkedIn is well above 100 million.

x, for some of my connections	z, for some of my connections
476	6
448	1
171	0
134	0
345	7
490	12
230	3
56	0
138	1
411	3
366	2
333	9
88	1
464	11

Figure 7-1: Table of sampled x and z parameters

Step 2: Compute x for a specific connection

Using the formula $x = (z \times N) / y$, if a LinkedIn member shares 200 connections with me, he probably has approximately 20,000 connections, using $y=10{,}000$ rather than 9,670, as an approximation for my number of connections. If he shares only one connection with me, he's expected to have 100 connections. You can compute confidence intervals for x by first computing confidence intervals for N, by looking at the variations in the above table. You can also increase accuracy by using a variable N that depends on job title or location.

▪ How would you proceed to reverse engineer the popular BMP image format and create your own images byte by byte, with a programming language?

Testing Your Own Visual and Analytic Thinking

Here are some exercises you can do on your own that will help to prepare you for job interviews. These exercises are aimed at assessing your visual and analytic judgment.

Detecting Patterns with the Naked Eye

Look at the three charts (A, B, and C) shown in Figure 7-2. Two of them exhibit patterns. Which ones? Do you know that these charts are called *scatterplots*? Are there other ways to visually represent this type of data?

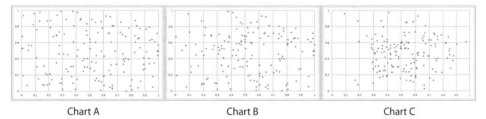

Chart A   Chart B   Chart C

Figure 7-2: Which charts exhibit no patterns?

It is clear that chart C exhibits a strong clustering pattern, unless you define your problem as points randomly distributed in an unknown domain whose boundary has to be estimated. So, the big question is: between charts A and B, which one represents randomness? Look at these charts closely for 60 seconds, then make a guess, and then read on. Note that all three charts contain the same number of points, so there's no scaling issue involved here.

Now assume that you are dealing with a spatial distribution of points over the entire 2-dimensional space, and that observations are seen through a small square window. For instance, points (observations) could be stars as seen on a picture taken from a telescope.

The first issue is that the data is censored: if you look at the distribution of nearest neighbor distances to draw conclusions, you must take into account that points near the boundary have fewer neighbors because some neighbors are outside the boundary. You can eliminate the bias by:

- Tiling the observation window to produce a mathematical tessellation.
- Mapping the square observation window onto the surface of a torus.
- Applying statistical bias-correction techniques.
- Using Monte Carlo simulations to estimate what the true distribution would be (with confidence intervals) if the data were truly random.

The second issue is that you need to use better visualization tools to see the patterns. Using + rather than a dot symbol to represent the points helps: some points are so close to each other that if you represent points with dots, you won't visually see the double points. (In our example, double points could correspond to double star systems—and these small-scale point interactions are part of what makes the distribution non-random in two of the charts.) But you can do much better: you could measure a number of metrics (averages, standard deviations, correlation between x and y, number of points in each subsquare, density estimates, and so on) and identify metrics proving that you are not dealing with pure randomness.

In these three charts, the standard deviation for either x or y—in case of pure randomness—should be 0.290 plus or minus 0.005. Only one of the three charts succeeds with this randomness test.

The third issue is that even if multiple statistical tests suggest that the data is truly random, it does not mean it actually is. For instance, all three charts show zero correlation between x and y and have mean x and y close to 0.50 (a requirement to qualify as random distribution in this case). However, only one chart exhibits randomness.

The fourth issue is that you need a mathematical framework to define and check randomness. True randomness is the realization of a Poisson stochastic process, and you need to use metrics that uniquely characterize a Poisson process to check whether a point distribution is truly random. Such metrics could be:

- The interpoint distance distributions.
- Number of observations in subsquares. (These counts should be uniformly distributed over the subsquares, and a chi-square test could provide the answer; however, in these charts, you don't have enough points in each subsquare to provide a valid test result.)

The fifth issue is that some of the great metrics (distances between k and its nearest neighbors) might not have a simple mathematical formula. But you can use Monte Carlo simulations to address this issue: simulate a random process, compute the distribution of distances (with confidence intervals) based on thousands of simulations, and compare with distances computed on your data. If distance distribution computed on the data set matches results from simulations, you are good; it means the data is probably random. However, you would have to make sure that distance distribution uniquely characterizes a Poisson process and that no non-random processes could yield the same distance distribution. This exercise is known as goodness-of-fit testing: you try to see if your data supports a specific hypothesis of randomness.

The sixth issue is that if you have a million points (and in high dimensions, you need more than a million points due to the curse of dimension), then you have a trillion distances to compute. No computer, not even in the cloud, can make all these computations in less than 1,000 years. So you need to pick up 10,000 points randomly, compute distances, and compare with equivalent computations based on simulated data. You need to make 1,000 simulations to get confidence intervals, but this is feasible.

Here's how the data in charts A, B, and C were created:

- Produce 158 random points [a(n), b(n)], n = 1,...,158
- Produce 158 random deviates u(n), v(n), n = 1,...,158
- Define x(n) as follows for n > 1: if u(n) < r, then x(n) = a(n), else x(n) = s × v(n) × a(n) + [1–s × v(n)] × x(n–1), with x(1) = a(1)
- Define y(n) as follows for n > 1: if u(n) < r, then y(n) = b(n), else y(n) = s × v(n) × b(n) + [1–s × v(n)] × y(n–1), with y(1) = b(1)
- Chart A: x(n) = a(n), y(n) = b(n)
- Chart B: r = 0.5, s = 0.3
- Chart C: r = 0.2, s = 0.8

The only chart exhibiting randomness is chart A. Chart B has significantly too low standard deviations for x and y, too few points near boundaries, and too many points that are close to each other. In addition, Chart A (the random distribution) exhibits a little bit of clustering, as well as some point alignments. This is, however, perfectly expected from a random distribution. If the number of points in each subsquare were identical, the distribution would not be random, but would correspond to a situation in which antagonist forces make points stay as far away as possible from each other. How would you test randomness if you had only two points (impossible to test), three points, or just 10 points?

Finally, once a pattern is detected (for example, abnormal close proximity between neighboring points), it should be interpreted and/or leveraged. That is, it should lead to, for example, ROI-positive trading rules if the framework is about stock trading or the conclusion that double stars do exist (based on chart B) if the framework is astronomy.

Identifying Aberrations

Pretend that I drew the picture shown in Figure 7-3, and then I told you that this is how Earth and its moon would be seen by a human being living on Saturn, which is 1 billion miles away from Earth. Earth's radius is approximately 4,000 miles, and the distance between Earth and its moon is approximately 200,000 miles. What would be your reaction? There's not a right or wrong answer; this simply checks your thought process.

Figure 7-3: Picture used for testing analytic reasoning

Potential answers include:

- The image is magnified. Earth is too small to be seen from Saturn with the naked eye, unless brightly illuminated by the sun. It is a false colors image.
- The distance between Earth and the moon seems too big seen from Saturn. Earth might not even be visible with the naked eye from Saturn. Maybe the sun would look as big and as bright as Earth on this picture from Saturn.
- The size of the moon is too big, compared to Earth.
- Why is the moon as bright as Earth and why is Earth brighter than any other stars?
- Where are all the stars?

Misleading Time Series and Random Walks

Many time series charts seem to exhibit a pattern: an uptrend, apparent periodicity, or a stochastic process that seems not to be memoryless, and so on. The picture shown in Figure 7-4 represents stock price simulations, with the X-axis representing time (days) and the Y-axis the simulated stock price.

Figure 7-4: Stock price simulation

Do you think there is an uptrend in the data? Actually, in the long term, there isn't; it's a realization of a pure random walk. At any time, the chance that it goes up or down by a given amount is exactly 50 percent. Yet, for short-term periods, it is perfectly normal to observe ups and downs. It does not make this time series predictable: you could try to design a predictive model trained on the first 1,000 observations and then test it on the remaining 1,000 observations. You would notice that your model is not better (for predicting up and down movements) than randomly throwing dice.

Another test you can do to familiarize yourself with how randomness and lack of randomness look is to simulate auto-regressive time series. One of the most basic processes is $X(t) = a \times X(t{-}1) + b \times X(t{-}2) + E + c$, where t is time, c is a constant ($-0.25 < c < +0.25$), and E is an error term (white noise) simulated as a uniform deviate on $[-1, +1]$. For instance, $X(t)$ represents a stock price at time t. You can start with $X(0) = X(1) = 0$. If $a + b = 1$, then the process is stable in equilibrium. Why? If $c < 0$, there is a downward trend. If $c > 0$, there is an upward trend. If $c = 0$, it does not go up or down (stationary process). If $a = b = 0$, the process is memory-free; there's no stochastic pattern embedded into it—it's just pure noise. Try producing some of these charts with various values for a, b, and c and see if you visually notice the pattern and can correctly interpret it. In Figure 7-4, $c = 0$, $b = 0$, $a = 1$. Of course, with some values of a, b, and c, the patterns are visually obvious. But if you keep both c and a + b close to zero, it is visually a more difficult exercise, and you might have to look at a long time frame for your brain to recognize the correct pattern. Try detecting the patterns with a predictive algorithm, and see when and if your brain can beat your predictive model.

From Statistician to Data Scientist

Recently a long thread grew on LinkedIn about why statisticians are not involved in big data and how to remedy the situation. You can read the entire discussion at http://bit.ly/197Jsfa. At the time of this writing, it had 160 comments from leading data scientists and statisticians. Here I mention those comments that I think will be most beneficial in helping you understand (particularly if you are a statistician) what you can do to make yourself highly marketable.

Data Scientists Are Also Statistical Practitioners

Statistics does not deal enough with applied computational aspects critical for big data, or with the business aspects that are critical for getting business value out of data. Statisticians should acquire business acumen, including being able to carry out tasks traditionally performed by business analysts, especially when working for a small company or tech startup. (The discussions on digital analytics in Chapter 6 show examples of this.) It will also be helpful for the statistician to acquire more engineering and computer science knowledge, including APIs, Python, MapReduce, NoSQL, and even Hadoop architecture—at least having a general understanding of these techniques and languages and how they impact data access, data storage, algorithm efficiency, and data processing.

Statisticians are well-equipped to make the transition to data science since they typically have critical skills that many data scientists lack, such as design of experiments, sampling, and R.

For those who believe that big data and data science are just pure engineering or computer science fields with ignorance of or poor application of statistics, you are now reading the book that will debunk this myth. In this book, you learn that data science has its own core of statistics and statistical research. For instance, in Chapter 2, "Big Data Is Different," you considered that in big data, you are bound to find spurious correlations when you compute billions or trillions of correlations. Such spurious correlations overshadow real correlations that go undetected. Instead of looking at correlations, you should compare correlograms. Correlograms uniquely determine if two time series are similar, which correlations do not do. You also learned about normalizing for size. You don't need to be a statistician to identify these issues and biases and correct them. A data scientist should know these things too, as well as other things such as experimental design, applied extreme value theory and Monte Carlo simulations, confidence intervals created without underlying statistical model (as in the Analyticbridge First Theorem), identifying non-randomness, and much more.

You can be both a data scientist and a statistician at the same time, just like you can be a data scientist and an entrepreneur at the same time—and actually, it is a requirement. It's certainly not incompatible; you just have to be aware that the official image of statisticians as pictured in ASA publications or on job boards does not represent (for now at least) the reality of what many statisticians do.

Still, data science and statistics are different. Many of the data science books can give you the impression that they are one and the same, but it's because the authors just reused old information (not even part of data science), added a bit of R or Python, and put a new name on it. I call this *fake data science*. Likewise, data science without statistics (or with reckless application of statistical principles) is not real data science either.

In the end, everyone has their own idea of what data science, statistics, computer science, BI, and entrepreneurship are. You decide what you want to call yourself. As for me, I'm clearly no longer a statistician, but rather a data scientist. (I was a computational statistician to begin with anyway.) My knowledge and expertise are different from those of a statistician. (It's probably closer to computer science.) And although I have a good knowledge of experimental design, Monte Carlo, sampling, and so on, most of it I did *not* learn at school or in a training program. The knowledge is available for free on the Internet. Anybody—a lawyer, a politician, a geographer—can acquire it without attending statistics classes.

NOTE Part of the Data Science Central data science apprenticeship is to make this knowledge accessible to a broader group of people. My intuitive Analyticbridge Theorem on model-free confidence intervals is an example of one "statistical" tool designed to be understood by a 12-year-old, with no mathematical prerequisite and applied in big data environments with tons of data buckets.

Who Should Teach Statistics to Data Scientists?

Statistics in data science can be built from within by data scientists or brought in by outsiders (those who don't want to be called data scientists and call themselves, for example, statisticians). I am an example of an insider creating a culture of statistics inside data science. Some people like contributions from outsider statisticians, whereas others like insider contributions because the insider is already familiar with data science, understands the difference between statistics and data science, and tends to be close to the businesspeople.

Hiring Issues

While many interesting positions are offered by various government agencies and large non-governmental organizations, the creative data scientist might face a few challenges, and might thrive better in a startup environment. Some of these challenges (also preventing employers from attracting more candidates) are:

- Bureaucracy often discourages people from applying. For example, security clearance requirements (eliminating Green Card holders and applicants from abroad; if you are an applicant, acquiring United States citizenship will open far more positions to you).

- The location is not desirable or flexible. If you apply for a position in a location that fewer applicants would like to relocate to, your likelihood of finding a job increases. Nowadays, a few employers offer telecommuting positions to increase their chances of attracting the best talent. (Employers take note: you might consider this option when hiring a data scientist.)

Data Scientists Work Closely with Data Architects

Statisticians should gain some familiarity with how to design a database: metrics to use (exact definitions), how they are captured, and how granular you need to be when keeping old data. This is part of data science. It involves working closely with DB engineers and data architects. Data scientists must have some of the knowledge of data architects and also of business people to understand exactly what they do and what they are going to capture. Data scientists should also be involved in dashboard design. Typically, all these things are tasks that many statisticians don't want to do or believe are not part of their job.

Who Should Be Involved in Strategic Thinking?

Discussing the question is the first critical, fundamental step in any project. Not doing it is like building a skyscraper without a foundation. But flexibility should be allowed. If something does not work as expected, how can you rebuild or change the project? How do you adapt to change? Is the design flexible enough to adapt? Who's in charge of defining the project and its main feature?

While business analysts (when present in your company, which is the case in larger organizations) and executives are eventually responsible for defining KPIs and dashboard design, the data scientist must get involved and communicate with these businesspeople (especially in organizations with fewer than 500 employees), rather than working in isolation. Data scientists should also communicate with data architects, product managers, and engineers/software engineers.

Such communication is crucial for several reasons: to help the data scientist to understand the business problem and gain business acumen and necessary domain expertise, to make technical implementations smoother, to influence company leaders by making recommendations to boost robustness and help them gain analytics acumen themselves, and so on. This two-way communication is useful to optimize business processes.

Two Types of Statisticians

In my opinion, there are two types of statisticians: those who associate themselves with the ASA (American Statistical Association), and those do not. Likewise, there are two types of big data practitioners:

- Those who know little about stats, but know far more than statisticians in other fundamental areas of big data.

- Those who know as much as the best statisticians in the world with statistical knowledge oriented toward data science.

I advise statisticians to apply for positions with teams that do not have strong statistical knowledge. (You can assess the team's level of competency by asking questions during the interview, such as what kind of statistical analyses they do.) You will better shine if you can convince them of the value of sampling, mathematical modeling, experimental design, imputation techniques, identifying and dealing with bad data, survival analysis, and sound confidence intervals, and show real examples of added value.

Also, when interviewing for a data scientist position (or when the interviewer is not a statistician), do not use excessive statistical jargon during the interview, but rather discuss the benefits of simple models. For example, the statistical concept of *p-value* is rarely used in data science, not because of ignorance but because data science uses different terms and different metrics, even though it serves a similar purpose. In data science contexts, many times there are no underlying models. You do model-free inference, such as predictions, confidence intervals, and so on, which are data-driven with no statistical model. So a data scientist interviewer will be more receptive to discussions of simple models.

> **NOTE** Instead of p-values, I invite you to use alternatives, such as the model-free confidence intervals discussed in Chapter 5. This equivalent approach is easy to understand by non-statisticians. In another context, I use predictive power (a metric easily understood by non-statisticians, as discussed in Chapter 6) as a different, simpler, model-free approach to p-value. Also, when talking to clients, you need to use words they understand, not jargon like p-value.

Data scientists also do EDA (exploratory data analysis), but it's not something done by statisticians exclusively. (See the section Data Dictionary in Chapter 5.) As a statistician, you should easily understand this data dictionary concept, and you may already be using it when dealing with larger data sets. Indeed, I believe that the EDA process could be automated, to a large extent, with the creation of a data dictionary being the first step of such an automation.

Using Big Data Versus Sampling

Sometimes you need the entire data set. When you create a system to estimate the value of every single home in the United States, you probably want the entire data set being part of the analysis; millions of people each day are checking millions of houses and neighboring houses for comparison shopping. In this case, it makes sense to use all the data. If your database had only 10 percent of all historical prices, sure, you could do some inference (though you would miss a lot of the local patterns), but 90 percent of the time, when a user entered an address to get a price estimate, he would also have to provide square footage, sales history, number of bathrooms, school rankings, and so on. In short, this application (Zillow.com) would be useless.

Examples of observational data where sampling is not allowed include:

- Credit card processing: each single transaction must be approved or declined.

- Book recommendations on Amazon.com: each book and each user must be a part of the data set.

- Price estimates for each house.

- High-frequency trading (trillions of tiny bins of data: the more data per bin, the better).

- Friends and other recommendations on social networks.

- E-mail categorization: spam, not spam. Each single piece of e-mail must be processed.

- Sensor data: higher resolution and frequency provide better predictive power.

- Customized hotel room pricing for each online request to book a room.

- Keyword bidding: each of 1 billion keywords must be priced right, in real time.

- Keyword correlations: find all keywords related to specific keywords. Needed in search engine technology or for keyword taxonomy, for billions of searches entered daily by users.

- Ad relevancy: matching an ad with a user and a web page, billions of times a day and individually for each page request.

- News feed aggregator: detection, categorization, and management of millions of microblog postings to deliver high-quality news to syndicated partners. Each posting counts.

Taxonomy of a Data Scientist

Understanding the taxonomy of a data scientist can help you identify areas of potential interest for your data science career. This discussion is the result of a data science project I did recently, and it is slightly more technical than the previous section. If you like, you can skip the technicalities and focus on the main conclusions of the discussion. But since this is a data science book, I thought it good to provide some details about the methodology that I used to come to my conclusions.

The key point of this discussion is to help you determine which technical domains you should consider specializing in based on your background. You can identify (with statistical significance) the main technical sub-domains related to data science (machine learning, data mining, big data, analytics, and so on) by attaching a weight to each domain based on data publicly available on LinkedIn.

Also provided is a list of several well-known, successful data scientists. You can further check their profiles to better understand what successful data scientists actually do. Finally, I explain cross-correlations among top domains, since all of them overlap, some quite substantially.

Data Science's Most Popular Skill Mixes

I present here the results of a study I conducted on LinkedIn, in which I used my own LinkedIn account, which has 8,000+ data science connections, to identify the skills most frequently associated with data science, as well as the top data scientists on LinkedIn. The following lists were created by searching for data scientists with 10+ data science skill endorsements on LinkedIn, and analyzing the top five skills that they list on their profile.

The statistical validity of data science–related skills is strong, whereas validity is weak for top data scientists. The reason is that you need to have at least 10 endorsements for your LinkedIn data science profile in the skills section to be listed as a top data scientist in the following list. Some pioneering data scientists are not listed because they did not add data science skills to their LinkedIn profile, for the same reason that you are not listed in top big data people lists based on Twitter hashtags if you don't use Twitter hashtags in your Tweets or if you do not Tweet at all.

Figure 7-5 shows the list of data science related skills (DS stands for Data Science). In short, you could write the data science equation as:

Data Science = 0.24 * Data Mining + 0.15 * Machine Learning + 0.14 * Analytics + 0.11 * Big Data +...

Skill	# People	Association with DS	Percent
Data Mining	10	139.54	27.3%
Machine Learning	4	58.79	11.5%
Analytics	6	69.69	13.6%
Big Data	7	53.82	10.5%
Predictive Analytics	3	33.27	6.5%
Data Analysis	4	29.86	5.8%
Predictive Modeling	2	24.13	4.7%
Hadoop	2	14.56	2.8%
Text Mining	1	14.33	2.8%
Statistics	1	13.09	2.6%
Natural Language Processing	1	11.67	2.3%
Start-Ups	1	10.43	2.0%
Algorithms	1	8.18	1.6%
Distributed Systems	1	6.50	1.3%
Map Reduce	1	5.56	1.1%
Data Warehousing	1	4.89	1.0%
Business Intelligence	1	4.29	0.8%
SQL	1	3.18	0.6%
R	1	2.83	0.6%
Scalability	1	2.72	0.5%

Figure 7-5: Top data science skills and related areas

Note that, surprisingly, visualization does not appear at the top. This is because visualization, just like UNIX, is perceived either as a tool (for example, Tableau) or sometimes as a soft skill, rather than a hard skill, technique, or field, and thus it is frequently mentioned as a skill on LinkedIn profiles but not in the top five. Computer science is also missing, probably because it is too broad a field, and instead people will list (in their profile) a narrower field such as data mining or machine learning.

Figure 7-6 shows how (from a quantitative point of view) related skills contribute to data science, broken down per skill and per person. (This is used to compute the summary table shown in Figure 7-5.) For instance, the first row reads: Monica Rogati lists data science as skill #3 in her LinkedIn profile; she is endorsed by 61 people for data science and by 106 people for machine learning. The machine learning contribution to data science coming from her is 106/3 = 35.33. The people listed in the following table (Figure 7-6) are data science pioneers—among the top data scientists, according to LinkedIn.

The full list, based on the top 10 data scientists identified on LinkedIn, can be downloaded at `http://bit.ly/1iRJXQC`.

Skill	Name	Endorsements	DS Skill Rank	DS Endorsements	Skill Association with DS
Machine Learning	Monica Rogati	106	3	61	35.33
Analytics	Vincent Granville	474	16	44	29.63
Data Mining	Vincent Granville	421	16	44	26.31
Data Mining	Monica Rogati	77	3	61	25.67
Analytics	DJ Patil	141	7	56	20.14
Predictive Modeling	Vincent Granville	292	16	44	18.25
Data Mining	DJ Patil	125	7	56	17.86
Data Mining	Kirk Borne	176	11	46	16.00
Predictive Analytics	Vincent Granville	252	16	44	15.75
Data Mining	DJ Patil	108	7	56	15.43
Data Mining	Gregory Piatetsky-Shapiro	137	9	24	15.22
Data Analysis	DJ Patil	102	7	56	14.57
Text Mining	Monica Rogati	43	3	61	14.33
Big Data	Monica Rogati	42	3	61	14.00
Big Data	Vincent Granville	223	16	44	13.94
Machine Learning	Kirk Borne	152	11	46	13.82
Statistics	Kirk Borne	144	11	46	13.09
Natural Language Processing	Monica Rogati	35	3	61	11.67
Hadoop	Milind Bhandarkar	194	18	10	10.78
Start-Ups	DJ Patil	73	7	56	10.43

Figure 7-6: Contributors to data science skill mix

Alternative Formula

If, for each skill, instead of summing Endorsements(person, skill)/DS_Skill_Rank(person) over the 10 persons listed in the spreadsheet, you sum SQRT{ Endorsements(person, skill) * DS_Endorsements(person) } over the same 10 persons, then you obtain a slightly different mix illustrated in the following:

Data Science = 0.22 * Data Mining + 0.12 * Machine Learning + 0.13 * Analytics + 0.11 * Big Data +...

Whether you use the first or second formula, you are dealing with three parameters, n, m, and k:

- You looked only at the top n = 5 skills (besides data science) for each person.
- You ignored people with less than m = 10 endorsements for data science.
- You looked only at the k = 10 top persons.

The most complicated problem is to identify all professionals with at least 10 endorsements for data science on LinkedIn. It can be solved by using a list of 100 well-known data scientists as seed persons, and then looking at first-degree, second-degree, and third-degree-related persons. "Finding related people" means accessing the LinkedIn feature that tells you "people who visit X's profile also visit Y's profile" and extracting endorsement counts and skills, for each person, using a web crawler.

> **WHICH IS BEST?**
>
> In your opinion, which formula is best from a methodology point of view? The first one, or the alternative? Not surprisingly, they both yield similar results. I like the second one better.
>
> A good exercise would be to find the equivalent formulas for data mining, big data, machine learning, and so on. It's important to remember that people can be more than just data scientists—for instance, a data scientist and a musician at the same time. This explains why the skill rank, for anybody, is rarely if ever #1 for data science: even I get far more endorsements for data mining or analytics than for data science, in part because data science is relatively new.

Skills Interactions

Machine learning is part of data mining (at least for some people). Data mining and machine learning both involve analytics, big data, and data science. Big data involves analytics, data mining, machine learning, data science, and so on. So how do you handle skill interactions? Should you have multiple equations, one for data science, one for data mining, one for big data, and so on, and try to solve a linear system of equations? Each equation could be obtained using the same methodology used for the data science equation. I'll leave it to you as an exercise.

Hilary Mason (at the time of writing) has data science as skill #4, with 49 endorsements and the following top skills:

- Machine Learning (104 endorsements)
- Data Mining (64 endorsements)
- Python (54 endorsements)
- Big Data (48 endorsements)
- Natural Language Processing (28 endorsements)

So she should definitely be in the top 10, yet she does not show up when doing a Data Science search using my LinkedIn account, although she is a second-degree connection. If you add her to the list, now Python will pop up as a data science-related skill, with a low weight, but above R or SQL.

Top Data Scientists on LinkedIn

Some of the top data scientists in the world and their areas of interest are discussed in this section. The list is summarized in Figure 7-7.

The 10 pioneering data scientists listed here were identified as top data scientists based on their LinkedIn profiles. For each of them, I computed the number of LinkedIn endorsements for the top four data science–related skills: analytics, big data, data mining, and machine learning (these skills were identified as most strongly linked to data science, as discussed in the previous section). Then I normalized the counts so that each is expressed as a ratio between 0 and 1, and for each individual the total aggregated count over the four skills is 100 percent. This approach makes the classification easier.

	Analytics	Big Data	Data Mining	Data Mining
DJ Patil	0.34	0.09	0.30	0.26
Dean Abbott	0.24	0.02	0.46	0.27
Eric Colson	0.28	0.38	0.27	0.08
Gregory Piatetsky-Shapiro	0.21	0.24	0.40	0.16
Kirk Borne (1)	0.00	0.15	0.45	0.39
Marck Vaisman	0.28	0.17	0.42	0.13
Milind Bhandarkar	0.09	0.54	0.12	0.25
Monica Rogati	0.09	0.17	0.31	0.43
Simon (Ximeng) Zhang (2)	0.53	0.14	0.32	0.00
Vincent Granville	0.38	0.18	0.34	0.10

Figure 7-7: Top data scientists on LinkedIn with skill mix

Note that the correlation between machine learning and analytics is very negative (–0.82). Likewise, the correlation between big data and data mining is very negative (–0.80). All other cross-skill correlations are negligible. Other notable items include the following:

- Kirk Borne's skill set is highly fragmented. Analytics is not listed, but many analytics-related skills are.

- Simon Zhang's profile experienced a spike in analytics endorsements when I completed the second part of this analysis. The spike could be a data glitch.

The big data/machine learning combo exhibits the strongest cluster structure among the six potential scatterplots. Milind Bhandarkar (Pivotal's Chief Scientist), and to a lesser extent Eric Colson (former VP of Data Science and Engineering at Netflix), are outliers, both strong in big data.

- Kirk Borne (Professor of Computer Science at George Mason University) and Monica Rogati (VP of Data at Jawbone) constitute one cluster, with strong machine learning recognition.

- DJ Patil (former LinkedIn Chief Scientist) and Dean Abbott (President, Abbott Analytics) belong to an intermediate cluster, with good machine learning skills but not known for big data.

- Simon Zhang (LinkedIn Director, previously at eBay, not a machine learning guy), as well as closely related—at least on the graph—Gregory Piatetski-Shapiro (KDnuggets Founder), Vincent Granville (Data Science Central Co-Founder), and Marck Vaisman (EMC), constitute the remaining cluster.

IS THIS BIG DATA ANALYSIS?

Yes and no. Yes, because I extracted what I wanted out of Terabytes of LinkedIn data, leveraging my expertise to minimize the amount of work and data processing required. No, because it did not involve massive data transfers—the information being well organized and easy to efficiently access. After all, you could say it's tiny data with just 10 observations and four variables. But that 10x4 table is a summary table. Identifying the data scientist with the most endorsements on LinkedIn isn't easy, unless you have domain expertise.

I performed what I would call "manual clustering." You could say that my analysis is light analytics. How much better (or worse!) can you do using heavy analytics: by extracting far more data from LinkedIn (200 people selected out of 5,000, with 10 metrics), and applying a real (not manual) clustering algorithm? Which metric would you use to assess the lift created by heavy analytics as opposed to light analytics?

Who Is the "Purest" Data Scientist?

I compared the four-skill mix of each of these 10 data scientists with a generic data science skill mix (Data Science = 0.24 * Data Mining + 0.15 * Machine Learning + 0.14 * Analytics + 0.11 * Big Data). In short, I computed 10 correlations (one per data scientist) to determine who best represents data science. The results are shown in Figure 7-8.

	DS Purity
DJ Patil	0.55
Dean Abbott	0.93
Eric Colson	-0.18
Gregory Piatetsky-Shapiro	0.83
Kirk Borne	0.70
Marck Vaisman	0.84
Milind Bhandarkar	-0.63
Monica Rogati	0.41
Simon (Ximeng) Zhang	0.20
Vincent Granville	0.43

Figure 7-8: "Purest" data scientists on LinkedIn

Dean Abbott is closest to the "average" (which I define as the "purest"), whereas Milind Bhandarkar (a big data, Hadoop guy) is farthest from the "center." Despite repeated claims (by myself and others) that I am a pure data scientist, I score only 0.43. (Sure, I'm also some kind of product/marketing/finance/entrepreneur guy, not just a data scientist, but these extra skills were isolated from my experiment.) Surprisingly, Kirk Borne, known as an astrophysicist, scores high in the data science purity index. So does Gregory Piatetsky-Shapiro, who is known as a data miner.

400 Data Scientist Job Titles

I looked at more than 10,000 data scientists in my network of LinkedIn connections and found that most data scientists (including me) don't use the title "data scientist" to describe their job. So what are the most popular job titles used for data scientists? Below is a list of many of the job titles I found for "director" and "chief" positions. But keep in mind that, for every director, there are multiple junior and mid-level data scientists working on the same team and, thus, they would have similar job titles (minus "chief" or "director"). Also remember that many data scientists are consultants, principals, founders, CEOs, professors, students, software engineers, and so on.

Chiefs:

- Actuary of GeoSpatial Analytics and Modeling
- Analytic Officer
- Analytics and Algorithms Officer
- Credit and Analytics Officer
- Data and Analytics Officer
- Research and Analytics Officer
- Scientist, Global Head of Analytics
- Vice President of Analytics
- Technology Officer, Enterprise Information Management and Analytics
- Client Director, Business Analytics

Directors:

- Analytics
- Analytic Science
- Analytics Delivery
- BI and Analytics
- Fraud Analytics and R&D
- Predictive Analytics
- Analytics and Creative Strategy
- Marketing Analytics
- Digital Analytics
- Advanced Analytics
- Analytic Consulting, Product/Data Loyalty Analytics
- Analytic Solutions
- Data Analytics and Advertising Platforms

- Digital Analytics and Customer Insight
- Health Analytics
- Innovation, Big Data Analytics
- Product Analytics
- Risk Analytics and Policy
- Science and Analytics for Enterprise Marketing Management (EMM)
- Web Analytics and Optimization
- Advanced Strategic Analytics
- Analytic Strategy
- Analytical Services
- Big Data Analytics and Segmentation
- Business Analytics
- Business Analytics and Decision Management Strategy
- Business Intelligence and Analytics
- Business Planning and Analytics
- Clinical Analytics
- Customer Analytics
- Customer Analytics and Pricing
- Customer Insights and Business Analytics
- Data Analytics
- Data Science and Analytics Practice
- Data Warehousing and Analytics
- Database Marketing and Analytics (Marketing)
- DVD BI and Analytics
- Gamification Analytics Platform, Information Analytics and Innovation
- Global Digital Marketing Analytics
- Group Analytics
- Forensic Data Analytics
- Marketing Analytics
- Predictive Analytic Applications
- Reporting/Analytics
- Risk and Analytics
- Risk and Business Analytics

- Statistical Modeling and Analytics
- Statistics and Project Analytics/Senior Analytic Consultant
- Strategic Analytics
- Web Analytics
- The full list can be accessed at `http://bit.ly/11WhOcu`.

Salary Surveys

This section provides data about salaries and the number of open positions for various big data skills in several major cities worldwide.

CROSS-REFERENCE Chapter 3, "Becoming a Data Scientist," presents a brief overview of salary surveys along with a link to comprehensive information (`http://bit.ly/19vA0n1`). Sample job descriptions and resumes, as well as companies hiring data scientists, are provided in Chapter 8, "Data Science Resources."

The following data was obtained in December 2013 from the job search website Indeed.com. (You can find the search results at `http://bit.ly/1dmCouo`.) Hadoop, a fast-growing data science skill listed in many job ads, is compared with other IT skills, including big data, Python, Java, SQL, and others, in different locales. Note that in these search results, an exact match is shown in quotes (for example, "data science") whereas a broad match does not contain quotes. The discrepancy between the results for "data science" and data science is huge because data scientists can have hundreds of different job titles, as seen in the previous section. The results for "big data" are 15 times smaller than the results for big data. Also note that San Francisco is the hub for big data, Hadoop, data science, and so on. But location #2 could be London, where there are more jobs and better salaries than in New York City.

Salary Breakdown by Skill and Location

The information presented here shows you what tools are available to help you find numerous job openings, where large numbers of jobs are located geographically, and the general salary overview for different data science skills. The numbers in parentheses represent the number of openings listed for each salary.

Hadoop – San Francisco, CA

- $60,000+ (2,196)
- $80,000+ (1,669)
- $100,000+ (865)

- $120,000+ (422)
- $140,000+ (210)

Hadoop – Seattle, WA

- $50,000+ (349)
- $70,000+ (248)
- $90,000+ (122)
- $110,000+ (47)
- $130,000+ (9)

Hadoop – New York, NY

- $60,000+ (781)
- $80,000+ (557)
- $100,000+ (358)
- $120,000+ (204)
- $140,000+ (121)

Hadoop – Chicago, IL

- $50,000+ (194)
- $70,000+ (150)
- $90,000+ (84)
- $110,000+ (40)
- $130,000+ (24)

Hadoop – Los Angeles, CA

- $50,000+ (320)
- $70,000+ (238)
- $90,000+ (113)
- $110,000+ (65)
- $130,000+ (29)

Hadoop – London, UK

- £40,000+ (619)
- £60,000+ (351)
- £80,000+ (170)
- £100,000+ (97)
- £120,000+ (37)

Big Data – San Francisco, CA

- $60,000+ (4,388)
- $80,000+ (3,268)
- $100,000+ (1,735)
- $120,000+ (867)
- $140,000+ (433)

"Big Data" – San Francisco, CA

- $60,000+ (2,630)
- $80,000+ (1,990)
- $100,000+ (1,075)
- $120,000+ (581)
- $140,000+ (296)

Data Science – San Francisco, CA

- $50,000+ (10,000)
- $70,000+ (7,739)
- $90,000+ (4,535)
- $110,000+ (2,060)
- $130,000+ (965)

"Data Science" – San Francisco, CA

- $50,000+ (320)
- $70,000+ (219)
- $90,000+ (152)
- $110,000+ (68)
- $130,000+ (24)

Python – San Francisco, CA

- $60,000+ (5,880)
- $80,000+ (4,024)
- $100,000+ (1,757)
- $120,000+ (761)
- $140,000+ (296)

SQL – San Francisco, CA

- $60,000+ (7,455)
- $80,000+ (5,206)

- $100,000+ (2,348)
- $120,000+ (1,040)
- $140,000+ (420)

Java – San Francisco, CA

- $60,000+ (10,266)
- $80,000+ (7,675)
- $100,000+ (3,527)
- $120,000+ (1,547)
- $140,000+ (649)

Perl – San Francisco, CA

- $60,000+ (3,850)
- $80,000+ (2,528)
- $100,000+ (1,119)
- $120,000+ (445)
- $140,000+ (187)

Statistician – San Francisco, CA

- $50,000+ (163)
- $70,000+ (111)
- $90,000+ (65)
- $110,000+ (33)
- $130,000+ (20)

"Data Mining" – San Francisco, CA

- $50,000+ (1,063)
- $70,000+ (772)
- $90,000+ (453)
- $110,000+ (257)
- $130,000+ (121)

"Data Miner" – San Francisco, CA

- No data available

A great source for salary surveys, some broken down by experience level, can be found at `http://bit.ly/19vA0n1`.

Create Your Own Salary Survey

You can use the same Indeed.com website, modifying the search keyword and location in the search box, to find the number of positions and salary breakdown in any locale, for any data science-related occupation. (See previous sections to identify potential job titles.) Many positions can be found on LinkedIn and AnalyticTalent, but competition is fierce (hundreds of applicants per opening) for jobs in the following companies: Google, Twitter, Netflix, PayPal, eBay, LinkedIn, Facebook, Yahoo, Apple—typically companies involved in data science since its beginnings—as well as Intel, Pivotal, IBM, Microsoft, Amazon.com, and a few others. Unknown companies or companies located in less popular cities (for instance, banks or insurance companies in Ohio) attract much fewer candidates—fewer than 50 per job ad. Startups are also a good source of jobs.

Other sources of career information include Glassdoor.com and Wetfeet.com.

Summary

This chapter focused on helping you get employed as a data scientist. It discussed more than 90 job interview questions, tests to assess your analytic and visual skills, guidance on transitioning from statistician to data scientist, top data scientists and data science–related skills, typical job titles for data scientists, and salary surveys. It also included a few small data science project examples.

In the next and final chapter, you can find several resources useful for current and aspiring data scientists: conference listings, sample resumes and job ads, data science books, definitions, data sets, organizations, popular websites, companies with many data scientists, and so on.

Data Science Resources

The previous chapter focused on helping you get employed as a data scientist. In this chapter, you will find numerous resources that will be of value to you in your professional life and your career-building efforts.

Professional Resources

This section provides information on resources to help you in your data science career, including data sets, books, conferences, organizations, websites, and important definitions.

CROSS-REFERENCE Chapter 3, "Becoming a Data Scientist," covers training programs, courses, and certifications.

See the sections History and Pioneers in Chapter 1, and The Big Data Ecosystem in Chapter 2 for details on vendors.

See the section Taxonomy of a Data Scientist in Chapter 7 for information on today's top data scientists.

Data Sets

Data Science Central has several data sets available at `http://bit.ly/W2HTJU`, including the following:

- Source code and data for your big data keyword correlation API (also see the section Source Code for Keyword Correlation API in Chapter 5).

- Great statistical analysis: forecasting meteorite hits (also see the section Forecasting Meteorite Hits in Chapter 6).

- 53.5-billion-clicks data set available for benchmarking and testing.

- More than 5,000,000 financial, economic, and social data sets.

- New pattern to predict stock prices and multiplies return by factor 5 (stock market data, S&P 500; see the section Stock Market in Chapter 6).

- 3.5 billion web pages: the graph has been extracted from the Common Crawl 2012 web corpus and covers 3.5 billion web pages and 128 billion hyperlinks between these pages.

- Another large data set: 250 million data points. This is the full resolution GDELT event data set running from January 1, 1979, through March 31, 2013, and containing all data fields for each event record.

- 125 years of public health data available for download.

You can find additional data sets at the Harvard University Data Science website at `http://cs109.org/resources.php`. I was particularly interested in their Linked Data resources at `http://linkeddata.org/`. Information on Harvard's data science course featuring these resources can be found at `http://bit.ly/1hU8O5l`.

KDnuggets is also a great resource and can be accessed at `http://www` `.kdnuggets.com/datasets/index.html` and `http://bit.ly/18U6fNw`. Additional resources include `http://data.gov.uk/` and similar initiatives in the United States (see `http://onforb.es/1mOW8cU`).

Books

Books useful for data scientists can be broken down into a few categories: visualization, big data/Hadoop, statistics/machine learning, pure data science, business analytics, data science for decision makers (recruiting and managing projects), and a few others.

Data Science Central lists 100+ books at `http://bit.ly/179em2h` and `http://` `www.analyticbridge.com/group/books`.

Following are some of the titles and references listed on these two web pages. These titles were recommended and acclaimed in data science circles such as KDnuggets, and are popular in the Data Science Central community. Details (book description, authors, date, and so on) can be found on the referenced web pages, along with direct links to resellers (Amazon.com in many cases) to allow you to find and buy the book quickly. Some of the listed titles are journals, and some are bundles (for instance, five books on data visualization), and quite a few are available for free as PDF documents.

These books are general, rather than being specialized for a specific industry or problem. A more comprehensive list, including specialized books, is available on the above web pages.

Business

- *Data Science for Business*, O'Reilly, 2013
- *Big Data Computing*, CRC Press, 2013
- *Past, Present, and Future of Statistical Science*, CRC Press, 2014
- *The Field Guide to Data Science*, free PDF document, by Booz Allen Hamilton, 2013
- *Implementing Analytics*, Elsevier, 2013
- *Automate This: How Algorithms Came to Rule Our World*, Portfolio Hardcover, 2012
- *Analyzing the Analyzers*, O'Reilly, 2013
- *Business Analytics: A Practitioner's Guide*, Springer, 2013
- *A Practitioner's Guide to Business Analytics*, McGraw-Hill, 2013
- *Delivering Business Analytics: Practical Guidelines for Best Practice*, Wiley, 2013
- *Building Data Science Teams*, O'Reilly, 2011

Technical

- *Practical Text Mining and Statistical Analysis for Non-structured Text Data Applications*, Academic Press, 2012
- *Data Mining*, Wiley-IEEE Press, 2011
- *Encyclopedia of Machine Learning*, Springer, 2010
- *Analyzing Data from Facebook, Twitter, LinkedIn, and Other Social Media*, O'Reilly, 2013
- *Ensemble Methods in Data Mining: Improving Accuracy Through Combining Predictions*, Morgan & Claypool Publishers, 2010
- *Causality: Models, Reasoning, and Inference*, Cambridge University Press, 2000
- Mining of Massive Datasets, download free copy at `http://infolab .stanford.edu/~ullman/mmds/booka.pdf`
- Applied Data Science, Columbia University course

■ *Forecasting: principles and practice*, 2013, download free copy at `https://www.otexts.org/fpp/`

■ *Alternative Methods of Regression*, John Wiley & Sons, 1993

Bundles

■ New computational statistics books for analyzing your data, eight CRC books, see `http://bit.ly/IUvPFu`

■ Two books on programming interviews, see `http://bit.ly/JZdgBn`

■ 60 statistics textbooks, see `http://bit.ly/1hnYZKa`

■ Five books on data visualization, see `http://bit.ly/1dtC8h0`

Programming Tools

■ *Big Data Analytics with R and Hadoop*, Packt Publishing, 2013

■ *Practical Data Science with R*, book in progress, see `http://www.manning.com/zumel/`.

■ *Predictive Analytics: Microsoft Excel*, Que Publishing, 2012

■ *Data Analysis with Open Source Tools*, O'Reilly, 2010

■ *Data Mining: Discovering and Visualizing Patterns with Python*, free download at `http://refcardz.dzone.com/refcardz/data-mining-discovering-and`

■ *Hadoop in Practice*, Manning Publications, 2012

■ *Hadoop: the Definitive Guide*, O'Reilly, 2012

Visualization

■ *Visualizing Data*, O'Reilly, 2007

Journals

■ *Big Data*, see `http://www.liebertpub.com/big`

■ *EPJ Data Science*, see `http://www.epjdatascience.com/`

■ *Journal of Data Science*, see `http://www.jds-online.com/`

■ *Data Science Journal*, see `http://www.codata.org/dsj/index.html`

■ *Decision Analytics*, Springer, see `http://decisionanalyticsjournal.com/`

■ *The R Journal*, see `http://journal.r-project.org/`

■ *Information Visualization*, see `http://ivi.sagepub.com/`

Conferences and Organizations

There are basically three types of organizations that are routinely involved in professional conferences: vendors, professional societies, and companies that organize conferences. Following are some of the key conferences and related organizations.

Vendors

SAS organizes the yearly Data Mining Conference. Pivotal organizes the Data Science Summit in partnership with VentureBeat and Data Science Central (`http://venturebeat.com/events/databeat2013/`). Other vendors such as Teradata, Hadoop (`http://hadoopsummit.org/`), Cloudera, Alpine Labs, and Hortonworks have their own events.

Professional Societies

There are two basic types of data science professional societies:

- Those such as IEEE or Direct Marketing Association (DMA, see `http://thedma.org`), with a focus much broader than data science, that recently started to organize analytics, big data, and data science events.
- Other societies more focused on analytics, such as INFORMS (operations research), American Statistical Association, Digital Analytics Association, and the International Institute for Analytics.

Conference Organizers

A few of the most active conference organizers include:

- IE Group organizes numerous big data, Hadoop, and business analytics conferences worldwide. (`http://theinnovationenterprise.com/summits/calendar`)
- O'Reilly organizes the "Strata" conferences. (`http://strataconf.com/`)
- Rising Media organizes various "Predictive Analytics World" conferences. (`http://www.predictiveanalyticsworld.com/`)
- FC Business Intelligence is known for its text mining conferences and others. (`http://www.datadrivenbiz.com/`)
- IQPC organizes "Big Data for Government & Defense." (`http://www.iqpc.com/`)
- White Hall Media organizes "Big Data Analytics" and other conferences. (`http://whitehallmedia.co.uk/wmconferences/`)

Websites

Data Science Central has put together a list of websites related to analytics, data science, or big data, based on input from Data Science Central members. (Each of these top domains was cited by at least four members.) The list includes vendors, publishers, universities, organizations, and personal blogs from well-known data scientists. Some of them are pure data science sites, whereas others are more general, but still tech-oriented with a strong emphasis on data issues at large, or regular data science content.

Since such a popular list is constantly evolving, it is available on the web at http://bit.ly/1ghDR7K so that you can always get the most current list. You might want to add your suggestions as well!

Definitions

Here are several selected terms that you need to understand and will likely use in your career. You can visit http://bit.ly/18UcD7c to find more details on them and names of the contributors to these definitions.

- **Adjusted R^2 (R-Squared)**: The method preferred by statisticians for determining which variables to include in a model. It is a modified version of R^2, which penalizes each new variable on the basis of how many have already been admitted. Due to its construct, R^2 will always increase as you add new variables, which results in models that over-fit the data and have poor predictive ability. Adjusted R^2 results in more parsimonious models that admit new variables only if the improvement in fit is larger than the penalty, which improves the ultimate goal of out-of-sample prediction.

- **Cluster analysis**: Methods to assign a set of objects into groups. These groups are called clusters, and objects in a cluster are more similar to each other than to those in other clusters. Well-known algorithms are hierarchical clustering, k-means, fuzzy clustering, and supervised clustering.

- **Cross-validation**: Cross-validation is a general computer-intensive approach used in estimating the accuracy of statistical models. The idea of cross-validation is to split the data into N subsets, to put one subset aside, to estimate parameters of the model from the remaining N-1 subsets, and to use the retained subset to estimate the error of the model. Such a process is repeated N times with each of the N subsets used as the validation set. Then the values of the errors obtained in such N steps are combined to provide the final estimate of the model error.

- **Decision trees**: A tree of questions to guide an end user to a conclusion based on values from a single vector of data. The classic example is a medical diagnosis based on a set of symptoms for a particular patient. A common problem in data science is to automatically or semi-automatically generate decision trees based on large sets of data coupled to known conclusions. Example algorithms are CART and ID3.

- **Design of experiments**: Also called experimental design. It is a methodology to sample, group observations, and test statistical models to detect root causes or influential predictive factors.

- **Exploratory Data Analysis**: Also called EDA. It is the first step in all statistical analyses after data has been gathered: looking at interaction, visualizations, and outlier detection, and summarizing the data using a data dictionary.

- **Factor analysis**: Used as a variable reduction technique to identify groups of clustered variables.

- **Feature selection**: A feature is a variable, and feature selection is about detecting, out of trillions of potential feature combinations, those that have a great predictive power and robustness (not sensitive to noise).

- **General Linear Model**: General (or Generalized) Linear Models (GLM), in contrast to linear models, allow you to describe both additive and non-additive relationships between a dependent variable and N independent variables. The independent variables in GLM may be continuous as well as discrete. (The dependent variable is often named *response*, and independent variables are named *factors* and *covariates*, depending on whether they are controlled or not.)

- **Goodness of fit**: The degree to which the predicted values created by a model minimize errors in cross-validation tests. However, over-fitting the data can be dangerous because it results in a model that will have no predictive power for fresh data. True goodness of fit is determined by how the model fits new data, for instance, its predictive ability.

- **Hadoop**: Open source framework that supports large-scale data analysis by allowing you to decompose questions into discrete chunks that can be executed independently, close to slices of the data in question, and ultimately reassembled into an answer to the question posed. It is a file management system more than a traditional database framework, though some SQL layers have been built on top of it.

- **Hidden decision trees**: Methodology designed to score transactional data. Blends linear and nonlinear classifiers, builds and blends multiple small decision trees (the nonlinear classifier) implicitly, and eventually merges and recalibrates two scores to produce a unique score. Fast and efficient but requires expertise in feature selection, though the process can be automated using the fast feature selection algorithm described in this book.

- **K-means**: Popular clustering algorithm where for a given (a priori) K, finds K clusters by iteratively moving cluster centers to the cluster centers of gravity and adjusting the cluster set assignments.

- **Logistic regression**: Regression used with binary data when you want to model the probability that a specified outcome will occur. Also used to describe a regression where the response is a probability.

- **Machine learning**: Set of techniques, usually described as algorithms, to classify data based on training sets. The training sets constitute the learning part, and much of the discussion is about designing automated or semi-automated learning systems.

- **Mahout**: Apache Mahout is an Apache project to produce free implementations of distributed or otherwise scalable machine learning algorithms focused primarily on the areas of collaborative filtering, clustering, and classification, often leveraging, but not limited to, the Hadoop platform.

- **MapReduce**: Model for processing large amounts of data efficiently. Original problem is "mapped" to smaller problems (which may themselves become "original" problems). Smaller problems are processed in parallel. Results of smaller problems are combined, or "reduced," into solutions to original problems.

- **Monte Carlo simulations**: Computing expectations and probabilities in models of random phenomena using many randomly sampled values. Akin to computing probability of winning a given roulette bet (say black) by repeatedly placing it and counting success ratio. Useful in complex models characterized by uncertainty.

- **Natural Language Processing (NLP)**: A set of techniques to automatically process text to extract insights, for instance, sentiment analysis, or to automatically produce taxonomies or abstracts. Evolved from word counts (bags of words) to more elaborate text mining techniques.

- **NoSQL**: "Not only SQL" is a group of database management systems. Data is not stored in tables like a relational database and is not based on the mathematical relationship between tables. It is a way of storing and retrieving unstructured data quickly.

- **Multidimensional scaling**: Reduces space dimension by projecting a N^2 (N = number of observations) similarity matrix onto a 2-dimensional visual representation. A classic example is producing a geographic map with cities when the only data available is travel times between any pair of cities.

- **Naive Bayes**: The Naive Bayes method is a simple method of classification applicable to categorical data based on Bayes theorem. It is fast and easy to implement, but it assumes that the variables (also called features) are independent. In practice, this is not the case and algorithms based on Naive Bayes (spam detection) perform poorly.

- **Nonparametric statistics**: Set of statistical techniques that process data without making assumptions about statistical observations. Also known as data-driven, versus model-driven, statistics.

■ **Pig**: Pig is a scripting interface to Hadoop, meaning a lack of MapReduce programming experience won't hold you back. It's also known for processing a large variety of different data types.

■ **Predictive modeling**: Set of techniques based on statistical models to make predictions (stock market, fraud risk, and odds for a user to convert into a sale), usually with confidence intervals for predicted values.

■ **Sensitivity analysis**: Process used to determine the sensitivity of a predictive model to noise, missing data, outliers, and other anomalies in the model predictors.

■ **Six Sigma**: Set of tools and strategies for process improvement, originally developed by Motorola in 1985. Six Sigma seeks to improve the quality of process outputs by identifying and removing the causes of defects (errors) and minimizing variability in manufacturing and business processes.

■ **Step-wise regression**: Variable selection process for multivariate regression. In forward step-wise selection, a seed variable is selected, and each additional variable is inputted into the model but only kept if it significantly improves goodness of fit (as measured by increases in R^2). Backward selection starts with all variables and removes them one by one until removing an additional one decreases R^2 by a nontrivial amount. Two deficiencies of this method are that the seed chosen disproportionately impacts which variables are kept, and that the decision is made using R^2, not Adjusted R^2.

■ **Supervised clustering:** Also known as discriminate analysis. Consists of classifying new data points when you already have a set (training set) of preclassified observations, that is, observations with a known cluster label.

■ **Time series**: A set of (t, x) values where x is usually a scalar (though could be a vector) and the t values are usually sampled at regular intervals (though some time series are irregularly sampled). In the case of regularly sampled time series, the t is usually dropped from the actual data and replaced with just a t0 (start time) and delta-t that apply to the whole series.

Career-Building Resources

In this section you can find information on the diverse companies that employ and routinely hire data scientists. This section also includes sample resumes and job ads, which can be a gold mine for identifying the hot keywords and skills mentioned everywhere in the data science world at this time (for example, R, Python, Hadoop, NoSQL, SQL, predictive modeling, machine learning, and so on).

Companies Employing Data Scientists

An enormous variety and number of organizations routinely hire data scientists, though each may use a different job title in its advertisements and organization. A few companies that you might not expect to be on such a list include Walmart, PwC, Electronic Arts, Boeing, and Starbucks. Companies at the top of the list (IBM, Microsoft) have a lower proportion of data scientists in their workforce than others such as Facebook, Google, FICO, eBay, or LinkedIn. Traditional industries, such as manufacturing, tend to use the title "operations research analyst."

Most jobs — particularly the senior-level roles — are still concentrated in the United States (New York City and the San Francisco Bay Area), but some places are catching up quickly, such as Singapore, Spain, Ireland, and London. Following is a list of the companies employing the largest numbers of data scientists. The list is based on my own 10,000+ LinkedIn connections, broken down by company and ordered by the number of connections. The top 20 companies represent approximately 10 percent of all data scientist positions, but the distribution has a long and unusually heavy tail. You can find a more comprehensive list of 6,000+ companies at http://bit.ly/19vRlNV.

- Microsoft
- IBM
- Amazon.com
- SAS
- Google
- Accenture
- Oracle
- LinkedIn
- FICO
- Bank of America
- Citi
- Tata Consultancy Services
- Facebook
- Cognizant Technology Solutions
- Wells Fargo
- Capgemini
- eBay
- Apple
- Hewlett-Packard

- EMC
- Pivotal

Sample Data Science Job Ads

This chapter would not be complete without providing you with information on what currently hiring companies are looking for in the data science arena, their requirements, and other useful information. Consider the sample (yet actual and recent) job ads found at `http://bit.ly/1hVAmr7`. The skills most frequently listed are: Python, Linux, UNIX, MySQL, MapReduce, Hadoop, Matlab, SAS, Java, R, SPSS, Hive, Pig, Scala, Ruby, Cassandra, SQL Server, and NoSQL.

CROSS-REFERENCE See Chapter 7, "Launching Your New Data Science Career," for more information on how and where to conduct job searches for different job titles, levels, and skills.

Sample Resumes

The following sample resume extracts are from actual data science practitioners who agreed to be featured in this book. In order to allow these professionals to delete or update their resumes, I've made the resumes accessible on the web at `http://bit.ly/1j4PNuP`. You can find more resumes and profiles by doing a search on LinkedIn with the keyword data science or related keywords, or by browsing Data Science Central member profiles.

Included in this list are people from different locales and backgrounds in an attempt to cover various aspects of data science. The emphasis is on providing a well-balanced mix of professional analytic people — both junior and senior, people with big company or startup experience or both, top stars and people with average resumes (sometimes the most faithful employees), and corporate or consultant or academia-related people. The purpose is to help you find one or more you can relate to. I also added mine to provide an example containing patents and classic big data science such as credit card fraud detection and digital analytics.

Typical skills mentioned in these resumes are: programming language R, Python, Matlab, MongoDB, SQL, MySQL, statistics/machine learning (KNN, decision trees, neural networks, linear/logistic regression), and finally Java, JavaScript, Tableau, Excel, recommendation engines, and Google Analytics. Of course, none of the resumes have all of these skills listed, but the most commonly listed skills are R in 50% of the resumes and Python in 50% of the resumes.

You should check these resumes to see career progression (lateral or vertical) and the degrees, ongoing training, and certifications these people have.

By comparing these resumes to the previously presented job ads, it seems that Human Resources departments are sometimes looking for a unicorn — a professional with a skill mix that does not exist. I encourage employers to seek out and hire people with strong potential and train them, rather than looking for the rare and expensive unicorn who often turns out to not be the best fit (and may only be happy running their own business).

NOTE A lot of discussion continues to occur in the data science industry about the ideal team structure for data science projects: is it better to have one or two "unicorns" who can do it all or a more diverse team? In reality, the diverse team structure is most common because it is just too difficult to find one individual who has all the required skill sets. But Human Resources should try, if possible, to hire someone with deep domain expertise, business acumen, coding experience (production code, unless the position is for prototyping algorithms), and an analytic background (real exposure to statistics, big data, and engineering/computer science), and have him/her learn statistics, Hadoop (as a user rather than an architect), or core data science or computer science techniques.

If a company can find all they want (minus data science core, which someone qualified can easily learn) in one person, they won't face competence silos and their drawbacks. But be aware that these skilled, polyvalent individuals may not stay as long as expected.

Summary

This chapter mentioned a number of useful resources for data scientists. Resources for practicing data scientists included data sets, data science books and journals, conferences, organizations, popular websites, and definitions. Career-building resources included information on companies with many data scientists, and sample job ads and resumes.

Index

SYMBOLS

+ (plus sign), bit.ly, 236

A

AaaS. *See* analytics as a service
A/B testing, 164, 176–178, 218–219, 223, 232, 239
aberration identification, 266
abnormal purchase pattern, fraud detection metric, 113
Access, 18
accidental fraud, 216–217
ACM. *See* Association for Computing Machinery
ActivePresenter, 120–121
ad relevancy algorithms, 49
ad rotation, 244–245
adjusted R^2. *See* R-Square
Adobe, 120
after-shocks, stock market, 208
algebra, 4

algorithms, 45. *See also specific types*
captcha, 215–216
e-mail encryption, 213
stock market API, 200–201
amateur data scientists, 79–80
Amazon.com, 27–29, 52–53
American Statistical Association (ASA), 32, 86, 271, 291
amusement park mobile app, 105
analytic software, 114–115
AnalyticBridge, 89, 178, 234
first theorem, 20, 32, 159–161, 191, 268
second theorem, 11, 127–128
third theorem, 192
analytics as a service (AaaS), 35, 178–183
analytics engineering, 33
analytics tools, 113–117

analytics versus seduction, sales boost, 20–21
analytics-to-data, in-memory analytics, 34
anonymous digital currency, 104
antimissile technology, 47
antispam, 101
Aon Hewitts, 247
APIs, 35, 38, 178–183, 200–203, 268, 288
arcsine law, 207–208
ARMA. *See* auto regressive models
ArmuredMail, 213
artificial intelligence, 32
ASA. *See* American Statistical Association
association analytics, 113
Association for Computing Machinery (ACM), 86
association rules, 154, 228–229
astronomical data, 46